If the Song Doesn't Work, Change the Dress

Photograph by Lucia Moffett; courtesy of Anstice Carroll.

Patricia Zipprodt at her drawing table in her King Street studio. Photograph by Lucia Moffett; courtesy of Anstice Carroll.

If the Song Doesn't Work, Change the Dress

The Illustrated Memoirs of Broadway Costume Designer Patricia Zipprodt

*Patricia Zipprodt
with Arnold Wengrow*

methuen | drama

LONDON · NEW YORK · OXFORD · NEW DELHI · SYDNEY

METHUEN DRAMA
Bloomsbury Publishing Plc
50 Bedford Square, London, WC1B 3DP, UK
1385 Broadway, New York, NY 10018, USA
29 Earlsfort Terrace, Dublin 2, Ireland

BLOOMSBURY, METHUEN DRAMA and the Methuen Drama logo are trademarks of
Bloomsbury Publishing Plc

First published in Great Britain 2025

Copyright © Estate of Patricia Zipprodt and Arnold Wengrow, 2025

The authors have asserted their right under the Copyright, Designs and Patents Act, 1988, to be identified as author of this work.

For legal purposes the Acknowledgments on p. 199 constitute an extension of this copyright page.

Cover design: Rebecca Heselton
Costume designs by Patricia Zipprodt

All rights reserved. No part of this publication may be reproduced or transmitted in any form or by any means, electronic or mechanical, including photocopying, recording, or any information storage or retrieval system, without prior permission in writing from the publishers.

Bloomsbury Publishing Plc does not have any control over, or responsibility for, any third-party websites referred to or in this book. All internet addresses given in this book were correct at the time of going to press. The author and publisher regret any inconvenience caused if addresses have changed or sites have ceased to exist, but can accept no responsibility for any such changes.

A catalogue record for this book is available from the British Library.

A catalog record for this book is available from the Library of Congress.

ISBN: HB: 978-1-3504-3065-5
ePDF: 978-1-3504-3068-6
eBook: 978-1-3504-3067-9

Typeset by RefineCatch Limited, Bungay, Suffolk
Printed and bound in India

To find out more about our authors and books visit www.bloomsbury.com and sign up for our newsletters.

CONTENTS

Preface vi
Foreword viii

1 Starting out in Chicago 1
2 College Days, a Puppet Show, a Fateful Meeting in Washington, Leaving Home for Good 13
3 Getting Started in New York 23
4 Making My Way on Broadway 37
5 Finding Myself Off Broadway 55
6 Hal and Jerry 75
7 *Fiddler on the Roof* 89
8 *Cabaret* 107
9 Mike Nichols, *The Graduate*, and Why I Hate Hollywood 115
10 Fosse 131
11 Dealing with Addictions, Buying God's Pocket 155
12 In Sum 161

Epilogue 163

Afterword: *Cat on a Hot Tin Roof* 179

The Designs of Patricia Zipprodt 185

Acknowledgments 199
Index 201

PREFACE

In May 1999, I was helping the theatre and film designer Tony Walton with his memoirs, and he sent me to interview the costume designer Patricia Zipprodt about their collaboration on the 1972 production of *Pippin*.

At Patricia's penthouse apartment on King Street in Greenwich Village, Whitney Blausen, one of her longtime assistants, escorted me to where Patricia was sitting in a wheelchair at a counter in the open kitchen. It was a bright spring day, and there was a view of a rooftop garden through a wall of windows. Although it was clear Patricia was ill, she was very animated and told me with great gusto the story of how she and Tony had hit upon the all-white color scheme for the costumes of the Strolling Players.

Then she leaned forward and said, almost accusingly, "Do you know the title of my memoirs? They're called *If the Song Doesn't Work, Change the Dress*." I didn't know what to say. Had I failed to do my homework? How could I not have known she had written her memoirs?

Then she instructed me to follow her down the hall to her open bedroom door. She pointed to some framed costume designs hanging near the bed. "Do you know who those are by?" Was this a test? I said, not confidently, "Leslie Hurry? Desmond Heeley?" She seemed satisfied. We said our goodbyes, and Whitney came to help her to bed and escort me back to the elevator. As we walked, she said, "Patricia wants to know if you would like to help her with her memoirs." Apparently I had passed the test.

Over the next few days, I learned that *If the Song Doesn't Work, Change the Dress* had never been published and had a contorted history. In 1988, Patricia's friend, the theatre director William Woodman had suggested they collaborate on a book about her life and career.

Bill and Patricia had first met at the American Shakespeare Festival in Stratford, Connecticut, in the 1960s, when they were both starting their careers. He was an assistant stage manager; she was an assistant to the costume designer Rouben Ter-Arutunian. They stayed friends as Bill went on to a distinguished career directing in regional theatres and in Europe. He was the artistic director of the Goodman Theatre in Chicago from 1973 to 1978.

Between 1988 and 1993, when Patricia moved to Virginia after marrying Colonel Robert O'Brien at age sixty-eight, the friends met at King Street to tape her recollections. Bill devised different drafts as they shopped the manuscript to contacts in the literary and publishing worlds.

Some of their publishing friends thought the book should be a coffee table book with lots of illustrations. Others thought it should be straightforward autobiography. Some thought it should emphasize Patricia's struggle as a woman to build a career in a male-dominated theatre. Others thought it should focus on anecdotes about her famous collaborators. No agents or publishers were willing to take it on.

Then, in 1995, Bill died after suffering a heart attack while dining at a New York restaurant. Patricia, meanwhile, was enjoying her new life in Virginia—until that life became one of taking care of O'Brien, as she always called him, during a long illness. After his death in 1998, she returned to New York and a year-long battle with a reoccurrence of cancer.

After my May 1999 meeting with Patricia, I went to London for a research project. I flew back on Sunday, July 18, expecting to call Patricia on Monday to begin work. When I opened the *New York Times* that morning, I saw her obituary. She had died on Saturday.

Whitney Blausen and Connie Zonka, Patricia's sister, asked me to revise and complete Patricia's memoirs. After Connie's death, Milo Zonka, Connie's son, and Harvey Stuart, Patricia's friend and former lawyer, encouraged me to continue.

Channeling Patricia's distinctive voice—buoyant, incisive, sometimes acerbic, always expansive—as she tells her story has been a great challenge and a great privilege.

Arnold Wengrow
Professor Emeritus of Drama, University of North Carolina at Asheville
Asheville, North Carolina
November 2023

NOTE: *Footnotes indicated by asterisks (*) are Patricia's own. Footnotes indicated by numbers ([1]) are my additions.*

FOREWORD

Joel Grey and Ann Hould-Ward talk about Patricia Zipprodt

The actor Joel Grey and the costume designer Ann Hould-Ward were two of Patricia Zipprodt's closest friends. Joel and Patricia first worked together in 1966 on Cabaret. *She was forty-one and had just had her first major Broadway success two years earlier with* Fiddler on the Roof. *He was thirty-four and about to create his first major Broadway role, the iconic Master of Ceremonies.*

Ann Hould-Ward was a twenty-four-year-old graduate of the University of Virginia's MFA program in costume design when she wrote to Patricia asking if she could come to New York to be her intern. She arrived in January 1978 only to discover that the production she was to work on had been cancelled. Patricia sent her to assist Rouben Ter-Arutunian at the New York City Ballet. She returned eighteen months later to become Patricia's second assistant, then to be her first assistant, and finally to be her co-designer for Sunday in the Park with George *in 1984, before launching her own career.*

Joel Grey and Ann Hould-Ward sat down in September 2023 to talk about Patricia's impact on them professionally and personally.

AH-W: Joel, you had a long-standing professional relationship with Patricia that turned into an enduring friendship. What are your first memories of Pat, the first time you saw her?

JG: Wild clothing, original, and the face to go with it. She was like a drawing or a painting. There was something that said art about her.

She was just so friendly. And I was so scared. *Cabaret* was my first real Broadway show, and I didn't know what I was doing. So I was hoping that the costume might tell me something about the character. And it sure did.

We went to Eaves Costumes on West Forty-sixth Street and got this terrible old tail coat that fit me to a tee. There was not any work that needed to be done. When we came back, everybody at the theatre said, "We'll make you a beautiful new one." And I said, "I don't think so, I like it like it is—old—and it smells funky, like mothballs." It fit my idea of who the emcee was. It was beat up, almost unwearable. But I thought it was right and so did Patricia and we won. We won that battle. Of course Hal [Prince, the producer and director] was for it and Ruthie [Ruth Mitchell, the production stage manager], but other people were saying, "You should really have a new suit. You really, really should."

I'm the kind of an actor who is off the beaten path in terms of my taste. And Patricia and I had that same kind of taste. So did Hal. Then we made the rest of the show out of all this dreck from the costume house.

AH-W: I've tried to go back and think historically, and I don't think anybody had done that before. You gave us the freedom to be able to have that eclectic nature. You changed the flavor of what we could do. It took courage to say we're going to use these old things and we're going to make it really tattered and torn, not fake tattered and torn. It had a poetic reality to it.

JG: She was like a kid. She had that delight in the surprise of everything new she was doing.

AH-W: Whenever I think about her, I think about how I loved it when our eyes met with a new idea. It was like a complete spark of fire and energy. Something had ignited. She had that kind of personality. I'd never experienced that in anyone before I met Patricia.

JG: I agree. And then to see the chaos in her mind that created that off, off, off, that was just so right, right, right. We did have a similar taste. Sometimes she was so specific about what she wanted that she was maybe difficult to get along with.

AH-W: Well, I think her brain was racing so far ahead in her ideas that sometimes it was hard for people to catch up. People had to catch up with her.

JG: And sometimes there wasn't time. And sometimes people got frustrated.

AH-W: I think that did happen. But from my intimate knowledge of her, I have to say that the ideas were always great ideas. In the theatre, we don't always have the time to get to that visual point.

I do know she taught me to look. She taught me how to look deeper and harder. She taught me to see shadows, for example, in a way I'd never seen before, especially in the theatre, and to see the way that light hits the figure. I think that was the instigation of the painting she did. She first wanted to be a painter, you know, and then came to the theatre from that. That whole reference in her life really affected everything she did.

Her sister Connie gave me a number of her paintings, and I find it so interesting looking at them daily, because they're all up in my house. The way she understood shapes and especially the human shape. She loved to paint the human figure. That in itself was such a part of a what she was as a costume designer. She lived many lives all around us.

JG: She was unexpected.

AH-W: What was it like as an actor when you got on stage the first time with the world she created?

JG: Dangerous! At the first preview of *Cabaret* in Boston nobody thought this was going to be easy or acceptable. And the end of "Willkommen," the opening number, stopped the show. They brought in Schneider's house for the next scene, but the lights hadn't come up on it. And the audience refused to stop applauding. I said to Ruth Mitchell, "What shall I do?" I thought maybe we'd have to do the number again, like in opera. Then I was caught in the light change as the show went on. That opening continued to stop the show.

AH-W: Joel, this is this is my last question for you. It's a question that's important to me. What did you love best about her?

JG: [After a long pause] She was like opening a bottle of champagne.

AH-W: She was like opening a bottle of champagne, yes—I thought about that question myself. One of the things I still have in my hall closet is a jacket she did for a show called *Swing* that I assisted her with. It never came in to New York. She had a show jacket made with black satin and rhinestones and "Swing" across the back. I loved it because it smelled like Patricia. It smelled like the Georgette Klinger perfume she wore. It smelled that way for years and years and years.

Every once in a while I would take it out of the closet just to smell it. After many years when I took it out, it didn't smell anymore at all. And I was so sad. When you knew Patricia, there was an all-encompassing world. It was smell, it was movement, it was energy. It was life itself.

JG: She was a true original.

1

Starting out in Chicago

Every so often someone asks me what a costume designer does. My answer is quite simple: I cover up bodies. And I've been doing this for some forty years. I am in a continual and very intimate relationship with performing artists—actors, singers, dancers—anyone who gets up on a stage and needs to be covered up.

It's often not easy. Once a prominent singer wailed during a fitting, "I just cannot sing in yellow." When I was costuming a rather noisy Wagnerian opera at the Met, a member of the chorus approached me in her little medieval outfit and complained that the orchestra was inside her hat. This I deal with.

And why do I deal with covering up these occasionally mad people? Why do I try to make them capable of presenting themselves as the beings they think they really are?

Because they go places emotionally that I haven't the courage or the talent or the knowledge to go. Places I need to go to make my life richer. I need to make that split-second, gravity-defying leap a dancer makes. I need to be in the presence of the beautiful sounds a singer produces. I need to know every conceivable human experience an actor portrays. And I want to be there, a fortunate member of their company.

How did I come to know I wanted to be in the company of artists? Looking back, I see that growing up in Kenilworth, a suburb of Chicago, I was blessed, and maybe cursed, with many experiences which set me on my path to becoming a costume designer, although I had no awareness of that path then.

My mother, Agnes Irene Turpin Zipprodt, was born in 1899 in Philadelphia, Pennsylvania. Her father, Edward Napoleon Bonaparte Turpin, was a French Catholic from the Isle of Guernsey. My mother claimed he was descended from one of *the* Bonapartes.

She was born into a well-to-do family with a lineage going back to the early shiploads that came over. She had in her life a grandmother, Rebecca Hicks, a harp-playing Quaker, who was a great influence. Mother always threatened my two sisters and me with making us join the Daughters of the American Revolution if we didn't behave ourselves. We could have done that because of Rebecca Hicks. We didn't do that.

Irene's mother died when she was five. I don't think she ever got over that sense of loss over her mother's death. She always envied the three of us, she said, that we had a mother. We weren't happy at all with the mother we had, so it was a stormy point.

Edward Turpin, her father, was quite a roué. He became very good friends with John Philip Sousa while the musician was living in Philadelphia, before he became the leader of the Marine Band. Edward Turpin was always running off to Washington whenever Sousa was performing there. After he had run out of all his money, he would come home in a taxi, collect, usually from Washington, in his frock coat with a boutonniere in his lapel. Mother's feelings toward him were always rather uncertain.

When she was seventeen, she was living in Germantown, Pennsylvania, a lovely suburb of Philadelphia, with her elder sister Leona. Aunt Leona had married Arthur Baruch, an Orthodox Jew who was a cousin of Bernard Baruch. Uncle Arthur had converted to Catholicism to marry Leona, so Mother was raised in a Catholic home under the tutelage of her sister and her brother-in-law, who became a strict but loving kind of stepfather, even though her own father was still alive.

When the United States entered World War I, Mother joined the Navy. I think she was underage but somehow managed to become what was called a Yeoman (F), for female. The Navy didn't supply uniforms for women. At that time, a dress or skirt was the only thing proper to wear. The Navy issued guidelines for regulation dress, and the Yeomen (F) were given money to purchase what they needed. Mother went to the best couturier in Philadelphia for her uniform and designed her own hat. She served in the medical division doing clerical work in the Philadelphia Naval Yard. She lived at home and arrived every day by car.

My mother was very beautiful. She posed for Liberty Bonds posters wearing great huge hats and holding the American flag. She was also a very theatrical person, a woman of great individuality, and, at her best, a woman of great independence. As a girl, she was a devout Catholic, convent educated, with her own little altar in her closet. Until she decided the Virgin Birth didn't make any sense, which prompted her to join the Navy.

After the war, she moved to New York and took up modeling. She always said she was in the Ziegfeld Follies. I've never known whether that was true or not, but I have a very deep feeling it was true because she was very tall and wore hats well.[1] Apparently sister Leona came and found her and dragged her out of the Ziegfeld Follies. Maybe that's when she switched over to modeling. This was in the early 1920s: a woman from a very proper family doing relatively radical things. She was always so proud of this time in her life.

She started modeling for a women's wear house owned by Maurice Rentner, a pioneer of ready-made clothing, who produced high-quality merchandise at high prices to match. Eventually she became a traveling saleswoman for Renter. A traveling saleswoman was unheard of in those days. She took the Rentner line to Chicago and made the first contacts with Marshall Field and Company.

In the process of being this traveling saleswoman to Chicago, with this elegant line of clothes, very beautiful in her own right, she ran across the man who was to become my father, Herbert E. Zipprodt.

---

[1] The 1981 obituary for Agnes Irene Turpin (Zippy) Zipprodt in the Fort Myers, Florida, *News-Press*, repeats the family legend that she was "an original member of the Ziegfeld [sic] Follies ... a traveling representative and a top model for a leading fashion designer of ladies clothing. She also served in the Navy in W.W.I."

My father had come up from his home in St. Louis and was serving in the Great Lakes Navy Yard. He was from a very religious family. His grandfather, Johann Jacob Zipprodt, was a member of the Swiss Brethren, akin to the Mennonites and the Amish, who came over from Switzerland around 1849. Johann Jacob had nine children. Two of the boys, Luke and John, and the two girls, Mary Elizabeth and Martha Magdaline, were given biblical names. Herbert's father was named Edward. They pronounced it "Zippro," because they were French-speaking.

My father's family was very poor because his father was much more concerned with preaching the word of the Lord than making a living. He handed out tracts on the street, wrote religious poems, and claimed he saved 10,000 souls. Maybe he did. But my father and his brothers had to stop school after the eighth grade to support his salvation work.

Out of this strict household came my father. The minute he got away from there, he did not put his foot back into any kind of church unless there was either a funeral, a wedding, or a baptism.

Mother thought he was a very difficult man. She went back to New York, where she was enjoying the life of a flapper. On several more of those business trips to Chicago, she saw more and more of Herbert E. Zipprodt until finally, one day, for some reason or other, they got married.

They had a very civil ceremony because they both came from extremely theologically overburdened families. Mother said he was late to the wedding. So ultimately I came into the world on February 24, 1925.

Family fable has it that my father, being violently anti-Catholic and anti-church, took me out of the St. Francis Hospital when I was about four days old for fear the nuns would baptize me. Away I went, safe and sound, to our apartment in Evanston, un-donated to any particular religion. I remained un-donated for years.

Growing up, I went to every kind of Sunday school. I went to all the little churches around Evanston. We moved to Kenilworth when I was nine, where my selection of Sunday schools was limited to two. One was the Unitarian Church and the other was Episcopal, both high and low, depending on which Sunday you went. It was called the Church of the Holy Comforter (we called it "The Holy Blanket") and Eugene Field, the "poet of childhood," was buried in its backyard. I didn't know which of the two to go to, but the people over at the Episcopal Church looked like they were more fun, and as a result, the entire family is now Episcopalian.

I arrived at the Holy Blanket in the fifth grade. When I was twelve I was baptized and confirmed the same weekend by a Bishop Stewart. He put holy oil on my forehead. When I went home and looked, nothing had changed. So I too, like my mother, was entering into my age of disillusionment with religious practice.

Our move to Kenilworth happened in May when I was four weeks shy of the end of the fifth grade. I had been in the Evanston schools, and apparently because I was bright, I had finished first, second, third, and fourth grades in three years. I was skipping right along, having a great time, reading and writing and doing my arithmetic. The principal at my new school, however, was worried that my social age, my physiological age, and my chronological age were not in sync. Here was a good time, he thought, to pause me and put me back to fifth grade again the coming year.

So I did Abraham Lincoln twice (in the State of Illinois you do Abraham Lincoln in the fifth grade). I did long division twice. My teacher had great sympathy with me, but

Patricia and Irene Turpin Zipprodt, 1925. Credit: Estate of Patricia Zipprodt.

she had to keep me alert and alive through this non-negotiable repeat year. I was put in the back of the room with special projects. I had to do a map of the United States with yarn going across it indicating the Lincoln Highway. I had potatoes growing.

In the meanwhile all the kids decided I had been kept back because I had flunked. Mortification overwhelmed me because I knew that wasn't the reason. It's annoyed me all my life.

My sister Barbara came along when I was about four-and-half. Then, when I was twelve, my youngest sister Constance was born. Barbara and I wanted a brother. When my father called from the hospital to say, "You girls have a beautiful baby sister," we hung up.

The baby had no name for six months. She was entered into the one of the social gazettes of the North Shore of Chicago as "No-name Zipprodt." We didn't know what to do because my mother and my sister and I had really planned on a boy. We had Peter and Charles and Michael, all the names that are popular now, for this fantasy male. My father, being a somewhat wise man, decided that he had a good harem going and was going to keep it going. He wanted a girl. He said, "God only sends girls to very careful places." I used to wonder about that, because ours was hardly a "careful" place.

Eventually she was named Constance. I was twelve and in the eighth grade when sister Connie was brought home from the hospital after the proper ten days that women stayed in the hospital then. A Swedish nurse named Inga May Nelson, who had taken care of Barbara, came and took care of Connie.

Inga May was thirty, very pretty, wore a white starched uniform and a little cap. She spent her life getting little babies started, even though she had two small children of her own. Mother could rest and stay in her bedroom for the three weeks or month Inga May was there.

Then she went away. Because the crib was in my bedroom, I now got Connie. At age twelve, I picked up where Inga May Nelson left off. I gave her her 10:00 p.m. bottle, her 2:00 a.m. bottle, and her 6:00 a.m. bottle. I bathed her and diapered her and got her dressed and put back in her crib. Then I would get myself dressed and go off to school.

I did that for many months, maybe a year. When I came back from school in the afternoon, I was Connie's entertainer. I pushed her around in the buggy and pushed her in the swing. She was sort of mine. She was mine because Mother had retreated from the role of an active mother and was deep into her problems. She was also getting deep into the effects of alcohol.

My relationship with Connie as a result is very complex. I don't think either one of us has gotten it

Barbara, Patricia, and Connie Zipprodt (five weeks old). Photograph by Herbert Zipprodt, "Our Lovely Girls." Credit: Heidi Zonka Sorensen.

resolved. It's mother–child, oldest and firstborn sister, and youngest and last-born daughter who became like a grandchild to my father. She was blonde, blue-eyed, and beautiful. I was brunette, green-eyed, and filled with god knows what. So today this relationship goes on, and we try to get across breaches of it as best we can. It has many, many levels.

When he was in St. Louis, my father made money selling lithographic plates for a printing firm. After the war, he had managed to save $1,000. After he got out of the Navy in Chicago, he set up his own lithographic advertising agency known as Zipprodt, Inc. They designed and printed colorful advertising posters and window displays. It became one of the biggest of its kind. He had all the big accounts in the city, like Ford and Heinz. He was a self-made man. He loved it. It was the great American Dream. The proper house, good sturdy brick and slate, the proper schools, and servants when they were needed.

Growing up, I remember looking at the women in the neighborhood, at my mother's friends and my father's friends' wives, and how they all seemed like such appendages. The men talked and the women acknowledged the conversation. In Kenilworth the men marched off to the train in the mornings to go to their high-powered jobs. Women were alone all day with the help in their big houses. When the children went away, the women were really alone. They always had fur coats, but they seemed unhappy. They seemed empty. They had everything that life was supposed to give them, but I always had a feeling of malaise. I knew then that I didn't want any part of it at all.*

My mother was officially a vice president in my father's company. She didn't do anything, but any time he needed official papers signed, he would put them on the desk and cover everything on them with both of his hands except the place for the signature. No reading allowed. "Sign here." It wasn't a woman's business. It wasn't that he was a dishonest businessman, it was just that business was none of her business. And she signed. She also got ulcers.

Mother had led a very active life before her marriage. After she married and had a home and children, she got involved volunteering with charities. Her favorite charity was the Mary Crane League. Jane Addams, the famous social worker-educator, had started the Mary Crane Day Nursery at her settlement, Hull House, and the Mary Crane League raised money for it. They worked all year to throw a lavish annual gala called the Snow Ball. It took elaborate preparations. Twelve women headed committees with five or six women each. The committees had names like Tickets, Reservations, Prizes, Music, Decorations, and Cigarettes and Flowers.

---

*A woman named Mrs. Smith-Williams-Story was a friend of my mother's. On the North Shore, the maid's day off was always Thursday. So robbers and burglars knew that was the day to find people unguarded. One Thursday the burglars came to Mrs. Smith-Williams-Story's house, and she was all alone. Marie wasn't there. The chauffeur wasn't there. They pulled a gun on her and said, "Give me your jewels." She said, "You don't understand, we've just come back from Europe and my jewels are all in the safe." "Give me your furs." "They're in the vault." "Give me your money." "We don't have money." They got more and more threatening, until finally they had poor Mrs. Smith-Williams-Story cowering underneath the dining room table. In her last effort to save her life, she said, "Well, perhaps I could write you a check." They were so completely astounded they left.

Mother, the wife of a prominent advertising man, was in charge of Publicity. She got the photographs of all the ladies taken. I was photographed on Jane Addams's lap at the age of five. Mother loved the Snow Ball.

My mother always responded passionately but erratically to pressure, and the pressure of this volunteer job struck my father as overwhelming for her. So he made her stop. *He made her stop.* He thought it was too much for her to handle along with the children, the house, a servant or two, him, and life.

Maybe he was right, maybe the pressure was too much. But the point was that he had control. She did not say, "On your life, I'll stop. I'll keep right on doing this."

Mr. and Mrs. Zipprodt, circa 1932. Credit: Heidi Zonka Sorensen.

No, she stopped. She was not a peaceful person, nor was she weak, but she stopped. That astounded me. It just horrified me. But that was Mother. And that's a helluva mother.

I've often toyed with the idea that her three daughters cast themselves in different scenarios to complete her lifelines. I took the work line. Barbara, the second child, took the family line. She eloped when she was eighteen, had four children, and just loved baking pies. Connie, coming later, looked upon both of us and decided to "have it all," family and career. Were we all three playing out an aspect of what was unfulfilled in Mother? That's my pop-psych analysis.

Men got to do all the exciting things. Before the days when fathers and now working mothers take their children to work to get an idea of what they do, my dad would take me down to Chicago to his office, which was on the eighteenth floor of the Tower Building on the corner of Madison and Michigan Avenues.

I adored it. I could look out the windows toward downtown along Michigan Avenue to the Art Institute and uptown to the lake and the Drake Hotel. It was my first vision of the city where I would look down and see little teeny cars riding on little teeny roads. It was my first glimpse of urban living. I loved the way the scale of things changed. I loved being way up in the sky looking out of the windows.

But the most fun was the art department. I would be let loose there for a couple of hours to play and draw and watch the artists do cardboard work and lettering and painting—all the things they did to prepare models for the lithographic advertising displays my father was commissioned to do. So at an early age PZ was going into the office, going into a man's world, going into a creative version of a man's world where people made things.

But I also noticed how low the positions of the women were there. They were either young and about to leave and get married or they were middle-aged ladies who hadn't gotten married. The men were sort of condescending to the older women but relied on them heavily because they knew they would never get married. They would stay there because they were stuck. They were nice-looking women. They wore suits, they sat at desks, they typed and said, "Yes, sir." But the men were having all the fun. The men had drinks at five o'clock; the men didn't have to wear their jackets in the art department.

They were great cartoonists. They would do cartoons of each other on birthdays. There was a very lively feeling in that art department, and it was one of my father's favorite places in the office. When he wanted to get a break from it all, he would always wander back into the art department.

To this day I still have one of the three-legged iron bases to the drawing boards from my father's office in my studio in New York. I've used it all my life. I got it when I was about ten. It was an old thing in the office. Dad brought it home as my table. So the Zipprodt office goes on.

I think my imaginative, artistic inner life began very early. When I was little, not more than six years old, because we were still living in Evanston, I would put myself to sleep at night by pressing my eyelids until I saw these wonderful spots. I'd go into that spot space and stay there till I went to sleep. I remember later in Kenilworth we had a lamp in the basement that had a translucent parchment lampshade with mottled tortoiseshell markings. I got absolutely transfixed by the light coming through it on more than one occasion because it was sort of watery. I would go downstairs and take off into this little watery world. In the early sixties, when I was a member of an LSD group, we would focus on a face or a stone, and a vision would come off of it. It was exactly the same process when I was a kid, except I was not taking acid. I was taking lampshade. It was similar to pushing my eyelids.

So I began to wonder where inner vision lives, where it comes from, and how you nourish it.

About the same time, I was going to a kindergarten near our house. One day, I woke up late, and my mother said, "Are you sure you want to go? It's raining out and you've got this little sniffle. And it's past nine o'clock." The art class began at ten o'clock. I said, "Oh, I want to get there in time for my drawing and painting class, Mommy," and I rushed to get dressed, get my big hair bow in my long curls, and I ran down the street. It was terribly important that I not miss this class.

I have some work that my mother saved, as all mothers do, from that period of my artistic career, and it seems I was consumed with a great desire to make expressions about African violets. I spent hours drawing African violets. They weren't realistically drawn. They were abstract, made with crayons and chalk, quite designed, really. My first formalized designs.

I always loved art during school. By the time I got to high school, I was really humming along with it. I had started taking drawing classes when I was about twelve. The Art Institute of Chicago had an Evanston annex where their teachers taught Saturday classes to suburban children. I was doing life drawing when I was twelve, thirteen, and fourteen, which is very early.

Saturdays consisted of 9:00 a.m. to noon at art school. Then at one o'clock to the braces dentist. Afterwards, I would take my drawings home to my dad, who loved to see them. He waited for them every Saturday because I was good at it. He was happy seeing this very young person drawing away with charcoal. He helped me blow the fixative across my drawings.

My mother started me out like a good mother with ballet class. I was five or six, but because I didn't do my barre work at home, that was discontinued. And then I got piano lessons. And I didn't practice for an hour every day, so that was discontinued.

What my mother was missing was that I would spend all weekend playing the piano. I'd go down to the basement, practice for an hour and then come back up and go out and play. Then I'd go down and practice again for an hour and come back up and go out and play. So over the weekend I might practice twelve hours intermittently. But I couldn't bear to sit down at the damn piano every day at five o'clock after school. I just couldn't do it. This is important to me because it's a rhythm that started very young and still holds. When I am designing a show, I cannot do an hour a day or get up early and design for a couple of hours, then do the other things of the day. I have to wait until Friday, when the week is over, and from Friday night until Sunday night I will jump in the hole, pull the lid in after me, and just go into a place several levels down where I can study the script or the ballet and start envisioning what is happening on the stage. It's usually very quiet. A lot of puttering goes on. And between the putterings I'm back in the basement playing the piano or looking at the lampshade for another hour and a half.

My mother started taking me to the afternoon children's series down at the Goodman Theatre. I was fascinated by it. She also took me to see the Humperdinck *Hansel and Gretel*, which was done by the Chicago City Opera every Christmas at the big Civic Opera House. The angels coming down the stairs transfixed me. As the little angels stepped down each step, which were quite high, each step lit up. I will never forget it. I would look forward to it every Christmas.

I started acting in plays as well. We did *The Merchant of Venice* in eighth grade. We actually started rehearsals in sixth grade, slowly, three hours a week. I learned to adore Shakespeare. I played Nerissa. I was miffed because I really wanted to play Portia.

At New Trier High School, I did a lot of acting. None of it was good as I was so shy. Once I was playing a wicked witch who had to faint. I never could faint during rehearsals. But on opening night when there was an audience, I crashed to the floor, just as they had told me how. I never could let my body go until that last moment. I really didn't have the makings of an actress.

As I was discovering my connections to art and theatre, I was inadvertently putting them together with a connection to clothing. My mother, having been a model, loved beautiful clothes and wore them with elegance. She always had fashion magazines around and magazines showing society doings.

On rainy days, when I was bored, I drew paper dolls. I painted them, cut them out, and mounted them on cardboard. They were maybe five or six inches high. They were mostly girls, although there were some boys. There was a blonde lady and a brunette lady and a red-haired lady, and they stood with one hand on hip, with their little toes going out in the classic model's pose. I had the men in their lives and their servants.

I penciled and crayoned a fabulous wardrobe for them and cut them out with little tabs. All their clothes were color coordinated, with parasols that matched the dresses or accented them. Their shoes changed, their parasols changed, even their hairstyles changed.

These ladies also had an environment they lived in. I would cut out wonderful pictures from my mother's magazines and catalogs: yachts, hunts, balls, beaches. Any room they needed I clipped for them, and they had little clothes for all these rooms.

I would dress my dolls with little tabs and march them around to their adventures. They would go to parties and put on their party clothes. They would go to the kitchen and put on their kitchen clothes. They had this whole life going. It was a great trip, and it lasted for several years.

When my mother and father sold our house in Kenilworth and moved to Florida, Mother cleaned out the attic. She found a batch of these paper dolls and sent them to me in New York. Suddenly, my past popped out of these envelopes, my childhood friends, these paper dolls, these funny little people with their yellow shoes and their matching yellow parasols.

And there I was sitting many years later doing exactly the same thing, telling stories with clothes, except that instead of cutting out things from Mother's magazines I was reading scripts that said, "Second act, they all go on to a ball."

I've thought a great deal about that. How I've observed people, particularly women who seem to me are looking at their lives very superficially. They aren't pulling from some inner core. They are pulling from a role and doing what the role said to do instead of what their core told them to do. My whole struggle has been to develop the core, the place where that inner vision lives and to stay away from the expected roles, because they can be so totally conflicting.

While my artistic inclinations were percolating, I was also discovering a kind of social conscience. My mother gave me a jolt in that direction when I was about ten. In Evanston, I came home from school and had lunch every day. I sat at the dining room table and lunch would be put in front of me.

One day I didn't like whatever it was. I didn't want to eat it, so I didn't eat it. My mother came by and said, "Young lady"—which was my name—"young lady, you must eat your spinach." "I don't want to eat my spinach," I said in my whiney voice. "You must eat your spinach."

She came by a little later, and the spinach was still there. "Young lady, if this spinach is not gone by quarter to one, we'll have to do something about it." She put a clock on the table. Tick, tick, tick, tick, tick, tick. Quarter to one came, and the spinach was still there.

"Very well," she said, and she popped me off the chair I was sitting on, popped me into my coat and hat, popped me out the back door and back to the garage, and popped me into the car. And we began a long, long auto journey from Evanston all the way down to Halsted Street in Chicago.

This was 1935, in the bottom of the Depression. It was winter. It was always winter in Chicago. She parked the car in the Hull House area, and hand in hand we walked up and down the alleys of the poorer sections of Chicago so I could see

Childhood paper dolls. Credit: Billy Rose Theatre Division, The New York Public Library for the Performing Arts; © Estate of Patricia Zipprodt.

children trying to find food in garbage cans. When I had seen enough of that, we got in the car and drove back to Evanston.

There were always hungry people at our back door. Anyone who came to the door who was hungry was allowed in. They were always sitting in the kitchen. My mother always had eggs and bacon for them. We had quite a little soup kitchen at the back of the house. It was that kind of house, to my father's consternation. Well, never mind, he wasn't home.

I found my high school years very difficult because I had an extremely destructive family scene. Alcohol was the base, and pandemonium was the rule. I had to go to other places for any sense of security or peace or quiet. I was terrified of becoming like Mother because I knew I had a lot of her wildness and temperament. I used to weep about this to my father in my teens.

By then, I was working on my painting seriously and taking classes at the Art Institute. Instead of going to college, I wanted to live in Chicago and take an art degree there. But my art teacher, Carl Scheffler, said, "If you are able to go to a regular college, do so. If you are really an artist, you will be an artist. But chances are very slim that you will go back and read Plato or take a course in physics. You won't do the kind of reading and studying and thinking that a college environment offers."

So I did what he said and promptly applied to college. I decided I had to get out of Chicago. I had been going to Philadelphia and New York all my growing years because my mother's family and my father's family were out there. So my place to look away from Chicago was Boston, New York, or Philadelphia. Because my high school grades were shaky, I applied to Bradford Junior College in Boston for a two-year degree. My plan was to get that liberal arts base and then come back and study painting at the Art Institute.

2

College Days, a Puppet Show, a Fateful Meeting in Washington, Leaving Home for Good

After the alcohol and arguments of my home life in Chicago, Bradford Junior College in Haverhill, Massachusetts, seemed like paradise. Thirty-five miles north of Boston, close to New Hampshire and the Atlantic Ocean, it had lawns, historic brick buildings, a pond (with fish), woods, and fields. It was considered an intellectual "Little Sister" of the high-powered Seven Sisters women's colleges.

It was a classy place. Daughters of socially prominent families went there. BJC women were served formal dinners in the dining room. They attended Sunday afternoon vespers and wore their class blazers into town. We were required to wear evening dress at the president's parties for faculty and students and to evening lectures and concerts.

Here were peace and quiet. All of a sudden I was making very high grades after my lackluster performance at New Trier. I may have been second in my class at Bradford.

I plunged into biology and zoology, thoroughly enjoying dissecting cats and dogs and making anatomical drawings. After all, I had studied life drawing at the Art Institute, working from a model, closely observing bones and muscles.

My zoology teacher my freshman year, Dr. Wolfgang Pauli, liked the way I drew up a storm from anything under the microscope. Amoebas especially came up as beautiful little pictures. He said, "You have a full career right here in your hands as a surgical artist." I said, "What's that?"

So I went home for Christmas and told my father and mother that I was going to be a surgical artist. My father scouted around and found a woman named Gladys McHugh, who was the head surgical artist at the University of Chicago Medical School. She was a pioneer of the medical illustration field and had just produced a beautiful book showing the eye in layers of transparencies.

He invited her to join us at his club, the Chicago Athletic Association. As we sat in deep tufted leather chairs in this elegant wood-paneled room, Gladys smoked constantly and flicked her ashes over her shoulder onto the oriental carpet. I was mortified. An attendant kept sweeping them up. She kept flicking.

"All right," she said, "if you're really interested, meet me tomorrow down at the University of Chicago at this address, and we'll go through the labs. If you genuinely like what you're experiencing, I would certainly consider taking you on as an apprentice when you finish your two years at school."

When I got to the address the next day, it turned out to be the morgue. We went through the labs, and she took me over to a bucket where there was half of a head, severed front to back, submerged in formaldehyde. She addressed it as Elmer. She picked it up by its hair and said, "Here, can you hold it?" I may have gulped, but I said, "Sure," and I did. So I saw what one was dealing with.

She knew I wouldn't be a surgical artist. I think I simply envisioned the drama of it all: surgeons in masks performing open-heart surgery, a highly theatrical version.

Another thing Professor Pauli said to me was, "You're too bright for this place. Get out." I knew I wanted to go to a four-year liberal arts college, and I knew I wanted to stay in New England.

So during spring vacation I went on a little tour of four colleges where I had friends from home: Smith, Vassar, Bryn Mawr, and Mount Holyoke. I made appointments with deans and took copies of my grades. Everyone said, "Oh, we'd love to have you as a transfer student. Your grades are wonderful. We like what you're interested in."

I had an extra day or two on my break and was to meet a friend at MIT. She said, "I'm going out to Wellesley to see a friend of mine later this afternoon. Why don't you come along?"

When I was at Vassar and Smith and the others, I noticed that they all seemed to have their cliques. If you ate with one table, you couldn't eat with another. It was exactly what I had been through in high school and I never wanted to do that again.

It seemed different at Wellesley. It was a beautiful campus, with handsome brick and stone buildings in a magnificent landscape of lawns, woodlands, and meadows. There was even a lake. As I walked around, people would give a nod or a "Good afternoon" or just acknowledge me with eye contact. I thought, "I like this place. It's human and it's beautiful."

I went over to the admissions office, where the dean was available to see me. She said, "Oh, no, Wellesley does not allow first year transfers. Your high school record is very weak. Keep up what you are doing at Bradford for another year, and we might be very interested in you at the proper time."

Of course I applied instantly only to Wellesley. When I was accepted, I think I may have been more excited than when I won a Tony for *Fiddler on the Roof*.

I went to Wellesley that fall intending to major in pre-med. But all the excitement of my studies at Bradford went out the window. Instead of the marvelous Professor Pauli who said, "Here, cut this up and draw it," the teachers here were giant ladies in white lab coats who spent their summers at Woods Hole looking at the world through a glass-bottomed boat. They had us running over the rustic acres with nets looking for snakes and spiders. And I just couldn't take chemistry.

At the end of my sophomore year, I ended up in an obligatory class in sociology, and I fell madly in love with the social sciences. Sociology and anthropology, the study of the family of man, became my majors. I minored in philosophy and theology. One of my assignments was filling out forms for Margaret Mead for interviews about the Irish in Boston and how they survived the potato famine.

Where was art? There was only one painting class, but it was already full by the time I enrolled. The only other art course that had any room for me was a history of

Chinese jade, and I didn't want to take that. I didn't get into art history until my late junior year.

I would occasionally set up still lifes in my room and paint. And I took a mural painting course my senior year because I'd never painted a mural. Four students in the class each chose a college tradition to depict on large Masonite panels to hang on the walls of the Well, a kind of café-soda-shop set up in Alumnae Hall during the war. The traditions were Tree Day, Step Singing, May Day, and Float Night. I chose Float Night, an event dating back to the 1880s, where girls set sail on floats on Lake Waban to sing, while other students paraded around the lake among trees hung with Japanese lanterns.

In the middle of my panel were four canoes forming a "W," surrounded by a crew race in full swing, pirates in big pirate hats, and spectators looking jaunty in their class caps. I still have the small sketch that I worked from. It was my one A for art.

I got involved with the Wellesley Dance Group, performing modern dance to Mussorgsky in the junior dance festival. My senior year I performed in something called "The Ballet of Unhatched Chicks" at Tree Day.

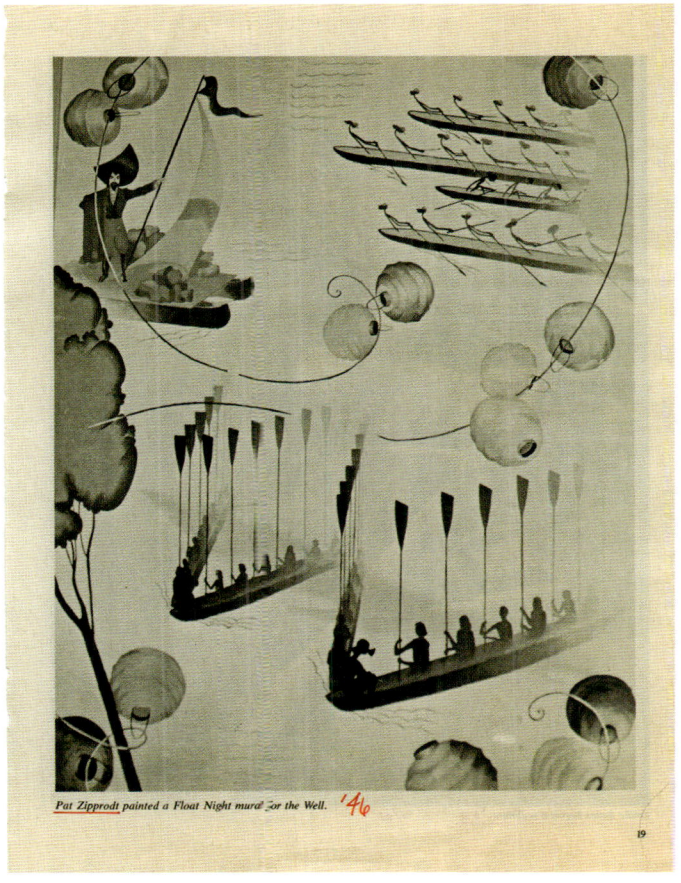

Wellesley mural. Courtesy Wellesley College Alumnae Association.

My senior year, I chaired the Senior Prom in April. My motto was to leave no stone unturned in making it a sweet dance with a romantic atmosphere and balloons. Two friends, Fuzzy Glassenberg and Barbara Chapline, and I danced a parody to the Andrews Sisters' recording of "Money is the Root of All Evil."

On Sunday after the Saturday dance, there were picnics and canoe trips with our dates who were able to stay over. This was our last fling at Wellesley, and then the class of '46 could be found locked in their rooms studying for what was called "the general"—our final chore.

There was no theatre at Wellesley, and I didn't go to plays in Boston at all. Theatre was not what I was pursuing in any way. I was only thinking I'd better finish and get out of this place first before I thought about a career.

Life was hard at Wellesley. Standards were high, and they just jammed us with work. I was always sort of cross-eyed. The men at MIT seemed to have more free time than we did at Wellesley.

If I wasn't thinking about theatre or even art then, it was because I was thinking about saving the world. Wellesley made a lot of noise in those days about how democratic it was because Madame Chiang Kai-shek graduated in 1917 and had addressed an assembly of students and faculty the day after speaking to a joint session of the US House and Senate. There were students from India and other Asian countries. There wasn't supposed to be any racial prejudice.

I found this just more than a little bit fake. All the women who came from overseas were from privileged backgrounds and dressed beautifully. To counteract that, I took a course in juvenile delinquency and spent the summer before my senior year working at Sleighton Farm School, a reformatory for girls in rural Pennsylvania. The girls' ages were twelve through nineteen, and their crimes ranged from truancy to attempted murder. We were never advised what any particular girl was guilty of so we would treat them all the same.

By my senior year, I had given up all notion of surgical drawing. It was just too boring to put up with. I was not temperamentally suited for it. But I still didn't know what I wanted to do.

So I came back home to Chicago after I graduated in 1946. The atmosphere was just as contentious as ever, if not more so. I had never fit, and I still didn't fit. All the men coming back from the war, the boys I had grown up with, the ones who were still alive, were not interested in what was going on in my head because I was not supposed to have anything going on in my head.

On Wednesday nights, the women played bridge and their husbands played poker. This was life on the North Shore. I was so bored with everything that I went down to our basement and set up shop with my drawing board and the little Corona typewriter that had been my present when I graduated from eighth grade, and I wrote long, long thoughts trying to figure out where I was going.

My father gave me presents whenever I graduated. My present from high school was a set of cream leather luggage, complete with hat boxes and shoe boxes, a fortune in the most gorgeous luggage. Even with this elegant ensemble, when I went off to Bradford, I didn't take the famous 20th Century Limited, which left La Salle Street Station at 2:30 p.m. and arrived in Boston the next day at 11:50 a.m., almost exactly twenty hours and twenty minutes. The war had started. I took a slower (and cheaper) train instead. I would be sitting with these pieces of luggage for almost fifty hours.

When it was time to graduate from Wellesley, I tried to anticipate the present they would give me. I didn't even want to stay for graduation because I thought that was an excessive activity. I wanted to go to the Cape.

I wrote to my father telling him my plans and said, "I don't know what you've got in mind, but what I would really like is some money put away so I could go on to graduate school." I've never gotten an answer to that letter. Or the money.

When I came home, my mother said, "You fool! He was going to give you a fur coat! I was instructed to take it back, so I took it back. Now you have nothing." My graduation present ended up being a fishing trip to Canada with my father, which was what *he* wanted to do.

I went through a nightmarish period realizing that I had used up four wonderful years of college directing myself completely off my first track. I had a wonderful time though. I adored what I studied. I adored my professors.

In the fall, a group of my college friends decided to visit Chicago and stayed at our house, to my father's horror. My father did not like company. We went in to Chicago to the theatre a lot, and my mother gave luncheons. One day, when we were scheduled to have lunch at the club, followed by a matinee, I woke up early and said to Camilla Tyler Lowman, my Wellesley roommate, "Let's get out of here! Let's look for a job."

We looked in the Yellow Pages under employment agencies and saw one called University Employment. I said, "That's it. We're fresh out of school, we've got our degrees; we will go to the University Employment Agency. We'll have a wonderful time this morning, and then we'll meet our friends for lunch."

We wore our little white gloves, which we would need for lunch and the matinee. We got to University Employment and sat down in front of a large woman behind a desk. "We're Wellesley graduates," we said, "and we can't do anything useful, but we want an interesting job where we can travel together, because we haven't been able to travel because of the war. We want to go to different wonderful places, and we want to make a good salary so we won't have to write home for money."

The woman stared at us. Then she said, "Will you both smile for me." We both went, "Cheeeese!" She said, "I think I've got just the thing" and pulled out a card from her little card file. "There is an opening for a pair of puppeteers at the Good Teeth Council for Children," she said. And she immediately dialed them and made an appointment for us. "Go!" she said. "It's in the Wrigley Building."

So we had to go. Off we went with the little card in our white gloves to the Wrigley Building, to the very top of the tower that sways in the Chicago winds, where Philip K. Wrigley, the son of William Wrigley Jr., the gum magnate, had set up the Good Teeth Council to promote the benefits of gum as a mouth exerciser and teeth cleaner.

As we got off the elevator, we heard music coming from a door painted with apples and carrots. Opening it, we saw a madhouse of puppeteers all preparing their shows for the road. Some had on smocks and were making little things with plasticine and paint. Some were washing little clothes. Others were talking in funny voices, saying "Hello, boys and girls," while they worked their puppets to a Victrola playing marching music.

We were ushered into the office of the lady who was doing the hiring. Scripts were thrust into our hands. My first reading consisted of "Bow wow wow." "Oh, you can do better than that," the formidable Catherine McAndrews, the assistant executive secretary of the Good Teeth Council for Children, boomed, repeating "Bow wow wow!" with great enthusiasm.

After a brief training period, we were signed up for a year's school tour.[2] We were the Jack and Judy team. We played all the characters: Jack and Judy, Grandpa and Grandma, and Dr. Parson, the dentist, who told the children about eating the right food and brushing three times a day. He would say to chew gum but not Wrigley's specifically.

Camilla played little Jack because her voice was in the right register. Little Jack would come out and say, "Hi boys and girls!" And they'd say "Hi!" because Jack and Judy came every year with a different story. My task was to jump out in front of the curtain and say, "Good morning, boys and girls, we're back again with another show, and you can read what it's all about by looking at the words up here on our lovely pink curtains. Now, what do they say?"

I would point, and they would say, "Good . . . teeth." I would say, "Oh, boys and girls, you can do better than that! Let's try it again!" Then this thundering crowd would say, "GOOD TEETH!!" It was quite wonderful.

Although the ladies at the Good Teeth Council admonished us to keep to the script as written, we milked our laughs and our applause. What started as a twenty-five to thirty-minute show we worked up to forty-five minutes just on laughs alone.

We went from Buffalo to Pittsburgh with lots of little towns in between and finally ended up spending three months in Washington, DC. Since all our expenses were paid, we chose to stay at the Hay-Adams House. Every morning I would open my French windows and look at the White House and Lafayette Park. Because our work day was only from 8:30 a.m. to 2:30 p.m., every afternoon I would go horseback riding in Rock Creek Park. It was lovely.

Then we got on the cocktail circuit in Washington, which was a very lively scene now that the war was over. Because our car was always loaded up with the scenery and the Victrola and the puppets and the props, we were afraid to leave it parked at the hotel. So we persuaded the men who were escorting us to carry all this puppetry stuff over to the apartment where the party was. After a while we set up the puppet shows and began to do Jack and Judy for the cocktail party circuit. I think we were even in the society columns. "Can it really be true that two women are going to cocktail parties giving puppet shows?"

---

[2] The Council issued detailed instructions: "When you arrive with your show and there is some apparent misunderstanding because the sponsor didn't thoroughly read or understand some communication from the Council office let the following points be your guide . . . We give only three shows a day—no more than three as long experience in observing the health of our field people has proved that this is the maximum load . . . We have learned that this . . . allows for keeping our field workers healthier, more energetic and less fatigued . . . It also takes into account those nerve-wracking moments when the electrical current won't come on, a curtain cord breaks and must be repaired, the stage is cluttered and must be cleared . . . 101 unexpected things which just may come up . . . We keep our script unaltered. No changes in teaching, story content, humor or business without first consulting the Council office. Please consider that *it only takes overnight* for an air-mail [sic] special delivery to reach us. In a letter you can tell a full, clear, accurate story and give us time to assemble files and information better than we could when an unexpected long distance call comes in. Thus we can help you with your dilemma, situation, tragedy or problem much more intelligently as well as economically."

Camilla Tyler Lowman and Patricia Zipprodt with puppet for the Good Teeth Council. Credit: Billy Rose Theatre Division, The New York Public Library for the Performing Arts; © Estate of Patricia Zipprodt.

Somewhere along the way at one of these parties, I met a dashing lieutenant colonel in the US Cavalry assigned to the Pentagon. His name was Robert O'Brien, but all his friends simply called him O'Brien. He was long and lean, had blue eyes and reddish sandy hair, and loved horses, as I did.

One Sunday we went out to Fort Myer to go riding. It was O'Brien and four or five other army men and me. I had on jodhpurs, which is not what they wanted to see at Fort Myer. We were on the polo fields, a long expanse of turf with no holes, not like the Midwest where I was used to riding.

With two polo fields of safe ground in front of me, I let go, really flying. I suddenly realized I was in very silent territory. I didn't hear any other hooves. I looked back, and there was this cool lineup of soldiers on horseback in the distance, very small, like a Kurosawa film. And among them was one face that was bright red, and that was O'Brien, dying at this woman in jodhpurs racing off the trail. I had to turn around and make my apologies.

After our tour was over, I returned to Chicago and considered doing what was called art therapy. I wanted to put my social consciousness together with art some way or other. After getting back on my feet from an almost year-long siege of mononucleosis, I went to the Art Institute in the mornings, frequented an empty drawing board in a little annex in my father's office in the afternoons, and did legal research two or three nights a week for Luis Kutner, who was doing pioneering work as a human rights attorney and was on the advisory body of Amnesty International USA in the 1960s. I then took a job in the research department of the J. Walter Thompson advertising agency, making charts and graphs. The office was in the Wrigley Building, where I had auditioned for the Good Teeth Council.

I kept thinking, "I'm a painter." But I never really put it first. Other things, including social life, got put first and second. Painting was always third or fourth.

During this time, O'Brien was assigned to the Fifth Army at Fort Sheridan, about ten miles from my home in Kenilworth. We were definitely connected and resumed where we had left off. He was courting hard and heavy. He would come down every weekend. My mother and father adored him. My sisters adored him. Everybody adored him. I rather adored him.

But the idea of getting married did not sit well with me. The marriage I had looked at all my life was not inspiring.

My father said, "You know what will happen if you continue seeing him. You'll end up marrying him." "No, I won't." "How do you know?" "Because essentially he bores me," I said. "He's interesting now, Daddy, but not for a lifetime."

The reason I thought I had to stay home was because in my head I was becoming my sister Connie's protector. My sister Barbara had eloped, and sister Connie, who was in high school by now, would be by herself with all the abuse there if I left. There was enormous conflict between my father and my mother. My mother would be one person during the day and another at night. Connie was literally getting knocked about.

I was beginning to understand that there was a line of depression in my family that began with my father and showed up most severely with my Uncle Bob, who took his own life around this time. Every time my father went out the door to take a walk, I was convinced he wasn't coming back, not to abandon us but to finish himself off.

Barbara suffered bouts of depression and made suicide attempts for the next fifteen years until she too succeeded.

Suicide has been a dark theme in my life. Besides my uncle and my sister, two men in my life killed themselves. I've felt hounded over and over by people taking their lives. Was I jinxed? Was I a jinx? It was hard knowing that I was very prone and very vulnerable to it.

In February 1949, a two-week trip to Washington, Baltimore, and New York made me finally realize I had to get back to the East Coast. An ambition to design for the dance, both ballet and modern, had begun to percolate in my brain the previous fall. While I was in New York, I attended and sketched the ballet as often as my purse would allow.

I discussed this notion in fruitless detail with Mother upon my return. The emotional upheaval was so strong that I took refuge at the home of my friend Anne

Meacham's parents for two days following. My father was out of town, and I didn't bother broaching the subject with him for fear of a repeat performance. I was not emotionally equipped to take it twice.

The level of my art work was declining. My home life was terrible. Commuting two-and-half hours daily was ridiculous. I had to move into an environment less hostile to the fulfillment of my needs. I would go to New York and hunt for a job that would satisfy some of my creative needs and my intellectual curiosity and let me meet my living costs.

Any ambitions to design for dance faded. I would become a painter. I would devote evenings to training and development in fine art. Maybe over ten or fifteen years I could see some genuine progress. My goal became to have a one-person exhibition on Fifty-seventh Street by the time I was forty.

Wrenching away from Chicago and my home was one of the hardest and most major things I have ever done.

3

Getting Started in New York

I extracted myself from Chicago and got to New York. Wellesley had not equipped me for any employment, but if there was one thing I could do it was write. At Wellesley we wrote papers day and night.

And if there was one world I knew, it was the world of publicity and advertising from my father's business and from working at J. Walter Thompson in Chicago. My Uncle Bob had gone to New York from St. Louis to work in advertising about the same time my father started in Chicago. Before he started his own agency, Uncle Bob had worked for O. J. Gude, the advertising man credited with bringing electric lights to Times Square and coining the term "The Great White Way."

I presented myself at various agencies. At Benton & Bowles, I was told they wanted me to keep in touch with them frequently. "Let us know where you are working," they said, "and we might be able to hire you away."

I had an excruciatingly tense interview at the William H. Weintraub agency with a mogul named David Karr. He was Drew Pearson's legman and the speech writer for New York Mayor William O'Dwyer. At age thirty-one he was generally acknowledged to be one of the hottest guys in Manhattan.

He led me into the secret conference room, deep in plush carpeting, upholstered chairs, and walls in several tones of cocoa. He leaned back in his chair behind his desk and said, "Tell me about yourself." I did, courtesy of a sudden supply of adrenalin.

He started to tell me who the various heads of departments at WHW were. The art director turned out to be Paul Rand, famous for his magazine page layouts and covers. I had spent two hours studying his work at the Museum of Modern Art the day before.

He said, "We at William H. Weintraub demand three things: Brains! Guts! Imagination!" I sweetly acknowledged in my most subtle way, "Oh, Mr. Karr, that is the most wonderful slogan." I also acknowledged that I had the corner in all three rarities. He said, "I hope to see you again soon." But he meant, "Don't hold your breath." David Karr turned out to be involved all kinds of shady business deals and political intrigues and was eventually outed as a Soviet spy.

A friend took me to meet Deedee Dobyns, a well-known publicity woman, at a party at her ancient brownstone where many Siamese cats, artists, and people with Scots accents were running in and out. Deedee and I clicked famously. "The tough part of any publicity job," she said, "is the contacts." She had contacts galore, she assured me, and was going to set them up for me and introduce me as her protégée.

Despite Deedee's contacts galore, I ended up doing publicity for Long Island University and Ruby Foo's canned Chinese foods. I wrote press releases and had photographs taken and sent out to newspapers. I had the great pleasure of seeing my own words in the *Herald Tribune*—with the food editor's byline. She had changed my first sentence and my last sentence.

Was I unconsciously replicating my mother's time as a flapper/career woman in New York before she married my father? I wrote to my family, "I am happily ensconced in life here. Very busy, very productive, making some money, and becoming more and more spoiled by the quality of people I keep meeting. Can you conceive of a more satisfactory basis for existence?"

I was lucky enough to inherit an apartment at 43 Carmine Street from Anne Meacham,[3] who had been in first grade with me in Chicago and was making her way as an actress. It was right in the heart of Greenwich Village and unheated—it stayed that way for the six years I was there—but the rent, $16 a month, was infinitely affordable. Water was coming through the ceiling, and the hall smelled of cats. But there it was. I quit my publicity jobs and begin painting again. I took some temporary jobs at art galleries during the day and enrolled in a painting class at the New School at night.

The plaster at 43 Carmine Street was falling off the wall, so I took it all off and exposed the bricks before that was fashionable. I put the plaster into bags, and when any of my visitors left, I asked them to take out a bag. The best place for dumping it was by Our Lady of Pompeii Church at the end of the block. No one ever complained, and I never got caught.

I sanded and refinished the floors, painted everything white except the brick and the floors, and even managed to create a fireplace by taking out a coal stove. I chopped away everything behind it and covered the opening with firebrick. Then I cantilevered a big piece of slate over it for a mantel. This, plus opening the oven door, was my only source of heat.

I needed some place to paint, so I found a space in the basement and knocked that around, whitewashed it, and made that my studio. I was a busy girl.

My only place to bathe was a clawfoot tub in the middle of my kitchen. When company came, I put a lid with four legs over it and brought out the tablecloth, the silver, and the candelabra.

Carmine Street seemed friendly and safe when I moved in. When I was low on funds and couldn't get to the bank to cash a check, I would dip into my precious stash of four silver dollars and ask a neighbor to hold them in exchange for paper dollars. I later gave my neighbor-pawnbrokers paper dollars back, and they would return my silver ones, frequently with a special polish.

One of the quality people I met was the photographer Gjon Mili, then working for *Life* Magazine. He had pioneered portraying dancers and athletes in motion

---

[3]Anne Meacham (1925–2006) studied at the Yale School of Drama and at the Neighborhood Playhouse and made her New York stage début 1952 in a World War II comedy called *The Long Watch*, winning a Clarence Derwent Award as the most promising new female performer. She was known for her work in the plays of Tennessee Williams, who became a friend. Her last stage appearance was in Tom Stoppard's *Rosencrantz and Guildenstern Are Dead* in 1968. She appeared in the NBC soap opera *Another World*, 1972–82.

using stroboscopic lights and even photographed Picasso making drawings in the air holding a strobe light.[4]

Gjon was shooting a photographic essay for *Life* on the New York City Ballet, the company that George Balanchine and Lincoln Kirstein had hatched in 1948 and was just beginning to dry its wings. He was going quite frequently, and he took me along. So there I was, fifth row center at City Center on West Fifty-fifth Street, seeing this extraordinary young company.

I became fascinated watching the costumes designed by Barbara Karinska and fabricated in her own shop, one of the finest costume shops in the world. Karinska, as she was known, had come over from Russia, via Paris and London, in that same flow of Russian talent that brought Balanchine to America.

One evening in February 1951, they premiered Balanchine's *La Valse*, set to Ravel's music. Out came Tanaquil Le Clercq, Balanchine's muse and later his wife, in the most ravishing costume I have ever seen. It had a tight fitted bodice and a huge Romantic tutu skirt in layers and layers of silk net in different tones of pink and white. The skirt floated and fell and caught the light as she moved. The ensemble also wore different tones of silk net, layer after layer after layer, floating and falling.

A little light bulb went off. There it was, I thought, it is actually possible to paint with fabric. Everything I was trying to put together, the painting, the paper dolls, clicked into place. I knew for the very first time that I wanted to be a costume designer more than anything else in the world.

Tanaquil Le Clercq performing La Valse, *photographed by Gjon Mili; © Shutterstock.*

---

[4]Gjon Mili (1904–84) was born in Albania and emigrated to the United States in 1923 to study electrical engineering at MIT. He became a staff photographer for *Life* Magazine in 1939 and kept an office in the Time-Life Building until his death. How he and PZ met is not known. Mili was friends with the photographer Lisette Model, who taught at the New School, where Patricia was taking art classes, and they may have met there. Whether PZ and Mili's relationship was romantic or not (some of her friends believed it was, others did not), it was of great importance both personally and professionally.

But how was I going to get the training I needed? I thought of the Yale School of Drama and Carnegie Tech, which had the best design programs at the time, but I knew they would not be interested in me, a complete novice. Besides, where would I get the money?

A few nights later, I was at my painting class at the New School and bemoaning my fate to a friend named Ernie. "I just need to go and do this so badly," I said, "and I can't get any schooling."

After class, we were at the Cedar Tavern, where our group used to hang out and sit at the feet of Franz Kline and Robert Motherwell. He said, "You know, there's

Karinska's costume for La Valse, *which inspired Patricia to become a costume designer. Courtesy The Museum of the Fashion Institute of Technology and Marc Happel, New York City Ballet;* © *The Museum at FIT.*

a funny school I've heard about over on Twenty-fourth Street, in the Central High School of Needle Trades. It's called the Fashion Institute. I think the tuition is free."

I was there the next morning.

At the admissions office, they told me they only took students right out of high school. But I insisted on taking an application form. I returned it with a letter declaring I was "relatively sure of my ability" and "absolutely positive of my goals," which were "to acquire a sound and basic training in fashion and costume design for direct application as a future designer of women's apparel" and a "hopeful application" to be a "theatrical costumer, with a special and high interest in ballet."

I went back and forth with them. No free tuition for someone with a Wellesley degree, which they assumed meant I was rich. No, most Wellesley students had fathers who were Presbyterian ministers or came from overseas on scholarships.

I asked to take tests to prove my ability. I laid siege to them. I wore them down. And finally they gave in. They took me and another older woman as an experiment, and they gave me a full scholarship.

Because I already had all my academic courses, I could concentrate on what I had gone there to learn: handcrafts. I learned how to cut. I learned how to drape. I learned how to make patterns. I learned how to set in a zipper. I learned how to put on a collar. I had been sewing since I was a girl but only on a home Singer. I learned how to run an industrial machine. I learned more and more and more and more. I loved it.

I walked the twenty-three blocks to school in the snow and the rain. I brought my lunch. I was surrounded by hot rod kids who had competition instilled in them in their baby beds. I knew I was going to be a theatre designer. And it all stemmed from that evening watching Tanaquil Le Clercq from that seat in the eighth row center, rather than way in the back in the cheap seats.

One of the teachers, Miss McTavish, had henna red hair and wore lots of floral prints and very high Joan Crawford sandals. She spoke in a rasping but rousing falsetto and would rise up on her toes when she addressed the class. "Remember," she said, "if you are a designer, you will not only design during the day, you will think design, you will bathe in design. You will sleep design. You will dream design. You will eat design. Design will be all for you. If necessary, to get started, you will pick up pins for designers."

I thought, "Not me! I'm from Wellesley. I won't pick up any pins. No way will I pick up pins!"

Classes at the Central High School of Needle Trades were on the seventh and eighth floors. I kept going down the "up" staircase and getting demerits. If I was sick (I had a lot of strep throat at that time) I had to bring a note from home. I became my own mother. I would write to the dean and say, "Patricia Zipprodt couldn't go to school today because she had strep throat. Signed, Patricia Zipprodt."

The summer between my second and third terms, I needed to make money, so I applied for a job I had heard about to make sample dresses at a company called Swirl, owned by a fabulous man named Jack Nachman.

He and his brother had started making wraparound dresses in Philadelphia in the 1940s and patented their technique: a band of shirred fabric on the back and a signature button at the neck. Swirls were made in wonderful cotton prints and decorated with all kinds of trims. The basic shape stayed the same, a bodice and sleeves cut in one piece and a full gathered skirt. They always had pockets. They came in street length and a hostess gown length for around the house.

Jack Nachman must have thought, "Who is this strange woman? She wants to be a sample maker? What is this? A Wellesley girl?" I had all these lovely drawings in my portfolio which had nothing to do with Swirl dresses. It amused him so. He said, "How much do you want?" I said, "Well, $50." He said, "Well, why not! Be here tomorrow." He became one of my great backers.

I had a little teeny office with two sewing machines, a big cutting table, and a phone. I could turn out one Swirl sample dress a day, which was then sent down to be manufactured in Philadelphia. Sometimes I worked until nine o'clock. I stayed there all summer until I had to go back to school in the fall. And I worked there again at Christmas.

That same summer of 1953 Anne Meacham was working with a group called the Artists' Theatre, which had just been founded by an art dealer named John Myers as a way to promote his artists. He and his business partner, Tibor de Nagy, were nurturing a group of young artists, including Morris Louis, Ellsworth Kelly, Frank Stella, and Joan Mitchell, who became known as the Second Generation of Abstract Expressionists.

They also represented people like Nell Blaine, Helen Frankenthaler, Red Grooms, Kenneth Noland, and Larry Rivers. It was Myers's idea to get these artists and a group of young poets he named the New York School of Poets—Frank O'Hara, John Ashbery, Kenneth Koch—to write plays which he would produce with scenery by his New York School of Artists.

Myers and a director named Herbert Machiz, his friend and lover (he was fresh from one of the first Fulbright Fellowships after World War II to study theatre in Paris) produced Kenneth Koch's *Little Red Riding Hood,* written in the style of William Butler Yeats. Anne played Little Red bantering with the Wolf in the woods like Rosalind and Orlando in *As You Like It.*

It was staged at the Theatre de Lys on Christopher Street. That building had just been converted from a movie theatre and in many ways helped kick off the Off Broadway movement. It was just around the corner—well, seven corners—from me on Carmine Street. They didn't have anyone to do costumes, so I was asked to run up Anne's cape and hood on the sewing machine which was always out in my apartment. My mother was in town visiting, and she pitched in to help stitch the other costumes. "Oh, give me that thing, dear," she said. That may have been the first play I ever costumed, although there was not a mention of costumes or my name in the program.

Thank heaven my mother wasn't around on the day I was asked on the spur of the moment to pose nude for one of Robert Rauschenberg's cyanotypes on blueprint paper. To my horror, it was printed in *Life* Magazine.

Here's how that happened. I had a friend in Chicago named Wallace Kirkland who was a photographer for *Life.* He was in town doing a story on the New York School artists and was shooting Rauschenberg's cyanotype sessions at the artist's studio. He invited me to go along. They had a nude model, and Kirk and everybody there was having the best time looking at this woman posing on blueprint paper.

When her time was up, they wanted to do some more. Kirk said to me, "Do you pose?" I said, "Pose? Me?"

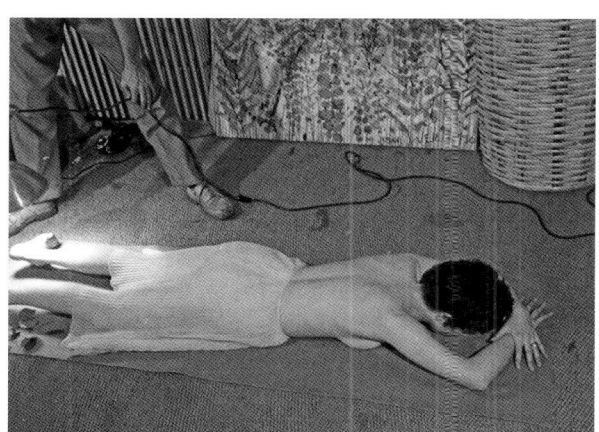

Patricia posing with Robert Rauschenberg for cyanotpyes, photograph by Wallack Kirkland; courtesy Wisconsin Historical Society.

I finally gathered up all my courage and lay myself face down on all these great sheets of blueprint paper while Bob Rauschenberg held this lamp above me. I kept thinking, "Oh, my god, what if my mother ever sees this and recognizes my feet, as only a mother would?" Rauschenberg liked my feet because they were triangular and very long. I got paid twenty-five or thirty dollars. That was my experience with the cutting-edge avant-garde.

Little Red Riding Hood wasn't my only foray into the fledgling Off Broadway scene. I helped Gerald Freedman costume an Equity Library Theatre production of *As You Like It*[5] in 1952 at a place called the Library Theatre in the Master Apartments, an Art-Deco skyscraper on the Upper West Side. Gerry was a recent graduate of Northwestern, where he studied with the brilliant acting teacher Alvina Krause. She ran a summer theatre in Eagles Mere, Pennsylvania, where she kept costumes in an old barn. We went and got what we needed, dragged them up several flights of stairs to my apartment. We washed and dyed them in my bathtub and spread them out on the fire escape to dry. The entire budget was around eleven dollars. At least this time I got a credit in the little mimeographed program.

One day, during my final term at FIT, I was walking down Fifth Avenue when I spotted the most elegant display in a corner window of Lord & Taylor's: three

---

[5] A talent scout from Columbia Pictures in Hollywood saw this production and recruited Gerald Freedman (1927–2020) to assist George Cukor on the film *It Should Happen to You* with Judy Holliday. When Holliday was cast in the Broadway production of *Bells Are Ringing*, she persuaded the director, Jerome Robbins, to bring Freedman back from Hollywood to assist him. This led to Freedman's career as a director, most noted for his productions of Shakespeare.

mannequins, just little gold knobs on the tops of dress forms, wearing the most beautiful camel hair coats I had ever seen. My eyes went out on stalks because they were so alive.

I thought, "Who did those?" They were three-dimensional. You could not detect any seams. I had been trying to do something like this at FIT by draping fabric on the bias and concealing the seams. I was not just painting with fabric, I was sculpting with fabric.

I went home, changed into my one best dress (a little black dress, of course), and went back to try on one of the coats. The label said "Charles James for William Popper." Charles James was an English couturier who had worked in Paris and London in the 1930s and by the 1940s had established himself as one of the most influential designers in New York. He won his first Coty Award in 1950.

My fourth and final term at FIT was meant to be an internship somewhere, probably unpaid. I was living on $900 a year. My rent was $16, I carried my sandwiches for lunch, and I didn't buy any clothes. I made fabulous soup out of anything I could get off the Bleecker Street market right around the corner. I was having a wonderful time.[6]

But I was running out of money, and I really needed something with remuneration. So I started a frantic campaign of writing letters to Charles James to get a job. I received frantic letters back from him. "Absolutely not! I have no money! I have too many people working for me now!" One of the problems was that people on the G.I. Bill who wanted to apprentice with Charles James were paying *him* to work there.

I was getting desperate. Gjon Mili sent me to see Sally Kirkland, the influential fashion editor at *Life* Magazine. She made calls to set me up with various women's clothing manufacturers. I drew up a whole line of clothes to show to them—dresses, coats, suits—and took my portfolio around to all these guys, although the last thing I wanted to do was work in one of those slave pits or have anything to do with Seventh Avenue.

A friend who worked at *Vogue* said, "Now don't go on any appointments until I find out what is happening for next fall." "I won't stir," I said. I would call her and say, "Do you know yet?" "No, I don't." Finally she called and said in ultra-hushed tones, "I've got it. I've got the news for fall. Can you hear me?"

"Yes, I can hear you."

"Remember this, though the news is not really out yet. *Red* is new."

Red is new? Red is a primary color, I thought. "Thank you very much," I said, as I hung up the phone.

This all must have happened around Christmas, because I was back working at Swirl. One day Jack said, "What is it that you want to do? Maybe I can help you. Obviously you're going to get where you want to get. What is your next step?"

---

[6]PZ's letters to her father during this time often included lighthearted but heartfelt pleas for funds. "All for now. Enough, I guess. Write me, send me MONEY! And tell me about you." "If you can see your way to it, I would like $150 as of April 1st. With heck & luck & good health, this might see me thru the better part of May." She always gave him a detailed accounting of her expenses and her income from temporary jobs. According to one of these accounts, she spent $16 a month on rent, $8.50 on electricity, and $11 on gas. When she had to see a doctor, it cost her $10. Despite her assertion that she bought no clothes (indeed she could have made them for herself), she did have shoes custom made, two pairs, one black, one brown at $75 a pair, which she paid for on time at $10 a month. So essentials were roughly $700, leaving enough for food and incidentals.

I said, "Jack, I've got to work for Charles James. I just have to work for Charles James." He said, "Well, you should work for Charles James." I said, "I've been writing him and writing him, and he says he has no money to pay me. He won't even see me."

Jack said, "How much will it cost you to live for six months?" I figured it up. He said, "I'll back you. You can work for him for nothing."

I found out where Charles James worked. His atelier was on Madison Avenue and Sixty-second Street. But he lived in a suite in the Sherry-Netherland a few blocks away, where he took two or three people to work for endless hours draping and pinning his original toiles.

I went there one morning about nine o'clock. I took my lunch and supper, my schoolbooks, and all seven newspapers of the time, the *New York Times*, the *Herald Tribune*, the *Journal-American*, the *World Telegram and Sun*, the *Mirror*, the *Daily News*, and the *Post*.

I knocked on the door. When someone answered, I said, "I am here to see Mr. James." "Do you have an appointment?" "No, I don't. I just want to see him. I'm Patricia Zipprodt. I've been writing to him."

Our writing had become voluminous because he was a passionate letter writer. He'd write to anybody. I had told him I'd work for nothing. I could hear Charles James say, "Oh, tell her there's nothing. I'm very sorry."

So I sat down on the carpet in the hall. I sat all day. I sat into the evening. People were passing in and out all day long. My presence was noticed. Charles James, however, wasn't passing in or out. Thinking back, they were very gracious to not just have me kicked out.

Finally, very late, the door opened, and Charles James peeked out. "Oh, all right, all right, come in." What was he going to do? "Be back tomorrow at eight o'clock," he said. "I don't know what you'll do, but until I decide, you can pick up the pins. Come back at eight o'clock." Instead of going home, I walked all night long. New York was mine that night. It was also still safe then. You could walk around all night in New York. I had a very peaceful night.

I must have stopped in a café somewhere. I know I bought a toothbrush and a lipstick in the pharmacy at the Sherry-Netherland the next morning, freshened up, and appeared at the door of Charles James's suite at eight o'clock in exactly what I had been wearing the day before. I was triumphant.

And I began my extraordinary year working for Charles James by picking up pins.

Charles scared me and all the other assistants. We always had to wait in line to get into the bathroom to throw up because he made us so nervous. I've never been so frightened in my life. I lost ten pounds.

I did progress beyond picking up pins. I progressed to the point where I was cutting and adapting Charles's clothes for Samuel Winston's mass-produced Seventh Avenue version. Charles was always changing, changing, changing. Every time he would change a seam by an eighth of an inch, I would have to rerecord it on the pattern. We were making changes so fast and so often, I needed a time record of each one. So I put the patterns with their notations into the time clock to stamp them. And we were always behind our deadline. I was quite active.

There sometimes would be eight of us sewing on one dress, like the famous Clover Leaf Dress. A new version was going under the machine for someone waiting to wear it to a ball. All eight of us would be following the hem around or pushing it under two machines at once to get it done. It was madness!

Charles would lock Miss Peel, the shop manager, in the closet a lot and then the key would go out the window onto Madison Avenue. The minute Charles left we would run down and get the key.

I left because I got fired by Samuel Winston. Charles, who was famously dismissive of mass-produced clothing, had contracted with Samuel Winston in 1954 for a collection of thirty designs over two years. But within a year Charles was convinced that Winston was stealing his designs and selling them unlabeled or with another designer's label. A huge lawsuit ensued.

So things were contentious between Charles James Inc. and Samuel Winston Inc. I was on the payroll for Samuel Winston, navigating between Charles's workshop on Madison Avenue and the Winston factory on Seventh Avenue.

I had worked until four in the morning one night and didn't get in to the Winston factory until five of nine. I was the last one in. Winston wanted to drop two people off the payroll, so they took the last two time cards for that day and mine was one of them. Charles wanted me back, but by that time I thought, "Enough of this craziness."

After I left Charles James, I decided I wanted to work with Pauline Trigère. Like Charles James, she was a great innovator and devoted to architectural silhouettes and punctilious tailoring. The Paris-born daughter of a Russian-Jewish tailor father and dressmaker mother, she had married a Russian-Jewish tailor who brought her to New York to escape Hitler. As well as liking her fabulous style, I liked her for having started out picking up pins in her parents' shop for a few pennies.

I didn't set up camp outside her door, but I did take measures to get to her. I was friends in Chicago with the brother of Ellie Rand Pope,[7] who was active in the Women's Board of St. Luke's Hospital and helped organize their annual benefit fashion show. Her husband was an investment banker, and she herself was a vice president of Stanley Korshak, Inc., the luxury goods department store that was one of the first to sell designer clothes. She was frequently nominated one of Chicago's ten best-dressed women. Naturally, she was friends with Pauline and usually wore one of her dresses to the show.

"Let me speak to Ellie," her brother said, "and maybe she'll speak to Pauline." So the introduction was made, and I went to see her. She couldn't believe that I had been paid by Charles. "He never pays people," she said. I think I finally brought her a pay envelope to prove it. I said, "See, he pays every other week at least." It was true. He was so busy paying lawyers to sue people that he used the funds he was supposed to pay us with to take Hattie Carnegie to lunch, and we'd have to wait.

Trigère put me to work as a sample hand in the sample room. What I wanted to do after my year with Charles James was to sketch for her or to assist her as she cut the actual fabric from bolts and draped and shaped it on live models. She was one of the few designers who did that. She never made preliminary toiles or paper patterns.

---

[7]The Rand in Ellie's name had transformed from her birth name Rosenbaum in a Chicago known for its discrimination against Jews. On her death in 1977, she was memorialized at the Fourth Presbyterian Church.

But that assisting job was occupied by someone who was really dug in. So I was back to being Bertha, the Sewing Machine Girl.[8] I was given little treasures like unmatchable chiffon plaids to cut into bias dresses, while Trigère gave instructions in French, even though she spoke perfectly good English.

There I was with pieces of chiffon floating around, with plaids that I could not make match on the bias or any other way, and I was not happy. The women in the workroom did not want me there. I wore earrings and lipstick and went out to smoke cigarettes. These ladies wore cotton smocks over their dresses and did beautiful handwork. They were working women in the old sense. I was not a sample hand and they knew it.

I got through about two weeks of this. Pauline was scheduled to go to the opera one evening after work. The women were running up a coat for her. It was getting near half past five and the others were leaving. She asked me if I would stay behind and put a hem in for her. Of course I said yes.

Now, I was a well-trained FIT person. I knew very well the difference between stone chalk and wax chalk and what you use them on. But here was someone who was scaring me, and after I picked the hem on this off-white silk moire full-length opera coat, I marked it with wax.

Now if you do not know, for silks you use stone chalk and for woolens you use wax, because the heat of the iron will make the wax just absorb. On silk it makes a grease mark. When I got home, I thought, "Oh, my god! What have I done?"

And I never went back. She still has my scissors. I wrote her a note saying, "Dear Miss Trigère, I have so enjoyed and learned so much from my time with you, but I do feel that since my interest is in the theatre and going into theatre design that I must now study theatre. Sincerely yours . . ."

After my abrupt departure from Pauline Trigère, I went down to visit my parents in Naples, Florida, where they had moved after my father retired. I suppose they still hoped that Little Patty would settle down with the right man, so they introduced me to a man named Bob Harris who had several occupations. One of them was wrestling with alligators in the Everglades. When movie producers needed some swamp work, they'd phone up Brother Harris.

He owned horses, and we used to ride together a lot. We went out into the swamps and spent days going from place to place in those wonderful glades. We fell madly and passionately in love. Bob wanted to marry me and have children.

I didn't really have time to be thrown into a quandary by this proposal because shortly after I returned to New York he was found dead in his home with a shotgun lying beside him. It was never clear if it were suicide or foul play, but suicide was strongly suspected.

I don't think I had thought through what married life with Bob would have been like. I might have become a buyer for a Miami clothing manufacturer. Who knows? In any event, this incident brought any thoughts of marriage and a family to a screeching halt. It strengthened my resolve to pursue a career on my own in Manhattan, whatever the odds were for a single woman. I became even more

---

[8] *Bertha, the Sewing Machine Girl* is a 1926 American film directed by Irving Cummings and written by Gertrude Orr, based on a 1906 play of the same title by Theodore Kremer.

convinced that what I really wanted to do was design for the theatre, so my next quest was, "How?"

Anne Meacham told me I needed to get into the scene designers' union, United Scenic Artists, known as USA Local 829, if I expected to work professionally as a costume designer. When I went to see them at their offices in the Hotel Belvedere on West Forty-eighth Street, I was told I had to take an all-day exam. There would be a thirty-minute break for lunch. I said, "What do I need to know?" They said, "The entire history of costume." I said, "Okay, and what else?"

Part of the examination consisted of making color sketches. I would have to bring a drawing board, watercolor paper, pencils, erasers, watercolors, brushes, a water container—in other words, everything I would need to design on the spot.

I wasn't daunted by the prospect of drawing then and there, but I hadn't studied costume history at FIT, the way students from Yale or Carnegie Tech had. I would need time to study. I went to Gjon Mili moaning, "What will I do? What will I do?" He said, "How long do you need to study?" "The exam's in June, two-and-a-half months away, and I'll need all that time." "How much will it cost you to live for two-and-a-half months?" "Oh, about $300." "Come to the studio tomorrow and get it."

When I got to Gjon's studio near the Flatiron Building, there were three one-hundred-dollar bills waiting. Much, much later, when I was able to get $300, I said, "Here, I want to pay you back." He said, "Oh, no, no, no! You do not pay me back. You do it for someone else." Since then I have said the exact same thing to other young people I've been able to help.

I went to the New York Public Library and started cranking my way through the history of costume. As I studied an epoch, I would draw all the garments and the accessories and the hair styles. I learned by drawing. This was what I got from Wellesley; I could pack it in. I started with the Egyptians. I got to the 1920s by the night before the exam. I thought, "If they ask for the thirties, forget it, I'll flunk!"

I needed references for the union committee. I went to Gus Tyler, who was vice president in charge of politics for the International Ladies' Garment Workers' Union. I had met him when I was at FIT and organized rental costumes from Brooks Costumes for a fortieth anniversary celebration of Local 91 in December 1953. It included a musical panorama, in the style of *Pins and Needles*,[9] of fashions from the previous four decades. That time my name was in the program. Gus wrote a letter saying I was always on time, responsible, and a good union person.

Gjon Mili called up his good friend Boris Aronson—in my presence—and asked if he would look at my portfolio and decide if he could write a letter. "You are under no obligation to do anything," he said. "If you do not like what you see, I will understand."

Boris Aronson was at this time one of the great masters of American stage design. The son of the chief rabbi of Kiev, he had come over in 1923 and started with the Yiddish theatres and then became involved with the legendary Group Theatre in the 1930s. At the time I first met him, he was one of the most important Broadway

---

[9]*Pins and Needles*, a musical revue by Harold J. Rome, Mark Blitzstein, Emmanuel Eisenberg and others, was produced on Broadway by the International Ladies' Garment Workers' Union in 1937; it ran for 1,108 performances.

One of Patricia's study drawings for the union exam. Credit: Billy Rose Theatre Division, The New York Public Library for the Performing Arts; © Estate of Patricia Zipprodt.

designers, having recently designed Arthur Miller's *The Crucible* and Tennessee Williams's *The Rose Tattoo*. I couldn't have imagined then that only a decade later we would be working together on *Fiddler on the Roof*.

I took my portfolio to his apartment on Columbus Circle, which was in complete disarray because he was in the midst of moving. He took a look, composed two sentences in pencil, and asked me if I would like to type it up so I could have a copy. I practically tripped over all the boxes and furniture rushing to the typewriter. Here's what he said: "I have studied the work-drawings and costume designs of Miss Patricia Zipprodt and I like them very much. They show talent and good professional craftsmanship."

When I brought it back, he couldn't find a pen. He rummaged around in the desk and brought out a bottle of red India ink and a drawing pen. It was an old bottle and in the process of dipping the pen, he spilled red ink on himself. I was standing there thinking, "I've done this to Boris Aronson!" The next day I sent him red carnations to say thanks.

First wax on Pauline Trigère's coat and then red ink on Boris Aronson. Would I leave a trail of destruction wherever I went?

When I applied to the union in the spring of 1954, I had to send a letter summarizing all my education and experience up to that time. It was very satisfying to think about all the paths I had traveled since I first started taking art classes at the Art Institute of Chicago as a twelve-year-old in 1937.

I had designed and executed costumes for myself and other girls for the annual dance festivals at Wellesley. I had painted a mural at Wellesley. I had organized costumes for plays and pageants at a Wisconsin girls camp during summers between my college years. I had flirted with medical illustration and art therapy. I had toured with a puppet show, which involved making costumes and painting scenery. I had worked as a freelance artist and illustrator in Chicago. I had studied painting at the Art Students League and the New School. I had those two decisive experiences: seeing Karinska's costumes at the New York City Ballet and Charles James's coats in the window of Lord & Taylor. I had barreled my way into FIT and the ateliers of

Charles James and Pauline Trigère. Although there had been detours and false starts, everything now was clearly leading me to a career as a professional costume designer in the New York theatre.

Most people who take the union exam fail it the first time around and take it a second and even third time. In the middle of the summer, I got a letter: "Dear Miss Zipprodt: It is with pleasure that the Costume Examining Committee informs you that you are one of three to pass the recent examination. Your average was 85.74%. On recommendation of the committee you were elected to membership in the Costume Associates of the United Scenic Artists at a meeting of the membership on July 6, 1954."

All I had to do now was borrow $500 to pay for my union dues, present myself for my obligation oath at the next meeting on August 2 at eight o'clock in the evening, and I was ready to join the ranks of officially unemployed theatrical labor.

4

Making My Way on Broadway

When people say to me, "After I get my union card, it will all be different," I say, "No, no, no, you'll just be out $500, and you'll be more unemployed than ever." After I was initiated into the union, I really was just floating. I didn't know what I was doing.

A friend told me about a possible job at ABC Television. Television was just starting to make its way into American homes and minds, and although some shows were being filmed in Hollywood, New York was headquarters for the three networks jockeying for dominance.

They all had seven or eight half-hour-slots to fill each night, usually with live studio shows. A fifteen-minute news segment at 7:00 p.m. or 7:15 p.m. led into the evening's lineup: musical and comedy variety shows, game shows, and wholesome family situation comedies like *Ethel and Albert*. Many of the shows had originated on radio. There were also hour-long drama anthology series, presenting either original plays or scripts adapted from Broadway or films. New opportunities were opening up for designers.

I made an appointment with James H. McNaughton,[10] head of the design department for ABC's studios in his office in the Paramount Building in Times Square. I knew I had to have a portfolio, but I had never done a show of any kind, only projects. So I scraped together whatever I could get my hands on: *The Country Wife*, my project for the union exam; lots of nontheatrical fashion stuff from FIT; the plates I had made to study the history of costume for the exam; and some watercolors from when I used to go around New York painting city scenes. That was all I had, plus a few letters of recommendation.

McNaughton didn't even look at my portfolio. He said, "Can you start Monday? We need somebody to help Al Lehman on *The Voice of Firestone*." Al Lehman had done some costume designing Off Broadway but was stepping more firmly into this new medium. He eventually made his way to Hollywood where he created Angela Lansbury's look as Jessica Fletcher in *Murder She Wrote*.

---

[10] James H. McNaughton (1912–79) studied architecture at Carnegie Tech and came to New York after graduation in 1935 to be a theatre designer. He began designing for television in 1945 and became ABC's first art director in 1954. He pioneered the use of illusionistic sets that created the effect of distance and height in a small studio space. He later settled in Palm Springs, California, where he designed mansions for wealthy clients.

The Voice of Firestone was broadcast live every Monday. It was wonderful fun because of all the famous Metropolitan Opera stars on it: Risë Stevens, Roberta Peters, Robert Merrill, Eleanor Steber, Patrice Munsel, Jerome Hines. I fell in love, at a distance, with Cesare Siepi. Its theme song, "If I Could Tell You of My Devotion," was written by Idabelle Firestone, the wife of the show's sponsor. It was quite popular in its day. I can still sing the opening refrain.

I only worked on Mondays, the day of the broadcast, for which I was paid $27.50 take-home, the union minimum. I actually lived on that for a while.

My job was quite simple. I made lists of clothing pieces we would need, collected shoes, and helped Al gather wardrobe from Brooks Costumes. There was usually a period of three hours in the afternoon when I covered for him at the studio while he was still at Brooks getting the last stuff out.

Union rules said I couldn't get the costumes ready for the performers until the people in the wardrobe union came on closer to air time. So if I didn't have anything to do, I would go to Durland's Riding Academy, which was in the same building, and go horseback riding in Central Park. That cost me about half my salary for the week. One time the producer and director, Charles Polachek, was looking out the door when I walked by on my horse. He said, "Oh, my god, don't fall off! We're on the air at 8:30!" Polachek was quite a figure in the opera world and was one of the founders of the NBC Opera Theatre.

I did this for about half a year. Every now and then Al would take a vacation or go to the coast for a week, and I would do *The Elgin Hour*, an anthology drama series sponsored by the Elgin Watch Company. I also worked on a series of five-minute commercials that Les Paul and Mary Ford, the famous husband-and-wife guitar and singing team, did for Listerine mouthwash. It was called *Les Paul and Mary Ford at Home* and was filmed at their home in New Jersey.

First there would be a scene of a suburban wife trying to make her marriage better by using Listerine to banish either her or her husband's bad breath. Then we'd be in Les and Mary's kitchen or on their patio. Les played the guitar, while Mary sang their overdubbed arrangements of "I'm Sitting on Top of the World" or "How High the Moon" as she put away groceries or arranged flowers. I would go pick out Les's coats and Mary's dresses from Ohrbach's or some place on Seventh Avenue who would work with us for the credit. One time I was doing hats, and I had both my hands full with Sally Victor hat boxes and couldn't flag a cab.

All this television work was big excitement. It was like opening a new show every week. I wasn't designing things; I was shopping things. But I was learning so much. It was another long apprenticeship, like working for Charles James or Pauline Trigère. One way or another, you're just picking up pins.

A few years later, I was invited to be in the NBC control booth in May 1956, when a live condensed version of the 1944 Broadway musical *Bloomer Girl* was broadcast. Barbara Cook played the daughter of a hoopskirt manufacturer in pre–Civil War Massachusetts, who rejects her father's product in favor of comfortable bloomers. She further defies convention by refusing to marry her Southern suitor until he frees his slaves.

The show was televised in what was then called "compatible color," meaning if you weren't one of the lucky few owning color sets, you could see it on your regular television in black and white. I couldn't believe how beautiful television color was in its pure and perfect state in the control room. The reds particularly came across so vibrant and juicy they gave me goose bumps. I saw that there was room for real design work in the eventual color medium.

By this time, however, I was picking up pins in the theatre, which is where I really wanted to be. Because I was in and out of the costume shops, I became visible, and people knew I was looking for work as an assistant. Once I started moving, I was moving, because good assistants are hard to find.

I had a little connection with William and Jean Eckart, a husband-and-wife design team who had been working on Broadway since the early fifties. They mostly designed sets but occasionally also did costumes and sometimes even lighting. Jean was from Kenilworth, and her sister and I had gone to New Trier High School together.

Jean took me on as her costume assistant for *Reuben, Reuben*, a musical by Marc Blitzstein with Eddie Albert. The influential producer Cheryl Crawford was mounting it. It got terrible reviews when it was trying out at the Shubert Theatre in Boston and closed there after about ten performances.

That was in the fall of 1955. The summer before I had my first real theatre job, assisting Robert Fletcher[11] at the first season of the American Shakespeare Festival in Stratford, Connecticut. Lawrence Langner, one of the founders of the Theatre Guild, had envisioned a home for Shakespeare in America after returning from a trip to the Shakespeare Memorial Theatre in Stratford-upon-Avon, England. And he was aware of what Tyrone Guthrie had started in Stratford, Ontario. He enlisted his heavyweight theatrical friends like Lincoln Kirstein and Roger Stevens to help fund it and commissioned a faux Globe to be built on the banks of the Housatonic River. It looked a little like an Elizabethan theatre on the outside, but on the inside it was a huge Broadway-style proscenium house.

It operated under a summer theatre contract, so we were working around the clock for nothing, although it didn't matter at the time. I worked eighteen hours a day for fifty dollars a week, my permanent salary for quite a while. I was getting good at being an assistant.

The theatre wasn't finished. The stage and lobby and box office were fine, but the roof over the backstage had mysteriously not gotten done. What are actors, anyway? Let it just rain on them. Their clothes were soaked. The Green Room was swamped.

The actors were wonderful: Raymond Massey as Brutus, Roddy McDowell as Octavius, and Jack Palance as Cassius in *Julius Caesar*; Massey as Prospero in *The Tempest*, with Roddy McDowell as Ariel. A young Canadian actor named Christopher Plummer played Mark Antony in *Julius Caesar* and Ferdinand in *The Tempest*. I remember thinking, "Who *is* this man?" He walked in a nimbus of light. He just radiated "star."

---

[11]Robert Fletcher (1922–2021) designed sets and costumes for Broadway, opera, ballet, and television productions in New York before moving to Hollywood to concentrate on television and motion pictures. He is best known as the designer of the first four Star Trek features: *Star Trek: The Motion Picture, The Wrath of Khan, The Search for Spock,* and *Star Trek: The Voyage Home*. His designs helped to establish the style for the Klingon and Vulcan characters in those films and beyond.

That first summer was ill-fated. It just never worked. But I went back the next season to assist Rouben Ter-Arutunian,[12] when John Houseman and Jack Landau had taken over. Rouben is one of the best. I loved his work; I adored him. We were a very good team. I was always good at interpreting his sketches. I had a great time getting swatches; I could really bring a wide range of things for him. I turned into a very good shopper for him.

Rouben was always back in New York working on the next show, leaving me to be what Boris Aronson in his Russian accent called "the wictim"—the person on every show who gets the blame for whatever isn't working. Boris's rule for the theatre was, "Don't be the wictim." I became the wictim in the basement.

One day, we were having a horrendous dress rehearsal, and I had just had it with John Houseman and Jack Landau. I couldn't stand one more minute. Someone said, "Why don't you take a tranquilizer?" Miltown, the first tranquilizer, had just been introduced in May and was becoming the thing, especially in Hollywood. I said, "I don't take tranquilizers!" "Are you sure? It will calm you down." "Give me a tranquilizer!" I said.

So I swallowed this tranquilizer and in about thirty minutes I began to think, "To hell with this, I don't belong here." I left the theatre, walked into Stratford, and headed to the only beauty parlor in town. I got my hair washed and set. I sat under the dryer. And then I returned to bedlam. And I have never taken a tranquilizer since.

Soon after finishing at Stratford, a huge package arrived at my door. Inside was the most beautiful handbag I had ever seen, a giant Italian model in a wonderfully buttery saddle-brown. It was from Rouben in thanks for the summer's work. I carried it daily and slept with it by my head so I could feel it and smell it. It was an unusual and totally unexpected gesture.

I was desperate to assist Irene Sharaff because she, like Karinska and Charles James, was the finest designer I knew at the time. I found her work stronger and more impassioned than either Motley or Lucinda Ballard, the other excellent designers of that period. But just for my own spirit I liked Miss Sharaff's sharp attack on what she was doing.

She had been working on Broadway since the thirties and in Hollywood since the forties. She won Academy Awards for *An American in Paris* in 1951 and in 1956 for *The King and I*, which she had originally designed for Broadway. She also designed for the American Ballet Theatre and the New York City Ballet.

I started another one of my letter-writing campaigns. She was very nice. She would always write back, which is not easy to do when you're busy as she was. She said, "No, I'm sorry, I have an assistant, thank you." This was back in the day when designers did only one show at a time, not like now, when they are juggling several

---

[12]Rouben Ter-Arutunian (1920–92) grew up in Paris and Berlin, studied art and music in Berlin and Vienna, and designed in Berlin, Vienna, Dresden, and Paris, before moving to New York in 1951, where he designed for Broadway, opera, ballet, and modern dance. He created the sets for George Balanchine's *Nutcracker* in 1964, when it moved from City Center to the New York State Theatre at Lincoln Center and became an annual winter attraction for the New York City Ballet.

projects at once. Ann Roth[13] was working with her all the time, out on the coast and in New York, so I couldn't get the job.

Gjon Mili had photographed two of Irene Sharaff's shows for *Life* in 1951, *A Tree Grows in Brooklyn* and *The King and I*. Now he was in Hollywood for *Life* photographing the film *Guys and Dolls* with Marlon Brando and Frank Sinatra while Irene was there working on the costumes. He took her to lunch and mentioned—at my prompting—that I had been bombarding her with letters. She said, "Oh, yes, I remember her, she came in first on the union exam." She had been one of the judges, and that's how I found out that I had made the top score.

In the fall of 1956, Irene Sharaff had taken on two projects despite her usual practice: Leonard Bernstein's *Candide*, which Tyrone Guthrie was directing, with sets by Oliver Smith, and *Happy Hunting*, a new Ethel Merman musical. Ann Roth would be assisting on *Candide*, so she needed another assistant for *Happy Hunting*. She remembered me from her lunch with Gjon Mili and called and asked if I would come by and show her my portfolio.

At that time, my hair was almost black, which I thought was a wonderful color for me, and I wore it long and straight back with an enormous bun. I was Miss Dancer, the ballet look. It was pouring rain when I went. Miss Sharaff opened the door, and there she was with her long black hair straight back and in a bun, looking like the Degas little dancer. We both looked at each other. She was dry, and I was wet and had the portfolio, but that was the only difference.

She looked at my portfolio and really liked it. She said, "I'm not altogether sure about the schedules. Do you have anything else that you might be doing if this doesn't work?"

As it happened, a good Chicago friend, Geoffrey Barr, who was working as Cheryl Crawford's personal assistant, had suggested me for a Broadway show Miss Crawford was producing called *The Girls of Summer* by N. Richard Nash, starring Shelley Winters. Geoffrey and I had reconnected when I assisted Jean Eckart on Miss Crawford's ill-fated production of *Reuben, Reuben*. I think he probably told her, "She's just getting started, she won't cost very much."

Soon after, Geoffrey went to work for CBS as head of their story department and then became a personal manager in Los Angeles for a number of stars, including Constance Bennett, Jean Simmons, Nancy Walker, Elaine Stritch, Charles Nelson Reilly, and Paul Lynde.

When I told Miss Sharaff I had been offered a Broadway show, but I'd really rather work for her, she said, "Are you crazy? You don't turn down a Broadway show." I said, "I've thought and thought and thought about it. If I'm going to do Broadway shows, I will get other offers. Once I start doing them, I'm not going to be working for you. If I don't get other Broadway shows, then I'd better be a good

---

[13]Ann Roth (b. 1931) studied theatre design at Carnegie Mellon and intended to be a scene designer until she met Irene Sharaff, who asked her to go to Hollywood to assist with costumes on five films. She then assisted Sharaff on five Broadway productions before starting on her own. As of 2021, she has designed 119 films and 112 Broadway productions. She has been nominated for an Academy Award for best costume design five times and won twice, for *The English Patient* (1996) and *Ma Rainey's Black Bottom* (2020). She has twelve Tony nominations, winning for *The Nance* in 2013.

assistant, and I should be working for you." I really felt working for Irene Sharaff was something I should do. Broadway would have to wait.

So she put me to work on *Happy Hunting*. It was to be Ethel Merman's triumphant return to Broadway after her two-year run in *Call Me Madam* had ended in 1952. David Merrick, on his way to becoming the most powerful and notorious producer on Broadway, had withdrawn as producer—apparently he didn't think it was going to be a big money-maker—so Jo Mielziner, who was to design the settings and the lighting, took over as producer as well.

Jo was one of the best-known and most prolific designers on Broadway at that time, probably rivaled only by Oliver Smith. His designs for such monuments as *A Streetcar Named Desire*, *Death of a Salesman*, *South Pacific*, *Carousel*, *Guys and Dolls*, and *The King and I* were legendary. At the time he was working on *Happy Hunting* he already had six shows running on Broadway.

But as I was soon to discover, even a designer who could write his ticket on Broadway periodically encountered tough financial sledding. Jo had an expensive studio and apartment to maintain in the Dakota on Central Park West. Although it was unusual for a designer to produce, Jo had to look for ways to provide himself with more income sources.

Working for Sharaff, I had to go to Mielziner's studio many times to check all the fabrics under Jo's lights and gels to make sure they were okay. I soon became friends with most of his young staff, many of whom would become important players in the theatre in their own right: Ming Cho Lee as a designer, Paul Libin as a producer and manager, Hugh Hardy as a theatre architect, and Word Baker as a director.

Word's first name was really Charles but when he came up from Texas he had to stop using it to avoid confusion with a well-known New York theatrical agent. So he took his mother's maiden name. Ming and Hugh did lots of drafting for Jo. Paul carried lots of coffee. Word was Jo's secretary as well as casting director on *Happy Hunting*.

Happy Hunting was a vehicle for Ethel Merman, and she was in the driving seat from day one. Howard Lindsay and Russel Crouse, who had written *Call Me Madam*, her big hit with songs by Irving Berlin, wrote it for her to bring her out of domestic retirement in Colorado with her husband Robert Six, the president of Continental Airlines. He had married a Broadway star, and he wanted her to stay a Broadway star.

Lindsay and Crouse's script was to capitalize on the hoopla surrounding the engagement and April 1956 marriage of Prince Rainier of Monaco and Grace Kelly, the Hollywood star originally from Philadelphia. Merman was to play a Philadelphia society hostess who is snubbed by not being invited to the wedding. She goes to Monaco anyway with a scheme to marry her daughter to a down-on-his-luck duke and upstage the princely nuptials.

Abe Burrows, one of the co-authors of *Guys and Dolls*, was the director. Fernando Lamas, the Argentine actor famous in Hollywood for his Latin-lover roles, was to play the Duke of Grenada.

Irene designed some magnificent high-society Philadelphia clothes for Ethel to wear in the scenes when she crossed the Atlantic on the *Queen Elizabeth*. Many of them were satin-on-silk gowns that went clear to the floor. They were all executed by Miguel Ferreras, who had been one of Charles James's assistants, in his own shop on Fifth Avenue near the Sherry-Netherland.

Ferreras was just starting out on what was to be to a major career before he got deflected by a series of dubious marriages to international heiresses. But at this point he was vibrant and knew how to cut fabric like an angel. These gorgeous clothes had such great style.

When they were completed, Ethel invited a very chic gathering to Ferreras's atelier to show off these gowns. Abe Burrows, Lindsay and Crouse, producers, lawyers, wives, husbands, secretaries, maids, everyone who was important in the theatre turned out for this great display. Champagne flowed. Irene and Miguel solved the dressing problems, while I ran around holding gloves and jewelry and watching it all.

There were "oohs" and "aahs" and "Oh, Irene, my god, you have outdone yourself!" I watched Burrows congratulate Sharaff over and over again. I thought to myself, "When I grow up, this will happen to me. My designs, my clothes, will receive this sort of acclaim."

It was clear that Irene's real interest was *Candide*, one of the most brilliantly designed shows I've known. Her number one assistant, Ann Roth, was working on it, and it was being built in the number one shop, Karinska's. Except for Ethel's, gowns, Brooks Costumes was cracking out *Happy Hunting* on a skimpy budget of $300,000 for maybe 300 costumes and 200 pairs of shoes.

Happy Hunting was trying out in Philadelphia, while *Candide*, a big heavy musical, was having trouble landing in Boston. Karinska was making such glorious costumes that they couldn't be ready in time. So Boston was hysterical to have Irene get there.

We were at the Forrest Theatre in Philadelphia having a most unhappy series of technical-dress rehearsals. Ethel and Fernando were on shipboard in their respective cabins, and there was a knee-high Art Deco railing between them. Abe Burrows didn't want Merman to open the little gate to visit Lamas. He wanted her to leap coyly over the railing. She could not manage this in the floor-length gowns, so Burrows ordered them to be cut off to street-length. Ethel went right along with this because she liked her legs. She had good legs.

These were the gorgeous ball gowns they had all adored in New York while they were drinking champagne, and now they were either being shortened or eliminated altogether. Every time somebody came on, something major had to be done to the costume.

Irene sat in the back of the house all by herself in her black hat and her black suit for three days and three nights listening and watching Abe Burrows destroy, cut apart, and decimate the entire wardrobe. I sat about six seats from her. No one would get near her while this was going on.

The show was in trouble. It wasn't gelling. Ethel knew it and was becoming difficult. Fernando was getting difficult. And he and Ethel were getting difficult with each other.

When a show is in trouble, the first thing people get their hands on are the costumes. They're much easier to destroy than the scenery, much easier to get rid of than a song. I learned the truth of this sometime later, and it crystalized into my mantra, "If the song doesn't work, change the dress."

Now I do everything I can to avoid those kinds of collisions. You have to get your nose bumped before you really learn it and understand it. It takes a long time of working before you can really get your ego out of it. You never can completely, but we have to accommodate so many people.

Irene sat there saying not a word. The space around her was getting wider and wider because of the vibrations coming out of this small person. The night before the last technical preview, she was leaning against a pillar in the back of the house on the stage left side. I was standing in the back near her.

Burrows, who usually sat on the aisle stage right of the house, came across the orchestra and was coming up the stage left aisle. Because Irene was slightly behind the pillar, he didn't see her until it was too late. He realized he would have to pass madame.

He had a kind of fleshy face, and it went white. As he went by, she said, "Abe, if I had a rusty razor, I'd castrate you." And that was the only thing I know that she said to him.

Irene went off to Boston the next day and left me to phone in reports to her every night. It was a nightmare. I babysat with that show night and day for three weeks. I babysat every change in Ethel's wardrobe, as her skirts went up and then came down again.

I found myself having to go out and get things and have them go on stage without any consultation with Irene. If someone wanted fly's wings on a suit, he got fly's wings. If Abe wanted anything, if Lindsay and Crouse wanted anything, if anybody who had any clout at all wanted anything, they got it. Because the show was so expensive, so big, so out of control, and so uninteresting that all the greatest talents of the Broadway musical theatre couldn't make it work. Anybody who wanted anything could get it, so long as there was money to pay for it.

Then Fernando started to get in on the action. If he saw that Ethel got a red dress in a scene, he would turn up the next day in pure untouched white shoes. Of course, all he had to do was to cross his legs and move his foot and he took the scene.

Ethel would see this, and she would get white shoes. Then Fernando wanted a blue jacket. I took him to Harry Fiorentino, whose tailoring shop was just a few blocks up from the Forrest Theatre on Walnut Street. Fiorentino had twenty-six tailors working for him and was famous for making clothes for Hollywood stars, business executives, doctors, and athletes. We got Fernando blue Fiorentino jackets. No one could control either Fernando or Ethel, and they kept putting everything on me.

By this time, Irene was hiding up in Boston because Karinska had delivered five days late and they were hardly able to open. She couldn't be found by phone. I was forced as an employee of all these people to undo what was left of Miss Sharaff's work.

Should I have resigned and just stranded everyone? I didn't. I stuck with it and tried to protect Irene's work and interpret it through me.

During the Philadelphia tryouts, Ming Cho Lee, Hugh Hardy, Paul Libin, Word Baker, and I attended the late-night sessions at the Warwick Hotel down the street on Rittenhouse Square, where everyone drank Scotch and ate chicken sandwiches on white bread with no crusts. We assistants sat without opening our mouths, taking notes for our elders, while Jo, Lindsay and Crouse, Abe Burrows, and Miss Merman's agent, and one time even her lawyer, went on hour after hour.

One night Abe Burrows turned to Lindsay and Crouse and said, "What this show needs is the best damn play doctor in the business. Unfortunately for you guys he's not available because right now he's sitting in this very hotel room trying to figure out how to direct your show!"

Ming, Paul, Hugh, Word, and I were flabbergasted. Here before us sat the gods of the Broadway Theatre, the giants who could do no wrong, and they couldn't figure out how to make this musical work. Of course we knew exactly what to do. When the meetings broke up, we would gather together and say, "Wait till we do this. We'll do it so much better, because we've seen how they do it wrong!"

After *Happy Hunting*, I realized I had to call a halt to my time of assisting. I had taken the cream of those experiences and was at the point where I was learning less and less for the amount of time invested. I had to go and do it myself.

What I didn't realize was that I had only been trained for very large shows, Shakespeare and huge musicals, because that's when designers hire assistants. They don't hire them for little shopping shows if they're going to Macy's to pick things out. This was where I would have to begin.

The summer before I went out-of-town with *Happy Hunting*, I was able to make one important improvement in my life. After six years on Carmine Street, I found a new apartment I could afford on Central Park South, near Columbus Circle. Carmine Street had served a good purpose, but it had had it, and so had I. There were too many drug dealers pushing to the kids on the street.

I had one terrifying experience when I was coming in late one night. A man followed me, pulled a switchblade, and held it against my stomach as he backed me against the wall. Giving myself up for dead anyway, I figured I had nothing to lose, so I swung at his face and screamed for my life. He ran away and disappeared into the subway.

It took me a week before I could sleep in my apartment. I stayed with friends and took something to calm myself down. The day after my escape I went into hysterics at Brooks Costumes. Jimmy Strook, the head of Brooks, had to give me a double shot of Scotch. And Jimmy Strook wouldn't give the time of day to his brother.

The new apartment had loads of work space for me and for an assistant, if I ever got enough work to hire someone. It was sizable enough for a good-sized cocktail party. It was chic enough to do some expensive dressmaking, should the opportunity arise. Garbage was actually collected, and there was heat and constant hot water. I could take a shower!

As I contemplated my next steps, I ran into Sherwood Arthur, a roaming director who was planting himself in the newly bustling Off Broadway scene. Sherwood always had a bunch of scripts under his arm, sat a lot in the Russian Tea Room, and seemed to know everything that was going on.

He was friends with Carmen Capalbo and Stanley Chase, a director and producer who had met as young story editors with the CBS drama series *Studio One*. They had scored a big success in 1954 by persuading Lotte Lenya, Kurt Weill's widow, to give them the rights to stage *The Threepenny Opera* at the Theatre de Lys, and they persuaded Lenya herself to star as Pirate Jenny. Now they were moving on to Broadway to produce the premiere of *The Potting Shed*, a play by the English novelist Graham Greene.

Sherwood Arthur was surprised to find out they still had no costume designer, even though the production was about to go into rehearsal. He said to me, "Why don't you go check up on that?" I got my portfolio together and trotted down to see Carmen Capalbo and Stanley Chase. But they didn't know my name, and they didn't want to see me.

This was on a Friday afternoon, so I did one of my sitting tricks. I sat and sat and sat until finally they said, "We'll see her, we'll see her. We'll have to see her to get rid of her."

I showed them my union project and things I had dreamed up for nightclub acts, things that had no relevance to the play whatsoever. Suddenly they seemed to realize that they indeed did not have a designer or even a costume supervisor. It was modern dress, and they figured actors just wore their own clothes. They were beginning rehearsals Monday, so they said, "Oh, well, I guess you might as well do it." It was rather vague.

I made an appointment with the general manager to sign my contract and get my first check. When I went to see him, he informed me that I was expected to kick back to the management some of my fee, which wasn't very large to begin with. This was the price one was expected to pay for the prestige of working on Broadway. He preferred cash, but I insisted on writing a check. I could have lost my union status, but in those days you would do just about anything to land that first credit on Broadway.

The Potting Shed is set in present-day England and concerns a middle-aged man, estranged from his family, who comes home when his father is dying. He needs to uncover a repressed memory of something that happened to him as a boy in the family potting shed.

The man's mother was played by Dame Sybil Thorndike, the great English actress for whom Shaw had written *Saint Joan* in 1924, when she was forty-two. She was now in her seventies. Her husband, Lewis Casson, was appearing in the play with her.

Dame Sybil and Lewis Casson were staying at the Union Theological Seminary up past Columbia University, where they had friends. One January morning, I had an appointment with her at Bergdorf Goodman's on Fifth Avenue to find shoes. It was bitterly cold and windy but very sunny and bright. Bergdorf's had agreed to let us in a hour before the store opened at ten o'clock.

Here came Dame Sybil walking towards me wearing a kind of a Queen Mary toque with a scarf underneath it and a scarf over it and a big old tweed coat that you could see was stuffed full of sweaters and scarves and vests. She had on two or three pairs of heavy cotton-wool hose, sturdy shoes, and gloves with mittens over them. She had walked from Union Theological on 123rd Street on the Upper West Side to East Fifty-ninth and Fifth. It must have taken her an hour and a half. She had a full day of rehearsal in front of her, and this was how she was using her energy.

She told me she had already been up at five o'clock to work on translating the New Testament from Greek. She was teaching herself Greek in the mornings, she said, because Sir Lewis was grouchy in the morning, and she didn't want to have anything to do with him. She'd provide him with his tea and go off to study her Greek.

Dame Sybil and I proceeded to the Delman shoe store in Bergdorf's, where we found a nice pair of walking shoes that elderly English ladies wear. But before we could leave, something caught her eye: some wonderfully wild-looking black satin sandals with very, very high heels. The heel looked like a twisted rose stem, with the rose blossom flattened over its back.

"I just have to put those on," she said. Before I could say anything, she had them on and was strolling around Delman's in her heavy stockings and layers of sweaters wearing these outrageously surreal sandals with dangerously high heels. It was one of the more bizarre sights I have ever seen, Dame Sybil Thorndike, this noble woman of stage and screen, having a bucket of fun before going off to work.

Our next morning treks were to Altman's, where I had friends who arranged for the store to get promotion credit on the show in exchange for providing Dame Sybil's wardrobe for nothing or at cost. Altman's still had a custom department then, so we choose the clothes from models. I picked the fabric in colors I needed, and they were made up or extensively altered from existing garments.

One morning when we were at the glove counter, the saleswoman looked up from writing the order and said "Aren't you Gladys Cooper?" Now Gladys Cooper was only six years younger than Sybil Thorndike. Dame Sybil pulled herself up very straight and said in her most haughty British tones, "No, no, Gladys Cooper is my mother." And that was the end of that conversation.

Sybil Thorndike spoiled me because she was such a gracious person. She was a star who was easy to work with. That was not always or even often the case.

My experience was very different with Leueen MacGrath, the English actress and playwright who was playing Sybil Thorndike's daughter.

Much has been written about Leueen MacGrath in the biographies of George S. Kaufman, whom she had married when she was thirty-five and he was sixty. They had collaborated successfully on the book for the Cole Porter musical *Silk Stockings* a few years before. By this time, however, Kaufman was unable to perform his husbandly duties and had encouraged Leueen to see other men. She was currently involved with Carmen Capalbo.

For the opening scene, the designer, William Pitkin, had created a living room with faded chintz and green walls that everyone thinks they have in England. So I put Miss MacGrath in a rust-colored dress with a fitted bodice and Peter Pan collar, long sleeves, and modest skirt. It was modified mid-fifties.

Leueen didn't like the color. In fact, she hated, loathed, and despised the color. She informed me that she looked wretched in it and absolutely couldn't wear it. I kept saying, "But look at the set. You're going to be marvelous. I've given you the best color. With this outfit and your lovely blonde hair, no one will be able to keep their eyes off of you."

So I stuck to my guns, and we had the dress made. Leueen arrived for the fitting. Tears immediately began to cascade down her cheeks at ninety miles an hour, and she sobbed uncontrollably, "I just cannot bear this color."

"Oh, now, now, Miss MacGrath, it is all going to be fine. You are going to be so very happy when you get up on the stage with the set." I was just going on my way, not hearing.

Ultimately, we came to the dress rehearsal and out came Miss MacGrath in her rust-colored dress looking absolutely splendid against the set. And the tears started flowing. "Carmen, Carmen," she wailed, "the dress, the dress . . ."

By the time the curtain went up for the critics on opening night, she was in navy blue. It was the same dress with a little accordion pleated sunburst skirt instead of the softly gathered gored one.

That is when I learned that you do not stuff people into colors they don't want to be in. If you do, they will do everything within their power to get out of appearing on stage in it. At this time, on my first Broadway show, I took this incident as an assault on my ego. "Where was the set designer when I needed him?" "Why does Carmen give in to her just because she's crying?" I really missed the point back then. I was busy being a young designer. I had little or no accommodation for anyone else.

I thought that when one made a commitment to a concept, one fought for it right down the line.

Quite a bit later I did think to myself, "Pat, what if you were about to appear before six or seven hundred people a night in a color that you felt made you look ugly? How would you feel? Admit it, you would be hysterical in a minute." It has nothing to do with being a star. Ever since this experience, I have always tried to ask my actors what colors they do not like and get those colors out of the way. It saves a lot of time and grief later on. I'm glad I got it out of the way early.

While I was working on *The Potting Shed*, I was recommended for another show, *Visit to a Small Planet*, a comedy by Gore Vidal, who was then making his living writing for television drama series like *Studio One*, *Philco Television Playhouse*, and *Goodyear Playhouse*. The 1955 television version of *Visit to a Small Planet* was now being expanded for Broadway for its original star, Cyril Ritchard, who was also directing.

Florence Klotz, a costume designer a few years older than me, steered me towards it after she turned it down. She was too busy working as a full-blown, grown-up assistant to Irene Sharaff and Lucinda Ballard, Broadway's other great, in-demand costume designer. We met, as people did, because we were in and out of the costume shops.

One of the producers was George Axelrod, a playwright and director who had a big success in 1952 with *The Seven Year Itch*, which was made into the 1955 movie starring Marilyn Monroe. He had a dreadful time remembering my name. Instead of even trying to say "Pat" or "Patricia" or "Miss Z," he always called me "The Girl" and addressed me as if I weren't in the same room. "Tell the Girl that we need a white dress for Sarah Marshall." "Tell the Girl that jacket doesn't look stylish enough." The Girl would be given these instructions by any number of flunkies, but mostly by his wife, Joan.

She was a very stylish, very well-coiffed blonde, an interior designer by profession, who became known as "designer to the stars" when she and George moved out to Hollywood. Because this was a modern-dress shopping show, and because she was the producer's wife, she assumed she knew as much as, if not more than, I did.

She would say, "I really think you and I should get together with George, dear, and have a little discussion. Perhaps we could meet Wednesday around noon at the Drake Hotel. Do you know where the Drake Hotel is, dear?"

I would smile and say "I know where the Drake Hotel is in Chicago, and I also know where it is in New York, thank you."

The budget on *Small Planet* was incredibly small, maybe $2,000, and allowed me only to shop at Macy's or Gimbels. Meantime, Joan would look for the same items at Bergdorf's, Bonwit's, and Bendel's. Her dress for Sarah Marshall would outdo my dress for Sarah Marshall because mine cost $23.95 and hers was $99.95. The budget miraculously swelled for her choices.

Oliver Smith, the scene designer for the production, used to hide out in the last row. Whenever there was a disagreement about a costume, he would say, "I know, I know, just do what you have to do, and we'll all get through it somehow. This really isn't designing, you know. It's just to make a little money while you wait for the right thing."

Cyril Ritchard, the director and star, had been half of a glamorous musical comedy duo with his wife Madge Elliott in the thirties and forties in England and Australia, their home country. He had relocated to New York from London after his wife's death, and he was now famous for portraying Captain Hook in Mary Martin's *Peter Pan* on Broadway and on television.

In *Small Planet*, he played an extraterrestrial from the future who lands his flying saucer in an American backyard. He arrives wearing clothes of the antebellum South because he has mistaken the 1850s for the 1950s. Finding life in the future on another world too perfect and boring, he's come to enjoy the drama and romance of the Civil War,

At six feet, two inches tall, and with an elegant manner—he was made for Restoration comedy and the plays of Oscar Wilde—Cyril Ritchard was a joy to costume and a pleasure to work with. I went up to see him at his apartment in the Langham on Central Park West. It was decorated by Mrs. Oscar Hammerstein II and had a fifty-foot living room with ceilings fourteen feet high. He fell in love with my fabrics and wanted to have all his footstools reupholstered in the one I had found for a dressing gown. Would I get him eight yards of that, please.

One day at a fitting for his antebellum clothes, the tailor at Eaves Costume Company informed me that my sketch was incorrect. I said that it *was* correct, but the tailor was determined to give a young designer a hard time. I had never argued with a tailor before. There was a lot of yelling and throwing bolts of fabric around the fitting room. Mr. Ritchard just sat quietly in his cubicle, waiting for us to calm down.

Shopping for the actors made me aware how woefully inadequate my own wardrobe was. Like the shows, my wardrobe was hobbled with a limited budget. I had to dress for famously drafty theatres in all seasons and temperatures, from initial meetings of casts through technical and dress rehearsals to opening night and the parties thereafter. I had to dress suitably to shop for costumes, be it at Macy's or Pierre Balmain, and to push a show through a costume house in all seasons and weathers. I had to be dressed for anything.

I'll never forget the horrible day in January 1957 while working on *Small Planet* when I had an enormous day of shopping work ahead of me. It was sleeting and wet, so knowing I would be out in the elements all day, I dressed in boots, slacks, an old coat, neck scarves, and a headscarf. Just as I was heading out, I got the message that I was required at one o'clock to meet Cyril Ritchard for lunch at Sardi's. And he was to be accompanied by someone really from another planet, the general manager of the Metropolitan Opera, Rudolf Bing. Oh, swell.

How did I protect myself against that sort of reoccurrence? By designing a special outfit for both hard labor and social occasions: black, fitted leggings; waterproof short boots; tunic tops; and smart shopping bags.

As if George Axelrod didn't have enough trouble with my name, the advertising staff for *Small Planet* was driven mad by it. The New Haven houseboards and handbills read "Costumes supervised by Patricia Ziprodt," leaving out the second *p*. They all had to be reprinted. And then the same thing happened again on Broadway. Perhaps I should have settled for "Clothes by The Girl."

My experiences with shopping shows on *Potting Shed* and *Small Planet* left me very shaken because I did not know how to do that kind of work. I did not know how to shop at Macy's. It was big, and it frightened me. I was always losing money because I kept losing my receipts. I couldn't afford taxis, and I got bursitis from carrying too many packages on the subway. I certainly couldn't afford an assistant.

Shopped shows didn't pay well. We were contracted on the basis of costume count, $50 per costume for the stars and featured players, $20 per costume for everyone else. With a cast of twelve in *Small Planet*, I grossed about $750. It took a minimum of four weeks, providing there was no trouble during out-of-town tryouts. So I averaged about $200 per week.

When I didn't have a show, expenses of course went on. Hunting new jobs cost money, and I was trying to resurrect my old middle-class living standards in my new apartment, unresurrected since my arrival in New York in September 1949. There I was in Macy's basement thinking, "I'm not getting anywhere here. This is not the American theatre I had planned on. Where is the ballet?"

My next show, *Miss Lonelyhearts*, was also modern dress, and it added to my depression about shopping shows. Howard Teichmann's dark adaptation of Nathaniel West's dark novel portrayed a young newspaper reporter assigned to write an advice-to-the-lovelorn column. He becomes caught up in his readers' miseries, with disastrous consequences. It was not a happy story and not a happy production, certainly not for me.

Jo Mielziner was designing the set and recommended me to Alan Schneider, the director. Schneider was already a Broadway director of note and was also working in the new experimental theatre going on Off Broadway. The previous year he had directed the American premiere of Samuel Beckett's *Waiting for Godot* and directed five of Beckett's American premieres subsequently.

My preliminary discussions with Alan Schneider were not fruitful. This was only my third play, and I was having an awful time trying to understand what directors wanted. Directors don't know how to talk to designers very well, particularly about modern clothes. They think there's no designing involved and that they, as well as everyone around them, know how to do it just as well as the designer.

It's called, "I'll know it when I see it." You shop and show stuff. Then you go back and shop some more and show more stuff. Everyone wants to get into the act—producers, producers' wives, agents, agents' wives. "Oh, it should be yellow." "No, it's the wrong color." "No, it's not the right dress."

Alan kept saying to me, "You're not communicating, you're not communicating." I kept thinking, "Well, I just don't know what you're talking about." He was hounding me to please get a bar mitzvah suit for Fritz Weaver, who was playing the reporter. Fritz was an up-and-coming young actor who had appeared in the early television drama shows. His Broadway debut two years earlier earned him a Tony nomination.[14]

When Alan said he needed a bar mitzvah suit, I hadn't been in New York all that long. What did I know, the Last of the Wasps from Kenilworth? "What's a bar mitzvah suit?" What he really meant was a blue serge suit, but he didn't say that and complained that I wasn't good at communicating. Poor Jo sat there, watching what I felt was a nightmare,

One of the best things to come out of *Miss Lonelyhearts* was my meeting Victor Samrock, the production's business manager. Victor was also the business manager

---

[14]His next two Broadway choices were not so fortunate. His second show opened one night and closed the next. *Miss Lonelyhearts* would close after nine performances. He did go on to have a distinguished career in the theatre, television, and film.

of The Playwrights' Company, a powerhouse producers group which had been formed in 1938 by five powerhouse American playwrights, Maxwell Anderson, S. N. Behrman, Sidney Howard, Elmer Rice, and Robert E. Sherwood. They averaged two or three shows a year, were a goldmine of work, and hard to crack into. Victor was the gun behind the guns. He had engaged Boris Aronson to design the set for their next production, *The Rope Dancers* by Morton Wishengrad, and on Boris's recommendation, he asked me to do the costumes. *The Rope Dancers* and my next project, George Bernard Shaw's *Back to Methuselah*, got me out of Macy's basement and let me do some period research and designing.

The Rope Dancers, a poetic drama set in a New York tenement at the beginning of the twentieth century, was the first Broadway play by Morton Wishengrad, who was well known as a scriptwriter for television and especially for the radio series *The Eternal Light*, produced by the Jewish Theological Seminary since 1944.

Siobhán McKenna played a poor Irish immigrant wife who blames her husband's sin of infidelity for their daughter's birth defect, a sixth finger on one hand. Art Carney was the husband. Joan Blondell was the woman of easy virtue downstairs.

It was a starry cast. Art Carney was famous from television as Ed Norton, the New York sewer worker to Jackie Gleason's bus driver on *The Honeymooners*. Siobhán McKenna, the noted Irish actress, had appeared on the cover of *Life* Magazine in September 1956, just before she opened on Broadway in Shaw's *Saint Joan*. Joan Blondell had been a movie star since the thirties.

Blondell had a brief and tempestuous marriage to the producer Mike Todd, which had ended seven years earlier. While we were in previews for *The Rope Dancers*, Mike Todd was killed in a plane crash. Everyone was worried how Joan would be feeling and tiptoed around her. Finally someone asked her how she felt. "Oh, about the same way I felt the day Hitler died, " she said. And that was the end of that conversation.

The director was a 27-year-old Englishman named Peter Hall. He was already prominent in the London theatre and a few years later would found the Royal Shakespeare Company in Stratford-upon-Avon. We met in the lobby of the Algonquin Hotel. First and foremost, he said, he wanted me to make Art Carney look sexy. "Sexy?" I thought. "He's playing a poor Irishman who has gone out whoring the night that his child was conceived." Even in his younger days, I don't think anyone would have described Art Carney as sexy. What was I to do? Put him in brown? In green? Give him tight pants? I fretted about this the whole production period. Here is another example of a director not making himself clear to me, and I could not figure out what was really on his mind.

Siobhán McKenna, like Sybil Thorndike, was heaven to work with. She would come to fittings with pictures of her mother to show me. "She didn't wear a cotton blouse, like you have here," she said. "She always wore silk, in a color like this." I was so inexperienced that I obliged Miss McKenna with a silk blouse of that very color.

When we arrived at dress rehearsal, Boris took one look and said "Ah, you never, never ever have a blouse like that." I headed back to Brooks Costume Company, my tail between my legs, and found a pastel-colored linen blouse of the right period in their stock, with a high collar and a little bit of cotton lace around it. Siobhán accepted it with no protest. She just put it on and wore it, and that was that.

The Rope Dancers was a very happy experience for me. It was the first time I felt I knew what I was doing.

This is when I first started putting all my sketches for all the characters on one big sheet so I could lay it against the basic scenic colors. I think I'm the only one who works like this, particularly with a small show. This way you could see what the inner relationships of the figures were right there. You could see what the different colors of white were, exactly what the color of red was, and just how gray the doctor's suit was.

Boris took me under his wings. He's very much a teacher. We had one color problem, in the scene where the little girl was sick in bed and was going to die. He said, "Now I want you to come to the scenic studio, and we will discuss the values."

I rode forever on the subway to get to the scenic studio, and there was Boris driving the painters mad: "No! Paint it more this way! Paint it a little that way!"

Our problem that day was that the actress, Beverly Lunsford, had very pale skin and very pale blonde hair. She was to wear a white nightgown with long sleeves because the tenement is cold. And she would be lying against a white pillow and a white sheet. What colors could we use so she wouldn't vanish in that frame of white? You put any kind of focus light on her and she's gone.

That's when I began to learn about value. I learned that there are maybe ninety-five whites, to say nothing of 3,000 reds. We ended up making her nightgown in a blue-white. We made the pillow and the sheet in a beige-white. She popped right out.

The Rope Dancers. *Credit: Billy Rose Theatre Division, The New York Public Library for the Performing Arts;* © *Estate of Patricia Zipprodt.*

If you didn't know what you were looking at, you wouldn't know what we had done.

That's why Boris called me up there, to get that across to me. He knew he was helping to shape me. He was my "Yale."

Brooks Atkinson gave me a little valentine of an opening night notice in the *Times*: "Patricia Zipprodt has provided costumes that portray character with remarkable insight."

Back to Methuselah is George Bernard Shaw's notoriously problematic play about the past and the future of the human race. Shaw's response to the disasters of World War I, it was really a cycle of five plays, stretching from the Garden of Eden in 4004 BC to AD 31920, meant to be performed over three long evenings.

The Theatre Guild had premiered it in 1922, and now Arnold Moss, a popular character actor known for his work in Shakespeare, movies, radio, and television, persuaded the Theatre Guild to produce it again in a version he adapted down to two acts.

Arnold had seen my work on *The Rope Dancers* and recommended me to the Guild. Besides preparing the text, he was also going to portray Shaw himself as a kind of narrator for the piece. Margaret Webster, an English actress and director from a long dynasty of English actors and managers, was set to direct. She had directed Arnold as Prospero in a highly successful production of *The Tempest* a dozen years earlier.

There was an immediate problem. Webster wasn't to arrive until the day rehearsals began. So Arnold was making most of the decisions about my costume designs. He was not very enlightening about the play, which had most of its scenes set in a futuristic world demanding plastics and DayGlo. I simply was not ready for it. I did not know enough about the craft of costuming. The Fashion Institute had been terrific, but it didn't teach me about a lot of the things I still needed to learn.

I was most definitely not ready for the production's stars, Tyrone Power and Faye Emerson. Miss Emerson had a moderately successful career in the early forties as a Warner Brothers star and was married briefly to Elliott Roosevelt, the son of the president. Now she was a glamorous television personality.

Mr. Power, a descendant of an Irish acting dynasty, had been a romantic leading man in the movies since the thirties. When he starred as Zorro in *The Mark of Zorro* in 1940, he immediately became pegged as a swashbuckler. He continued to do theatre and had made a strong stage impression just a few seasons before in *John Brown's Body*, a concert-style reading of the Stephen Vincent Benét poem that toured nationally.

The Adam and Eve costumes were, naturally, the most challenging. Ernest Adler, the star hair stylist for Broadway and Hollywood, designed a long blonde wig for Faye that went clear down to her calf. I obliged by designing a sort of net union suit with leaves in appropriate places to cover her commodious figure.

I devised a similar arrangement for Mr. Power, but at our first fitting I was in for a rude surprise. When Mr. Power stepped out of one of his gorgeously tailored suits, he revealed a very unprepossessing body. There was a forward tilt to his pelvis, and now, in his early forties, he had a little bit of a pot. His shoulders were slightly slumped, and he always walked with his head a little bit forward.

Movies can hide many of an actor's physical defects, but on stage, five-eighths of the view we have of a performer is from the side. We never see them full front except when they make their entrances. We designers can do optics that will help the front and the back, but the side shows a silhouette, and there's not much we can do about that.

The production was scheduled for a three-month, forty-city tour before its late March Broadway opening. Tyrone Power apparently enjoyed touring. The stars would be traveling by limousine. The company and crew were to go by bus. Faye Emerson and Mr. Power were photographed in heavy coats with turned-up collars—Miss Emerson's a full-length fur, of course, with a hood—as they boarded a plane at Idlewild Airport to fly to Orlando, Florida, where we would open.

We began at the big Orlando city auditorium. I was there without any assistant, only a disgruntled wardrobe mistress who was not even minimally responsive to my needs. I kept waiting for the wardrobe trunks to arrive from New York, but there was no sign of them. The company manager wasn't riding herd over the missing costumes, so I constantly trekked out to the air freight section of the airport myself, only to find that the trunks were too big for the propeller cargo planes. Instead they were being sent by rail.

When the trunks finally did start to arrive, one by one, I would try to piece together all the past, present and futuristic costume elements. Most of the plastic was broken, half of it was useless, and many pieces arrived days late, not even in time for the dress rehearsal. There may not have even been a dress rehearsal. The actors only got to wear their costumes going into the opening performance.

When Tyrone Power walked out on the stage in my Adam costume, I was standing in the back of the house next to Armina Marshall, one of the Guild's co-founders with her husband, Lawrence Langner. She grabbed my arm and murmured, "Oh, my dear . . ." I muttered "I know."

I had to cover both Power and Emerson up quickly. I rushed around to decorating shops on the Florida coast to find coir, the meshy brown covering of coconuts. I started covering the net union suits and leotards with it. The outfits now became opaque, but a new problem arose: they itched. Tyrone Power complained first. "Do I really have to wear this?" he pleaded with me.

Eventually Mr. Power appeared on Broadway in brown tights with lots of fig leaves, and Miss Emerson wore yards and yards of cheesecloth. But it was to no avail. This time Brooks Atkinson did not give me a valentine. "It seems to this theatergoer that the performance that Margaret Webster has staged is unhappily earthbound," he wrote. "Marvin Reiss' settings are not really imaginative, nor are Patricia Zipprodt's costumes."

It was episodes like this that made me realize that I really didn't know anything. Even if the shows I did looked good, I was really out there without any experience. I had to go to Off Broadway to put it all together.

5

Finding Myself Off Broadway

With *The Potting Shed*, *Visit to a Small Planet*, *Miss Lonelyhearts*, *The Rope Dancers*, and *Back to Methuselah*, I had tried to emerge as a grown-up Broadway designer, like Athena from the head of Zeus, without really knowing what I was doing. I didn't know what my style was, because I hadn't worked to find it.

By the time *Methuselah* opened in New York in March 1958, however, I was beginning to realize my real place as a designer was Off Broadway.

Word Baker and Paul Libin, two of my assistant friends from Jo Mielziner's office, wanted to go out on their own as producers, and Word was determined to be a director. Watching our elders like thieves on *Happy Hunting*, we all said "We can do it better." So we went off and did it better with a revival of Arthur Miller's *The Crucible*.

The Crucible has ascended to the status of a classic, but when it premiered on Broadway in 1953, it was a deeply troubled production. Miller, despite the acclaim and the Pulitzer Prize for *Death of a Salesman* in 1949, wasn't yet, at age forty-three, the modern master. The production's director, the Broadway veteran Jed Harris, had given the play a static, tableau-like production that neither critics, audiences, nor the playwright liked. Miller had taken over the production after it was running, eliminated Boris Aronson's setting, changed the script, and tried, without success, to bring the play back to life.

Jo Mielziner had designed the setting for *Death of a Salesman*, so he put Word in touch with Miller. Word was able to persuade Miller that his directorial ideas for the play, staging it in an intimate space without scenery, could restore the passion and human feeling the playwright had intended.

Paul and Word didn't even have a theatre yet. While Paul was running some errands one afternoon, he saw a sign at the old Martinique Hotel at Broadway and Thirty-second Street that a ballroom was available for rent. The manager wasn't enthusiastic about these young fellows turning his ballroom into a theatre. So a few days later Paul invited Arthur Miller to see the space, and Miller brought along his wife, Marilyn Monroe. The hotel manager suddenly became very enthusiastic, and by the time Paul got back to Jo's office on the Upper West Side, there was a message from the manager wanting to make a deal.

The designer Ming Cho Lee, another one of Jo's assistants, transformed the ballroom with the simplest of elements—director's chairs on bleachers, folding screens, overhead lighting pipes—into a beautifully functional three-quarter-round acting space.

Part of Word's agreement with Arthur Miller was that Ming and I had to present our concepts directly to the author. I had talked my ideas through with Word, but articulating them to Mr. Miller was another matter. We all went over to his apartment on East Fifty-seventh Street. There were pictures of Marilyn Monroe all over the foyer.

Miller sat behind the desk in his study, facing away from me as he listened to Ming's ideas. Then he turned directly to me. Blinding sunlight came through the window behind him. He looked like Michelangelo's Moses.

I have a great weakness for strong male necklines, and I found Arthur Miller's neck absolutely beautiful. "This is one of the most gorgeous men I have ever seen in my life," I thought. When it was my turn to describe the costumes, I couldn't open my mouth. Word finally broke the silence by saying, "What she would like to say is this . . ."

The look that I wanted for the Puritan inhabitants of Salem was a bit of an Abstract-Expressionistic quality. I achieved this with felt and rubber sheeting for the collars. They would be flat and sculptural, and they would be easy to keep clean. Make-up would wash right off the rubber. I made the buttons out of felt as well, four layers glued together and cut into circles of various sizes. Each character had his or her own button size.

The teenage Salem girls who start all the frenzy wore A-line dresses, very fitted under the bust. In the mad scenes, when they claim to see the witches and are all whirling around, the fullness of the skirts went flying like dance skirts.

All the costumes were made in my apartment with my Singer sewing machine and a three-quarter-inch plywood sheet on wooden horses for a cutting table.

The Crucible, *John Proctor. Credit: Billy Rose Theatre Division, The New York Public Library for the Performing Arts; © Estate of Patricia Zipprodt.*

Miller and Monroe would come to rehearsals all the time. It was very sweet the way they would just sit quietly in the bleachers and watch. She had on her little scarf and dark glasses so no one would know who she was. After a while he'd get her to take her scarf off and then her dark glasses. They would just watch, an hour here, a half-hour there, just watching it build and grow.

The Crucible became a hit and ran for 633 performances. The Broadway production had closed after 197 performances. This was our generation moving.

In the fall of 1958, Sherwood Arthur, my agent provocateur for *The Potting Shed*, introduced me to David Hays, the resident designer at Circle in the Square, a theatre-in-the-round that two others of our generation on the move, the producer Theodore Mann and the director José Quintero, had created out of an old nightclub on Sheridan Square in the Village.

The Crucible, *Putnam*. Credit: Billy Rose Theatre Division, The New York Public Library for the Performing Arts; © Estate of Patricia Zipprodt.

The Crucible, *John Proctor in court*. Credit: Billy Rose Theatre Division, The New York Public Library for the Performing Arts; © Estate of Patricia Zipprodt.

The Crucible, *Elizabeth Proctor*. Credit: Billy Rose Theatre Division, The New York Public Library for the Performing Arts; © Estate of Patricia Zipprodt.

The Crucible, *Abigail*. Credit: Billy Rose Theatre Division, The New York Public Library for the Performing Arts; © Estate of Patricia Zipprodt.

The Crucible, *Betty Parris, Mercy Lewis*. Credit: Billy Rose Theatre Division, The New York Public Library for the Performing Arts; © Estate of Patricia Zipprodt.

David had designed Tennessee Williams's *Summer and Smoke* for Quintero in 1952. That production made Geraldine Page a star and is often said to be the real beginning of the modern Off Broadway movement in the American theatre. David also designed the 1956 production of Eugene O'Neill's *The Iceman Cometh* for Quintero, sparking an O'Neill revival. That in turn led to the Broadway premiere of *Long Day's Journey Into Night* six months later, also designed by David.

At the time I met him, David was designing sets, costumes, and lighting for Quintero's production of Brendan Behan's *The Quare Fellow*, a comedy-drama set in a Dublin prison. David had gotten himself in a mess with the costumes. Scenic people on the whole should not do costumes. They know about lumber; they don't know about fabric.

David had found the prisoners' clothes, white cotton dishwashers' jackets and pants, at a restaurant uniform supplier. He dyed them blue, but they looked like dishwashers' uniforms dyed blue. As the actors appeared on stage at the dress rehearsal, Quintero kept saying, "David, David, they all look like they're in pajamas."

David phoned me in a panic for help the day before Thanksgiving. The play was opening the next week. What could we do to make these uniforms look like they had been worn a long time and handed on from prisoner to prisoner?

That's when I started to teach myself how to age fabric. In those days we referred to the process as distressing clothes. I arrived at the theatre early Thanksgiving morning, when the place was closed, and began to hunt up any caustic elements I could find—sandpaper, steel wool, wooden rasps, vegetable graters—anything that would break down the fabric. I worked them through the jackets and trousers, and then I washed them with salt, softener, and lord knows what else. I spent all weekend doing this.

At the next rehearsal Quintero was enchanted, and David felt that I had saved the day. And six years later I would apply this baptism by fire into the aging process on another show that would have a profound effect on my career, *Fiddler on the Roof*.

This was my pass into the inner sanctum of Circle in the Square and Off Broadway, an association that was one of the happiest and most fruitful of my early career. Unlike Broadway with its ever-changing places and personalities, Off Broadway became a home base. I could take my little Singer sewing machine and my plywood table on wooden horses and go anywhere and make you a show. And I did!

Over the next five or six years, I designed and built nine shows at five different theatres. Like a nomad in the night, I would raise my tents, setting up shop wherever I could find the space. There was a whole underground of costume people who were willing to work through the day and into the night, stirring dye pots over electric burners, running here and there, and having a fabulous time.

We always had very loving workrooms. I insisted on that. Everyone who worked there was there because they wanted to be. There wasn't any money, and we all ate a lot of sandwiches, but we built some wonderful things.

After I became David Hays's ager and distresser on *The Quare Fellow*, he and José Quintero invited me to design costumes for a revival of Thornton Wilder's *Our Town* in March 1959. I knew the situation: I would have to do all the buying and lugging of fabrics to the theatre and all the cutting and sewing and fitting myself.

I had a wonderful scheme. I put everyone in abstract clothes of the period of the play, 1901–13, made out of raw denim—a hard, unsoaked denim that was on the market then. It came in different hues, with the same dark thread running through it. It was very inexpensive and so wide you could get a lot out of each yard.

The women had simple, high-neck blouson tops with puffed sleeves and a fitted lower arm. They were belted at the waist with skirts with fullness in the back. Each woman had some special accessory, like her hat. It was all very subtle and never got noticed by the critics.

Many months later, there was a party for the cast and crew. One of the actresses in the graveyard scene came up to me and told me that her sleeve was still too tight. I thought, "Actors, I can't stand it; she hasn't seen me in months to say hello and she gives me a costume note at a party." I was so depressed.

My struggles with *Back to Methuselah* and shopping shows so soured me that for a time, when nothing further came my way on or off Broadway, I made the difficult decision that I could just not stay in the theatre. I would have to find another way to make a living, something that I would enjoy.

So I returned to painting in earnest. I found three or four artist friends, and we all chipped in to rent a studio and hire some models. I started to feel much, much better. It was a total delight to sit at an easel and not worry if anyone was looking over my shoulder. And I relished the fact that I did not have to read anyone's mind. Rouben Ter-Arutunian once said to me that ninety percent of designing is mind-reading what the producer, director, writer, and actors want.

One person who stayed with me during this difficult period was Jo Mielziner. In the fall of 1959, he was designing sets and lights for a new play by Jerome Lawrence and Robert E. Lee, the playwriting team who had had big successes with *Inherit the Wind* in 1955 and *Auntie Mame* in 1956.

The play was *The Gang's All Here*, a fictionalized telling of President Warren G. Harding's 1923 Teapot Dome Scandal. It was produced by Kermit Bloomgarden, who had produced *Death of a Salesman*, *The Most Happy Fella*, and *Look Homeward, Angel*, three recent successes designed by Jo. It was directed by George Roy Hill, a television director who had made his Broadway debut with *Look Homeward, Angel*. George Roy Hill went on to Hollywood and is now remembered for pairing Paul Newman and Robert Redford in *Butch Cassidy and the Sundance Kid* and *The Sting*.

Jo asked me to design the costumes. *The Gang's All Here* was a wonderful show for me. It was well cast, well directed, and beautifully designed by Jo. It was a period show with strong characters, so I could do real designing.

I was lucky to have Jean Dixon in the cast. She had been well known on Broadway since 1929 for her comic roles, especially in plays by George S. Kaufman. She was in Hollywood comedies of the thirties, where she often played the witty friend of sophisticated leading ladies like Claudette Colbert, Katharine Hepburn, and Irene Dunne.

Miss Dixon was an extremely elegant woman who had been dressed in the twenties and thirties by the House of Worth, the historic Paris couture firm. I called her "Miss Dixon" for two weeks into rehearsal until she finally said, "Would you mind calling me Jeannie?" I said, "Well, with your permission . . ." Jean played the wife of the president, Griffith P. Hastings, played by Melvyn Douglas, who looked like my father.

I had a lovely time researching Jean's clothes at the Brooklyn Museum Costume Collection. Robert Riley, the curator there, had studied set design at Yale, so he always welcomed theatre designers. He would say, "We're closed for the summer, but if it's for the theatre, come on out anyway. We're doing conservation work, so we're here."

Bob Riley had special rooms for designers. His staff would set you up in your own little room with books and some clothes on dummies and get you started. One time I had a room right next to Norman Norell.[15] He was studying a little sequined jacket from the twenties which he later produced.

Melvyn Douglas's clothes were the challenge. One of his basic outfits was a blue blazer and white flannels that the president wore on informal occasions. I got little swatches from different blue flannel fabrics and took them up to Jo's light room, something I had learned to do with Irene's swatches. Jo's lighting was different from

---

[15]Norman Norell (1900–1972), sometimes called "the dean of American fashion designers," helped make New York a rival to Paris for fashion after World War II. He also occasionally designed for theatre and film. In 1956, he designed Marilyn Monroe's wedding dress for her marriage to Arthur Miller.

anybody else's. It was very heavy on the ambers. It always seemed like the air in his settings was thick with light.

His colors could destroy fabrics or enhance them. I'd call him up and say, "Jo, I'm working on a scene, I'm coming up." He'd put the gels in and the light would be ready for me to check my colors. I could go back and either buy it or dye it.

I picked two blues and two white flannels that worked under the lights. When I got out in daylight, however, the blue, a royal blue, was too bright. And the pants fabric looked like sandy mud. So I went back in the booth and turned the lights on again. The same two that looked wrong in daylight still looked right.

Jo said, "Those two colors will work very nicely." I went back to Brooks, which was building the clothes, and I said, "These two colors." Someone said, "These two colors? That blue makes my teeth itch." Nevertheless, they went and bought the fabric. When I looked at it on the bolts under the fluorescent shop lights, I was horrified. It was so gauche, so harsh. I grabbed these two big bolts of fabric and took them up to Jo. He said, "They look just fine." I said, "I know they look wonderful in here, but, Jo, look at these two pieces of fabric. I have to put these on Melvyn Douglas." He said, "Well, they work here in the light booth. And these are the gels that I'm going to be using. I'm all set on that. I am not going to change." "Okay," I said.

I went back to Brooks and said to George, the tailor, "Let's not cut this today." I was absolutely shaken by this. I went back up to Jo's again, under the ruse of another errand but really to look again. Then I said "Okay, George, I guess we just cut these things and hope for the best."

I tried to not look at it while it was on the tables being worked. But the day came when I had Mr. Douglas in for a fitting. First of all, I could tell he didn't like the tailoring. George was Hungarian, and he always made very big shoulders, like the suits made by Adrian, the Hollywood costume and fashion designer. The arm started two inches off the shoulder, so you always got a strange little snugness. It didn't matter what period, that's the way George cut.

Mr. Douglas put on this outfit with these strange caramel-colored pants and this bright, almost DayGlo royal blue jacket, and he looked at himself in the big three-way fitting room mirror. He didn't say anything. He just kept looking. Then he began to talk about his tailor in Spain who was such a wonderful tailor and who made him such beautiful clothes and bought such beautiful fabrics that they had there.

And I'm dying. "I've checked these under Mr. Mielziner's lights," I said, "and he also looked at these colors with the color scheme of his scenery. These will read like this sketch I've painted, which is a blue blazer and cream-colored pants."

Melvyn Douglas looked at the sketch and looked in the mirror, and I knew he was thinking, "This woman is absolutely demented, but what can you do." So he patiently went through the fitting, still talking about his tailor and the lovely fabrics in Spain, obviously miserable with our tailor and our fabrics. And I'm ever mindful that this is the man Garbo adored and one of the major stars of our world.

Then came the dress parade at the costume shop, with Kermit Bloomgarden, Lawrence and Lee, George Roy Hill, and the entire cast in attendance. Everyone was there except Jo, who didn't go to dress parades.

Jean Dixon showed her lovely clothes, which were fine. Then Melvyn Douglas came out, and they said, "What, that's the blue blazer?" I went through my whole story about the lights, and I knew they were thinking, "Who is this woman?" I didn't sleep when I got home that night. I'm seeing this thing on stage which is going to ruin my career. Jo is going to be wrong.

Eventually we got to the first dress rehearsal under Jo's lights. Out came Melvyn Douglas in the most beautiful dark blue blazer and cream-colored pants you have ever seen. Everyone looked at me. I became an instant genius. Lawrence and Lee took me to dinner afterwards and said, "We can't tell you what we were expecting." I didn't want to tell them I was expecting it too.

Jo was the only designer I've known who had a light booth where you could go and check your colors. He lit his own way for mood. Because of his palette, heavy amber and blue, you could not work on his sets without checking everything. Jo believed that you should never have a color on human beings lighter than their skin. He said the lightest thing should be the teeth and eyes and skin, because that's what you're looking at. If you put a pure white shirt on someone, the light is going to hit the shirt first. If I had white shirts to do for Jo, I'd always put them in French blue. That was the lightest register that really worked on his sets.

I was learning this from Jo the way I learned from Boris when he made me go up to the paint studios with him on *The Rope Dancers* to see what shade of white the nightgown needed to be so the little blonde girl's pale face could emerge against the white of the pillows. All these subtleties we're working with all the time.

The Gang's All Here. *Credit: Billy Rose Theatre Division, The New York Public Library for the Performing Arts;* © Estate of Patricia Zipprodt.

In the spring of 1960, I was offered two shows Off Broadway. Word Baker asked me to design costumes for a little six-person musical he and two friends, Tom Jones and Harvey Schmidt, had concocted when they were students at the University of Texas. It was called *The Fantasticks*.

I did not do *The Fantasticks*.[16] I've often thought, "Oh, god, twenty-five dollars a week for the rest of my life might have made a difference." I never got a royalty at the Circle. I barely got my expenses back. When they had some bad weeks, they'd stop paying people altogether.

Instead, I accepted José Quintero's offer to design *The Balcony* by the radical French writer Jean Genet. The play takes place in an upscale bordello in an unspecified city where an uprising is taking place. Madame Irma lets her clients act out fantasies of being men of high status—Bishop, Judge, Executioner, General, Chief of Police—while her ladies play whatever roles the men desire: penitent, thief, the general's mare. When the real bishop, judge, general, and chief of police are killed by the revolutionaries, their brothel mock counterparts assume their places. Nancy Marchand played Madame Irma, with Betty Miller, Salome Jens, Grayson Hall, and Sylvia Miles as the ladies.

Genet called for the Bishop and the other archetypes of authority to be larger than life, with inordinately broad shoulders, and towering on cothurni, the platform shoes worn by actors in ancient Greek tragedies.

The cothurni that I made probably had no relation to their Greek originals. They were constructed from old men's shoes, the kind that hook up very high above the ankle. Then I glued layers of cork together and glued that sandwich to the soles of the shoes. I used cork so the shoes would be lightweight enough for the men to move with relative ease. Still, it was a terrifying sight to watch the actors walk around for the first time on these cothurni.

For the English production, Genet had complained that the actors, who had to play with seven-inch lifts on their shoes, had not had sufficient time to rehearse. He insisted three months were needed. In an interview in the *New York Times* before the show opened, José said, "We have only four weeks, I hope none of the actors will fall off their heels on opening night."

The shoulders for the men's clothes were constructed out of football shoulder pads, with aluminum wiring added to make them almost like croquet hoops. I wanted the Bishop's robe to be wonderfully grand and grotesquely large. I found some marvelous heavy upholstery fabric in hammered satin with a dimpled surface, and I dyed it a deep purple. Then I thought to myself, "What can I find to really make this robe stiff?"

I had just recently discovered Sobo Glue, similar to Elmer's Glue, which was new on the market. If I applied large amounts of Sobo to the backside of the robe and let it dry very carefully, it would be like a piece of sculpture, which is exactly what I wanted.

I added ecclesiastical trim, with different gold papers marking the edges on the center front. Everything was very three-dimensional against this beautifully dimpled satin. This gorgeous robe practically stood by itself.

Then came dress rehearsal. The actor playing the Bishop got into his robe, walked around the stage a bit, said a few lines, and finally tried to sit down on his throne.

---

[16]*The Fantasticks* opened May 1960 and closed January 2002, after 17,162 performances.

The Balcony, *The Pony Girl*. Patricia used this image as the logo for her personal stationery. Credit: Billy Rose Theatre Division, The New York Public Library for the Performing Arts; © Estate of Patricia Zipprodt.

BANG! The hard Sobo was cracking. It sounded exactly like one of those old-fashioned theatrical thunder sheets. "Help! Help!" the poor actor cried, and there was much chortling out front. José Quintero gave me a look. "What do we do with this noisemaker?" he asked. "We will not be able to hear a word of dialogue." And I thought, "Oh, lord, now what do I do? Me and my high-tech ideas."

I knew that dry cleaning wouldn't get the Sobo Glue out of the robe. I had to soak it in water. But where do you go to soak a robe that has been cut long enough to fit over the actor's cothurni? I took it up to the bathtub in my apartment. I'd soak awhile, then pull out the stopper, refill the tub, and start the process all over again. I do not know how much the reservoirs of the Catskills contributed to the soaking and rinsing of the Sobo out of this robe. Half the pipes of the New York sewer system must still have remnants of that glue stuck permanently in them.

Money was always a problem in those days at Circle in the Square. Ted Mann, the managing director, had his office on the second floor at 159 Bleecker Street, our new theatre after we moved from Sheridan Square. It was very near where I was constructing all these wild costumes. I would wave frantically in his line of vision when I needed some petty cash to go shopping for fabric so I wouldn't have people sitting around with nothing to do, looking at me. Many times he would just sit there, either on the phone or talking with someone, staring at me without acknowledging me.

The Balcony, *The Bishop*. Credit: Billy Rose Theatre Division, The New York Public Library for the Performing Arts; © Estate of Patricia Zipprodt.

One day I put on a pair of those cothurni, pulled down a sign from the wall that certified me as a bona fide Kentucky Colonel, grabbed a long black umbrella left over from *Our Town*, marched up to his desk, and loomed over him. I seem to recall that our financial affairs were in better order after that. I couldn't resist. I just couldn't resist.

The Balcony was a huge critical and popular success. It played 672 performances and ran for over a year.[17]

While *The Balcony* was running at the Circle, Ted Mann and José Quintero produced a revival of Tennessee Williams's *Camino Real* at an upstairs theatre called St. Mark's Playhouse on Eighth Street and Second Avenue. The play is a surreal fantasy about lost souls gathering at a dusty plaza with a dry fountain at the literal

---

[17]Stuart Little, a friend of PZ's who was writing a theatre news column for the *New York Herald Tribune* when *The Balcony* was running, wrote in his 1972 book *Off Broadway: The Prophetic Theatre*: "The costumes by Patricia Zipprodt were extraordinary—each an extension of and a further insight into the character. Salome Jens played 'The Pony Girl.' Patricia costumed her in a tight low-cut top with leather puffing, curving around the upper part of her thighs—and what a pair of legs and what a performance! She was the human embodiment of an independent self-willed horse. José gave Sally the key to this characterization and led her through the role like a groom gently taking her reins showing her the way. Patricia's costumes for 'The Pony Girl' and 'The Slave' all had elements of leather in the design. Within the next few years and to this day, leather as clothing has become the fashion rage and I think Patricia started it."

Camino Real, *Inhabitants of the Camino Real*. Credit: Billy Rose Theatre Division, The New York Public Library for the Performing Arts; © Estate of Patricia Zipprodt.

and figurative dead end of the royal road. Among these transients looking for some kind of salvation are Don Quixote, Casanova, Marguerite Gautier, otherwise known as the Lady of the Camellias, lord Byron, and an American boxer called Kilroy.

As I started sketching for this otherworldly assortment, I simply could not come up with an image of Marguerite Gautier. I sketched and sketched, but she just never felt right. I would show some of my designs to José, who would look, shake his head, and say, "Oh, no, no, no . . . Not really . . . Not quite." He would talk and talk and I could not hear a thing that could really help me.

Finally one I day I went by his apartment and said, "José, if you would be so kind as to get up and go out of the living room into the back hall and re-enter as Camille, I think that would help me." "Wonderful," he said and left the room immediately. As he returned through the French doors that separated the two rooms, there before me was Camille. He didn't really have to walk a step further. I ran home, dashed off a sketch, brought it back to him, and he said, "Yes, that is Camille."

José was the ideal person to work with in this way. He is such a physical and expressive man. What he could not always say with words, he could achieve brilliantly with his body. This is one of his prime directing tools.

Once again we constructed, bleached, and dyed the clothes on the second floor at 159 Bleecker Street. By this time, I had an assistant, Connie Wexler, who was married to a young scenic and lighting designer named Peter Wexler. She did a lot of assisting, including helping Irene Sharaff on *Funny Girl* a few years later. She did her own designing for television and won a Daytime Emmy for the soap opera *Search for Tomorrow*. She would work again with me on *Fiddler*.

Camino Real, *Camille*. Credit: Billy Rose Theatre Division, *The New York Public Library for the Performing Arts*; © Estate of Patricia Zipprodt.

One day I asked Connie to go outside and buy the clothes off of one of the homeless men who hung around the Bleecker Street area, particularly near the old Bleecker Street Hotel. Connie thought I was kidding. I thought I was absolutely serious until she suggested that I go out and ask him myself. That was the end of that conversation.

Brooks Atkinson in the *Times* liked our *Camino* better than the Broadway original, particularly José's version of the script. "By eliminating many characters and cutting the text, it concentrates the elements of the story that matter the most." And he gave the designers some credit: "Both the physical production and the mode of the performance reflect Mr. Quintero's understanding of the theme. Although the stage resources of Off Broadway theatres are limited, Keith Cuerden, scene designer, and Patricia Zipprodt, costume designer, have visualized the torpor, sleaziness and callousness of the Camino Real, with its violent contrasts between impotent wealth and impotent poverty. And Patricia Collins' lighting plot boldly dramatizes the fugitive moods of the drama."

After *The Balcony*, I took on two more shopping shows. Although it was against my better judgment, I needed the money. The first, *Period of Adjustment* by Tennessee Williams, let me work again with Jo Mielziner and George Roy Hill, with whom I had enjoyed myself on *The Gang's All Here*.

And it gave me the chance to work with Tennessee Williams, probably America's most important playwright along with Arthur Miller. Tennessee knew my work from *Camino Real* at Circle in the Square. He liked the production and came and watched it a lot. So everyone was used to me, and they wanted me very much to do it, which was lovely.

The play, which Williams called "a serious comedy," was about the tribulations of marriage. After an unsuccessful wedding night, a newlywed couple seeks advice and comfort at the home of the husband's army buddy, who is himself having marital difficulties. Barbara Baxley was to play the still-virginal wife. James Daly was the army buddy. Baxley had played Esmeralda in the 1953 Broadway production of *Camino Real*. Daly was a regular on Broadway and in the early live television dramas.

I thought *Period of Adjustment* would be simple. It was a one-set, one-dress show: a living room, over a long Christmas Eve, the bride staying in the same suit she was married in.

It wasn't simple.

First of all, James Daly had to change into pajamas, and he kept insisting they be pure white. I had a dreadful time with that man. "Ah, white's white!" he'd say. And I'd say, "Go look at a painting of white flowers, go look at a Renoir." It was the same argument over and over again. I have to figure out how to put pieces of well-related colors under certain colored gels against certain color backgrounds. It's a very sophisticated form of color work. Most people have no idea about it, particularly actors.

Secondly, the pajamas I found at Bergdorf Goodman in the right shade and the right fabric to hold up under the lights cost $350. The producer wanted to know why I couldn't find some pajamas for $125. And when the show went on its tryout tour, and something happened to the pajama bottoms, the wardrobe people went out and bought another set and used the new bottoms with the original top, so they didn't match. White isn't white.

Barbara Baxley's dress was the key to the show. I dressed her as a bride on her honeymoon in an Empire dress with a little bolero jacket and a hat. Barbara was very broad in the shoulders, so I had to play that down. I got the form of the dress right for her small frame.

I looked at Jo's set very carefully and figured that a beautiful color for the bride would be salmon. It would look good on Barbara's blonde coloring. Everyone else would revolve around that color. I took swatches of salmon, peach and rose in a whole range up to Jo's light booth again, and we looked at them under the lights for three or four scenes. She had to move from room to room. The lights changed over the course of the play's time span, and Jo's colors changed. But the dress had to stay the same.

There was one color that would do it, a pink salmon in a very soft middle-value color. No matter where I moved it, no matter what light cues were going on, it was the only one that survived, the only one that didn't go boom or sink. It survived every place it had to go. I was thrilled. And it was a pleasant-looking color even out of the stage lights, not like Melvyn Douglas's blue jacket.

The dress was constructed by a young costumer, Barbara Gray, who had just arrived from London to work with Ray Diffen Stage Clothes, a highly regarded costume house started by another Englishman. After she married Arthur Matera, Barbara would establish her own shop and go on to create costumes for American Ballet Theatre, New York City Ballet, the Metropolitan Opera, and hundreds of Broadway shows.

The dress was beautifully made in wool crepe with a little print bodice top. But during her fittings Miss Baxley did nothing but shed tears all over it. I thought, "This is Leueen MacGrath all over again."

Period of Adjustment, *Barbara Baxley as Isabel. Credit: Billy Rose Theatre Division, The New York Public Library for the Performing Arts;* © Estate of Patricia Zipprodt.

The first stop on our tryout was Wilmington, Delaware, where we would have final dress rehearsals and a four-night engagement at the Playhouse Theatre, a charming place in the equally charming and historic Hotel DuPont. DuPont executives had built the theatre specifically to compete as a tryout venue with Philadelphia and Washington.

When we unpacked the costumes, Barbara's dress didn't fit. Somehow in the finishing, the bodice got tightened up. She couldn't zip it closed. I was hysterical. I called Ray and I said, "Send someone down to Wilmington, I need help." "Oh, it's only one dress" he said, "I can't. I'm very busy. Deal with it yourself, honey."

I opened up the center seam to see how much fabric I needed. It would take a triangle about three inches wide. All I had was little tiny pieces, so I had to sew them up myself by hand. I spent one long night putting these fragile pieces together. I made the dress fit.

As a comedy, *Period of Adjustment* was not all that funny. George Roy Hill knew he had not got it where it should be yet. Barbara Baxley was nervous carrying a Tennessee Williams play on her back. Tennessee, who was having difficulties with his lover, Frank Merlo, was half in and half out of it.

They all started to pick on Barbara's dress. The design was wrong. The shape was wrong. The cut was wrong. The sleeves were wrong. The bodice was wrong. The length was wrong. And of course the color was wrong.

We all began shopping up and down the Northeast Corridor for a new dress. Tennessee and Frank Merlo went off in one direction. Cheryl Crawford, the producer, headed off in another, while I hunted through the very limited selection of clothing stores in Wilmington. The teams arrived back at the theatre late every afternoon, and Barbara tried on our findings. When she came out on stage, someone would say, "No, that's not it."

Sometimes Barbara collapsed from nerves and exhaustion, and a doctor was rushed in to give her a B-12 shot. We did this every day in Wilmington. We did this every day that show was out of town. They finally decided that the shape of the dress was all right, because they couldn't get any shape that made her look better. Now it was down to the color.

Jo was sitting very quietly all the way through this, not saying this is the only color that will work, although he knows it. It's my problem. I didn't have any backup, and I needed it, because the situation was getting out of hand. The costume designer is not in a strong position. The producer, the director, the playwright, the star all have the power.

When we got to New Haven, I went back to New York and had the dress remade in ivory. I thought, "She's going to look like a nurse." I came back and put it on her. It fit beautifully. She walked on just to have it checked, and George said, "Won't do. Put the other one on." For the rest of the tryout period, she played in the original salmon dress.

One night in the Shubert Theatre, George and Tennessee were standing in the back watching. I looked at them, and I had really had it. I walked up and said, "Excuse me, gentlemen, but you know something? You're putting your problems on my dress."

They looked at me silently for a long moment. George gave Tennessee a glance, turned back to me and said, "Yeah, you're right." There was an eleven-o'clock train to New York. I was on it and never came near the production again.

A few weeks later, my phone rang. "Pat, it's Cheryl Crawford speaking," she said in her deep gravely voice. "You know that salmon dress that Barbara's been wearing? I'm wondering if you could see to it being copied again so it will be fresh for the New York opening?" I still spoke my mind those days, and I remember saying, "I expected this to happen." That's why I say, "If the song doesn't work, change the dress."

Sunday in New York, my other shopping show in this period, was by Norman Krasna, known for his light comedies filled with one-liners and farcical situations. He was also well regarded as a screenwriter. He was one of the writers of the enormously successful 1954 movie *White Christmas* and was considered by some the equal of Frank Capra and Preston Sturges.

David Hays was designing the sets and the lighting, so there was that nice connection. The director was Garson Kanin, the writer and director of *Born Yesterday*, which made Judy Holliday a star. With his wife, the actress Ruth Gordon, he had written four screenplays, including *Adam's Rib* and *Pat and Mike* for Katharine Hepburn and Spencer Tracy.

The producer was David Merrick, who was turning out Broadway hits in rapid succession. Did I think working with these luminaries would be good for my career? It didn't turn out that way.

The heroine of the slender plot of *Sunday in New York* is an earnest young reporter from Albany, played by Pat Stanley, who comes to New York to ask her airline pilot brother if she should compromise her virtue as her fiancé is urging or save herself for marriage. Although the brother himself has a girl in every port, he advises her to wait.

The comic complications arise when the girl has a meet-cute encounter on a bus with a handsome newspaper reporter, played by Robert Redford in his first starring role on Broadway, and has to rethink her options.

I went through tortures trying to dress Pat Stanley, who had won a Tony for her role in a musical called *Goldilocks* a few seasons back. At one of the dress rehearsals in Wilmington, Delaware, where we were trying out, neither Garson Kanin nor Ruth Gordon liked the pink suit I gave her for the opening scene, when she arrives at her brother's apartment.

"Darling," Miss Gordon said, "she just doesn't look stylish enough. and the color makes her look far too mature. I have a suitcase with me that is just full of old Chanel dresses. Let's try one of these." The suitcase was duly fetched. I never saw so many old Chanels in my life.

Fortunately, Miss Gordon and Pat Stanley were about the same size. We kept putting them on the actress, which had the effect of making her look even more sophisticated and more mature. Eventually, we found something we could use, and I ended up redoing Pat's wardrobe out of these old Chanels.

It wasn't just the lack of stylishness in Pat Stanley's clothes that the Kanins objected to. There was a great calling together in the Brandywine Room of the Dupont Hotel. Everyone was there: Garson and Ruth, Norman Krasna, his wife, who was Al Jolson's widow, and various agents and attorneys. We were seated at a big circular table. For some reason, there was an empty chair next to mine.

"I think we should start off by saying that the clothes really have no humor to them," said Mr. Kanin. Ruth Gordon, who always sat next to him and was the kind of woman who still wore black satin pumps in the daytime, nodded vigorously.

I sank lower and lower into my chair and munched on a crabmeat cocktail to get myself through this ordeal. I was about to speak when I bit into the little membrane that comes with crabmeat. It got caught in my throat and I could not utter a sound. I was convinced I was going to choke and die right in front of all these illustrious people.

Just then I heard a low voice next to me. I turned to see David Merrick, who had slipped quietly into the chair to my left. He smiled at me and said with a slight chortle, "Well, let's just see if the play is funny before we do anything about the costumes. Okay?" "Oh, my god, I thought, "I have a friend!"

The next day, after a respectable first performance, I received a memo from Mr. Kanin: "The costumes are starting to appear funnier." I had not touched any of them.

One day I got a call from Gene Frankel asking if I would be interested in working on the American premiere of Genet's *The Blacks* which he would be directing at the St. Mark's Playhouse. I had done *Camino Real* at St. Mark's, and I had a gorgeous time doing *The Balcony*, so I said yes.

Gene had started out as an actor but became active as a director just as the Off Broadway movement was getting started. In 1957, he won one of the early Obie Awards, which the *Village Voice* had started in 1955 to recognize good work there. St. Mark's had the height Gene wanted for a two-level set and raked seating suggesting a Greek amphitheatre. Gene saw the play as a kind of Dionysian ritual.

In *The Blacks*, a troupe of black players is re-enacting the murder of a white woman before a kind of court of white colonial archetypes—The Queen, The Missionary, The Governor, The Judge—all played by black actors wearing white masks. A sculptor was originally supposed to design and fabricate the masks, but about two weeks before dress rehearsals were to begin, he withdrew, and I was asked to step in. I had never made a mask in my life.

What did I do? I bought a book on how to make masks. It said to put Vaseline on people's faces. So I got this group of wonderful actors—Maya Angelou, Godfrey Cambridge, Raymond St. Jacques, Charles Godrone, James Earl Jones, Cicely Tyson, Louis Gossett, Roscoe Lee Browne—to lie down, and I put straws up their noses, smeared Vaseline on them, and made plaster casts of their faces. I took my plaster molds, made positives, and then began to build the masks with Plasticine.

After about a week of doing this day and night, I noticed that when I got home late at night (I was always getting home late at night or early in the morning) my left hand always had the Plasticine on it, and my right hand was always clean. I realized that although I was a right-handed person, I was using my left hand to model. Somehow a different hemisphere of my brain had become engaged. When I've done masks since then, I've used my left hand. My left hand is my sculpting hand.

A fabulous woman who was in Karinska's millinery department covered the masks with kid leather and satin and long ostrich feathers for eyelashes. It was white upon white upon white. We had a wonderful time working on them.

Opening night was the first time that I was able to see the play from the very beginning. I had always been down in the basement fixing one last item on somebody's costume. As the performance started, I was unprepared for what was to follow. The lights came up on the second level of the set, and there were four of the characters in my masks dancing a Mozart minuet.

Suddenly, with no warning, the music changed to a wildly pulsating march tempo, the entrance door to the theatre flew open, and the most spectacular parade of masked figures swirled past the audience and up the curved ramp.

One by one they went by, acknowledging the audience. It was almost like a dream. Though I had seen their costumes and masks in bits and pieces in fittings, this was the first time I saw them all together. Everything that I had envisioned in my imagination was parading right before me now. Working Off Broadway, I had found my style. *The Balcony* had come right out of my head, and now *The Blacks* came right out of my head.

The Blacks, *The Captain*. Credit: Billy Rose Theatre Division, The New York Public Library for the Performing Arts; © Estate of Patricia Zipprodt.

All those modern Broadway shopping shows, working with people who couldn't remember my name, let alone spell it correctly, all the persons who questioned and doubted my styles and colors suddenly were seen in perspective. I would be able to put up with any of them in the future, because I now knew that I had once again caught that inspiration from watching *La Valse* at the New York City Ballet dancing in Karinska's colors. I knew once again that I could indeed paint with fabric. That opening night of *The Blacks* I certified myself to myself once and for all.

The Blacks ran for 1,408 performances and was the longest-running Off-Broadway nonmusical of the decade. It opened on the very day that the first Freedom Riders left Washington, DC on two public buses for Alabama to test the Supreme Court's ruling that segregation in interstate bus and rail stations was unconstitutional. During rehearsals the actors were very outspoken that the play was expressing their cause, and there were meetings, sometimes tense, voicing their concern that the producer, the director, the designer, and the crew were white.

The Blacks, *full cast on stage. Courtesy of* Whitney Blausen.

It was a difficult time for Gene Frankel. But the play's success made it all worthwhile. In many ways, *The Blacks*, although by a white author, and a Frenchman to boot, marked the beginning of the modern Black theatre movement in America. Many black actors who later became important figures rotated through its cast during its three-year run. Was it a coincidence that the Negro Ensemble Company was founded a few seasons later at the St. Mark's Playhouse?

6

Hal and Jerry

I met Jerome Robbins and Harold Prince within a few months of each other in 1961. Both men were to play important roles in my future career. Our first meetings were not auspicious.

I met Hal first. Harold Prince was one of those wunderkind producers who had his first Broadway hit, *The Pajama Game*, in 1954, when he was only twenty-six. Other hits followed quickly, including *Damn Yankees* in 1955 and *West Side Story* in 1957. Now he was trying his hand at directing with a musical called *A Family Affair* by a young composer named John Kander and a pair of playwriting brothers, James and William Goldman. He had engaged David Hays, my pal from Circle in the Square, to design sets and lights.

David recommended me for costumes. I got called over to the office in Rockefeller Center which Prince shared with an older producing partner, Robert Griffith, and his mentor, George Abbott. Mr. Abbott, as he was always called, had first appeared as an actor on Broadway in 1913 and had so many hits as a writer, director, and producer he was sometimes known as "Mr. Broadway."

I arrived with my sizeable portfolio filled with sketches and photos of *The Rope Dancers*, *The Crucible*, *Period of Adjustment*, *The Blacks*, the three Circle in the Square plays, and a show called *Laurette*, which had closed in New Haven when its star, Judy Holliday, was diagnosed with breast cancer.

Prince, Griffith, and Mr. Abbott sifted through my material. The room became very quiet. "Not much color here," said Mr. Abbott, looking at *The Rope Dancers*. "Well, yes," I said, as my heart began to sink, "that's true. But it's a play about poor Irish immigrants." I pointed to another photo from *The Rope Dancers*. "There's color in that red velvet jacket," I said. "Siobhan McKenna sewed on it throughout the play." "But it's on a dress dummy," said Griffith.

"Oh, that was the one about the little girl with six fingers on her left hand," said Prince. Dead silence. "I don't think I saw that one," said Mr. Abbott. "Wasn't Art Carney in it?" More silence.

"These sketches are awfully dark and gloomy," said Prince. "We want this musical to be very bright and full of color." I turned to some of *The Blacks* sketches. "There's color in these costumes," I said, pointing to one stunning long dress worn by Cicely Tyson. "But most of them are wearing masks," said Griffith.

"Well, I do have photos of the costumes I did for *Laurette*." "Oh," said Prince, "wasn't that when Judy Holliday was taken ill? Do we really want to see those?"

I shook my head, thanked them for seeing me, packed up my portfolio, and made for the door. I imagined them behind me looking at each other and thinking, "Who *is* that woman?" My first thought as I hit the street was, "Boy, have I ever gotten David Hays into trouble with my gloomy portfolio."

One Friday a few months later, the phone rang, and this dulcet, cultivated voice said, "This is T. Edward Hambleton from the Phoenix Theatre. Would you be interested in doing a show up here?"

Now even though *The Blacks* was still running and all kinds of important people in the New York theatre were seeing it, I had never gotten a call about another job as a result. So when this gentlemanly person spoke, I got a little twittery. "Oh, yes," I twittered, "I really would!"

He said, "Perhaps you could come and meet with our director." "Oh, yes," I twittered again, "I'll be there as soon as I can." I didn't even think to ask who the director was. And I forgot my portfolio and had to go back and get it.

The distinguished T. Edward Hambleton, a Yale graduate from a Baltimore banking family, was a veteran theatre producer who had teamed in 1953 with another Ivy Leaguer, the veteran producer Norris Houghton, a Princeton graduate, to found the Phoenix in a former Yiddish theatre on Second Avenue in the East Village. Like Ted Mann and José Quintero at Circle in the Square, they were really among the inventors of Off Broadway. Now Hambleton and Houghton were in the process of moving to a new, more intimate space on East Seventy-fourth Street.

After I met Hambleton—I would eventually call him T. like everyone else—I was introduced to Norris Houghton, who led me to a chair, handed me a script, and said, "You have an hour to read through this before you see Mr. Robbins. It's not a long play, but please read fast."

And that's when I discovered I would be meeting the famously difficult Jerome Robbins.

Now it takes me as long to read a script as it does for the script to play on stage. I should be hired out to estimate running times, because if a play is going to run two hours and twenty-two minutes, I can tell you. I tried reading this all the way through in one hour, but I couldn't.

The play had an extravagant title, *Oh Dad, Poor Dad, Mamma's Hung You in the Closet and I'm Feelin' So Sad,* and it was by a recent Harvard graduate, Arthur Kopit. It's a farce about an overbearing mother, Madame Rosepettle, and her nebbishy son who check into a Caribbean hotel carrying a coffin with her taxidermied dead husband inside. And, yes, she does hang him in the closet.

This was the time when a kind of playwriting called Theatre of the Absurd was making its appearance, with Genet one of its first exemplars. Young Kopit's play, his first, used many Theatre of the Absurd devices, but he was also making fun of the genre. The hour's worth I got to read was tremendous fun, and I could see why Robbins might choose this as his first nonmusical to direct.

I was ushered into a large rehearsal room where Mr. Robbins was sitting at the far end. He was just as gloomy and formidable as I had heard from any number of friends. After glancing at some of my material, he said, "We're beginning rehearsals on Monday. You'll go home and do some sketches for me, and I'll see you Sunday." I said, "Well, okay."

When I got home, I thought, "I'm not going to do that." I had done all the clothes for Judy Holliday on *Laurette*, from Laurette Taylor's childhood to her elegant twenties and thirties dresses and to her drunken bathrobe before she made her comeback as Amanda in *The Glass Menagerie*. Because no photos had been taken of Judy Holliday in the clothes I'd designed, I got them all together and took them over to Gjon Mili's studio, put them on myself—Judy and I were about the same size—and modeled them for Gjon to shoot. My favorite was a black velvet coat with sablesque tails for sleeves. I knew there were elements in the wardrobe for *Laurette* that were dead right for Madame Rosepettle.

I looked absolutely wonderful in these costumes, and I learned something important from that experience: the clothes really tell you what to do.

I went back to the theatre on Sunday afternoon for my next meeting with Mr. Robbins and brought out the *Laurette* photos which I hadn't got to show Hal Prince. He studied them for a long, long time. Dead silence. Then he finally said, kind of under his breath, "Well, I suppose, you'll do." So he *supposed* me into the job. I didn't mind. I was glad to get the work.

I found out later that Jerry had gone through every designer's portfolio in New York. Bill and Jean Eckart were doing the sets (I had assisted them on *Reuben, Reuben* in its ill-fated Boston tryout), and they said to Jerry and T., "Oh, there is that girl who did that weird thing down at St. Mark's, *The Blacks*." Jerry had seen it and said, "Let's see her." Being Friday before rehearsals began, they didn't have much choice but to deal with the last person down the pipe, which happened to be me. So T. Edward Hambleton had called me.

Jerry's cast included Barbara Harris, Austin Pendleton, and Jo Van Fleet. Barbara was a gifted comic and dramatic actress who had just appeared on Broadway in a revue called *From the Second City*, with the revolutionary Chicago improvisational troupe. Austin was making his New York debut after graduating from Yale and spending several summers at the Williamstown Theatre Festival.

Miss Van Fleet was at the crest of a distinguished career that included creating the roles of Marguerite Gautier in the original *Camino Real* and Eliza Gant in *Look Homeward, Angel*. She won an Academy Award in 1955 as best supporting actress for playing James Dean's mother in Elia Kazan's film *East of Eden*.

And she was about to make my life a living hell.

I launched into what I came to call The Sketching Exercises. I would show a sketch to Jerry, and he'd approve. Then I would show it to Miss Van Fleet, who would disapprove. I would then do more sketches and show them to Miss Van Fleet first, and she adored them. I showed them to Jerry, and he hated them.

I sketched Madame Rosepettle whirling around in one after another variation of a ball gown. I sketched her heading for the beach at night in a floppy straw hat with a flashlight in hand, where the character kicked sand in the faces of all the lovers lying there.

Finally I caught Miss Van Fleet and Jerry on a day when they both liked the same sketches. Jerry wanted everything made at Karinska's shop, since he knew her from the New York City Ballet. I popped the sketches into a bag and ran off to meet for the first time my idol, Karinska, the woman whose work had inspired me to become a costume designer.

She looked at my drawings and loved them. She even called up Jerry to say what a talented lady I was. Then she said, "Madame, Madame, these things are wonderful. I wish I could do them, but I am very busy and I cannot." She kissed me on the cheek. "Goodbye, darling! Good luck!"

"I launched into what I came to call The Sketching Exercises." Credit: Billy Rose Theatre Division, The New York Public Library for the Performing Arts; © Estate of Patricia Zipprodt.

Oh Dad, Poor Dad, Mama's Hung You in the Closet, and I'm Feelin' So Sad, *Madame Rosepettle*. Credit: Billy Rose Theatre Division, The New York Public Library for the Performing Arts; © Estate of Patricia Zipprodt.

I ended up having the costumes built at Grace Costumes, a new shop just opened by Grace Miceli and her sister Maria Brizzi. Grace had been a protégée of Karinska's and was now going out on her own. I was one of her first customers and she became one of my frequent collaborators.

Jerry was notorious for not being able to make up his mind. At the opening of the show, the hotel bellboys bring in a white coffin with travel stickers. Every day during dress rehearsal, Jerry would say, "Oh, it's too long." So the coffin would disappear, and the next day it would come back shorter. "Oh, it's too short," and it would get longer. This poor coffin went in and out like an accordion for days on end. I finally discovered the carpenter's secret. Downstairs he had all these intermediate slices of the coffin on hooks and numbered. When it was too long, he would take out two of them and put in one. When it was too short, he'd add another slice. He had it organized, "Any size you want, Mr. Robbins. A little shorter this time? Okay, just give me a minute." And no one ever knew the magic which was going on down in the basement with all these little slices of coffin hanging up on hooks along the rafters.

Meanwhile, rehearsals were becoming explosive. T. Edward Hambleton had to stop some sessions when Van Fleet and Robbins were throwing chairs around. One day Jerry was seen stomping out and muttering, "I think I've finally met my match!"

Fittings with Miss Van Fleet were a nightmare. She would come into the costume shop early on the days when she wasn't rehearsing and would still be going hours later. "This isn't right." "Pull this up." "Let me try it this way." "Let me sit down in it." It went on and on and on.

It all came to a climax with Madame Rosepettle's ball gown. I had designed it in black with a very wide opening in the back. When she twirled around, a beautiful section of red satin covered with handmade roses would be revealed. It had taken Grace and her staff hours to construct and attach those roses.

Miss Van Fleet did not approve. "I don't like the shade of red on the roses," she announced. "It is not becoming to me." "But it is exactly the shade Mr. Robbins approved," I protested. "I don't care," said Miss Van Fleet, "I want a different shade of red." Was this Leueen MacGrath yet again?

The first dress rehearsal was two days away. After Miss Van Fleet left, I coached Grace and her assistants to explain, if necessary, that it would be very costly to replace these roses. The next day at the theatre, I coached T. Edward Hambleton and Jerry Robbins to stand by me.

Came the dress rehearsal, and afterwards we all went down to the basement where the dressing rooms were. T. Edward and his wife, Merrill, who helped raise funds for the theatre, were there. Mr. Robbins and his assistant, William Daniels,[18] were there. I was there with my assistant, Nancy Azara. Grace Miceli and Maria

---

[18] William David Daniels (b. 1927) is an American actor known for his work in theatre, television, and films. He would work later with PZ when he played Mr. Braddock, Benjamin Braddock's father, in *The Graduate*, and John Adams in both the Broadway and film versions of *1776*, for which PZ designed costumes. He was very aware of the problems between Jerome Robbins and Jo Van Fleet. As an acting colleague, Daniels tried to get Ms. Van Fleet to listen to Mr. Robbins and to mediate between them. But, he recalled, she was a terrible bully and could get the upper hand with Robbins. Daniels worked with Barbara Harris and Austin Pendleton while Robbins and Van Fleet battled it out in another room.

Oh Dad, Poor Dad, *Madame Rosepettle ball gown. Credit: Billy Rose Theatre Division, The New York Public Library for the Performing Arts; © Estate of Patricia Zipprodt.*

Brizzi were there with their assistants. We were all there, the whole group, facing Miss Van Fleet. She was adamant: that color red was not right for her.

I said, "But this is the color Mr. Robbins wanted. To replace these roses will be absolutely prohibitive in cost." Miss Van Fleet looked at T. Edward Hambleton. "Oh, I guess it won't cost so very much that we couldn't find the money to do it," he said. I looked over at Jerry, who was clearly fading out on me.

I was young and untried in those days. I took what I saw as a betrayal to heart and just steamed. Today I'd give a philosophical shrug and say, "So, red, what's red?"

We finished up down in the basement and went our ways. I saw Jerry sneak by to get out by a big fire door. All of a sudden I just started running after him. I chased him through the door and into the back alley. I grabbed him and shook him so hard his hat flew off. And then he started to laugh. He knew he'd been bad. The next day he sent me a bunch of tulips. Not roses. I don't remember if they were red.

Oh, Dad was a success and ran at the Phoenix for over a year. About a month after the show opened, I received a letter from Lucinda Ballard, who had been designing costumes on Broadway since 1937. She had designed the original production of *A Streetcar Named Desire* as well as the film version and won the first Tony Award given for costume design in 1947. "I saw 'Oh Dad, Poor Dad' on Sunday," she wrote, "and I was mad about it. I am sure everyone has told you what a brilliant job you did, but I *know* what it is to make things in a basement with no money—and these don't show the agony you went through. They are just wonderful and you are very much to be congratulated." Praise from someone who understood everything like that was praise indeed.

Oh, Dad was one of the first Off Broadway productions that moved to Broadway, where it opened in August 1963 with Hermione Gingold replacing Jo Van Fleet and a young Sam Waterston making his Broadway debut replacing Austin Pendleton. It was not as successful there, however, and closed after forty-seven performances.

Meanwhile, T. Edward Hambleton and Norris Houghton were so pleased with me that I was taken on as a sort of in-house designer at the Phoenix for their next five productions. One of them was Thornton Wilder's *The Matchmaker*, which the Phoenix was producing for a five-week, twenty-one-city tour of New York State sponsored by the New York State Council on the Arts.

T. invited me to meet the director and in walks Hal Prince. "Oh, my god," he said, "it's the girl with the gloomy portfolio and the play about the little girl with six fingers." His tone was light-hearted, but I could tell he was uncomfortable. This was his first nonmusical directorial effort. He was using it to try out, just as Jerry had done with *Oh, Dad,* as his first dramatic show. This was a period when the Phoenix was a place for new directors to experiment.

T. came to the rescue by reminding Hal I'd done the clothes for *Oh, Dad* and *The Blacks*. "Oh," he said, "you did *The Blacks* and *Oh, Dad*." I could feel the atmosphere lightening.

Hal cast Sylvia Sidney as Dolly Levi, Sada Thompson as Irene Molloy, and Ralph Dunn, who had played the manager of the pajama factory in Hal's production of *The Pajama Game,* as Horace Vandergelder. I came up with bright, funny clothes for all the women, and we had a field day finding wonderful hats for Mrs. Molloy's millinery shop. It was a wonderful little production which toured happily all over the state. When we opened in Poughkeepsie, and Hal saw all these colorful clothes come on, he said, "I have found my designer for life."

This production of *The Matchmaker* inspired David Merrick to ask Hal to direct a new musical he was developing based on Thornton Wilder's comedy. It was first to be called *Dolly: A Damned Exasperating Woman,* then *Call on Dolly,* and finally *Hello, Dolly!* Hal declined.

The Matchmaker, *Sada Thompson as Mrs. Molly.* Credit: Billy Rose Theatre Division, The New York Public Library for the Performing Arts; © Estate of Patricia Zipprodt.

The Matchmaker, *Minnie Fay.* Credit: Billy Rose Theatre Division, The New York Public Library for the Performing Arts; © Estate of Patricia Zipprodt.

The Matchmaker, *The Hats.* Credit: Billy Rose Theatre Division, The New York Public Library for the Performing Arts; © Estate of Patricia Zipprodt.

Instead, he began work producing and directing a new musical called *She Loves Me*, with music by Jerry Bock, lyrics by Sheldon Harnick, and a book by Joe Masteroff, based on a 1937 play by the Hungarian playwright Miklós László and the 1940 Ernst Lubitsch movie *The Shop Around the Corner*, with Margaret Sullivan and Jimmy Stewart.

She Loves Me is a charming romance about a shy assistant manager of a perfume shop in 1930s Budapest named Georg and a nervous, newly hired clerk named Amalia. Neither realizes they are anonymous pen pals known to each other in their letters only as "Dear Friend." At work, they are constantly getting on each other's nerves, but love flourishes in their letters. The complications are of course resolved happily.

Hal put together a superlative cast: Barbara Cook, still a size eight, the original Cunegonde in *Candide* and Marian the Librarian in *The Music Man*, as Amalia, and Daniel Massey, a versatile classical actor known at the time mostly in London, as Georg. Barbara Baxley, whom I had worked with on *Period of Adjustment*, Ludwig Donath, a Viennese-born actor well known for character roles in films and television, and Jack Cassidy, active on television as well as Broadway, were other perfumery inhabitants with their own romantic complications.

She Loves Me had a very complex costume plot, mostly because the story progresses through all four seasons. The show concluded with a wildly inventive Christmas sales sequence choreographed by Carol Haney[19] and a gorgeous snowfall scene, as the two lovers finally realize their true identities. The beautiful settings were by my friends Bill and Jean Eckart.

When I was designing *She Loves Me* I took Barbara Cook and Barbara Baxley out to the Brooklyn Museum's Costume Collection. My friend Bob Riley pulled out good dresses of the thirties and let them put them on. We studied photographs of the period, how people actually stood, so the clothing would drape properly. With all the bias cutting, you have to stand leaning back a little so the dress drops slightly back. They were able to see for themselves in the mirrors how it worked. They took all that information back to Carol Haney, who got it incorporated all the way through the show. This is what research is about.

When I first started designing *She Loves Me* in January 1963—we were scheduled to open in April—the challenge was color again, getting colors that would please both me and Hal. He wanted things lighter and brighter. I took some of my initial sketches to his office one gray, blustery Thursday morning, and when I left I could tell he wasn't happy. He went off to lunch. He was leaving with his wife for a sunshine break in San Juan, Puerto Rico. After lunch, he tried and failed to reach me by telephone, so he dictated a long letter before he left for the airport.

---

[19]Carol Haney (1924–64) began as a dancer in Hollywood musicals when she was fifteen and became an assistant to Gene Kelly on *An American in Paris* and *Singin' in the Rain*, among others. She danced with Bob Fosse in the film of *Kiss Me, Kate* (1953). Fosse cast her in his first Broadway choreographic assignment, *The Pajama Game* (1954), and her performance in "Steam Heat" and "Hernando's Hideaway" made her a star. She then concentrated on choreography with *Flower Drum Song* (1958, directed by Gene Kelly), *Bravo Giovanni* (1962), *She Loves Me* (1963), and *Funny Girl* (1964), which had been running two months when she died at age thirty-nine.

She Loves Me, *Amalia*. Credit: Billy Rose Theatre Division, The New York Public Library for the Performing Arts; © Estate of Patricia Zipprodt.

"The costumes for the shoppers in the summer scene are perfect," he said, "they are all prints; they have color; they seem in some way to blend and make a statement and to be part of a musical. This is not quite so of the winter costumes."

The problem, he said, was that most of the play takes place in the winter, and the ladies on the street would be seen for most of the evening in clothes he called "dour." Could we find some way to find more lightness that would not distract from the inhabitants of the shop, yet keep the stage alive when we get out on the street?

"See what you can do," he closed, "with some adjustment in color to assuage my feeling that the winter clothes may well be depressing in the street. Redundantly, and hastily, and affectionately, Hal."

I pondered all this and sat down on Sunday and wrote him a long letter. "I agree," I said, "and will go further to say that my entire basic conception was off, due to the feeling that it was a play with music rather than a musical, and due to misleading myself by concentrating too heavily on the 'shabby' quality, the poorness of the people in the shop that we talked about. Thus I headed up a blind alley and ended up being too literal."

She Loves Me, *Shoppers in summer. Credit: Billy Rose Theatre Division, The New York Public Library for the Performing Arts; © Estate of Patricia Zipprodt.*

I assured him I was going over the entire show. "Do cheer up about this," I said, "I appreciate your letter and I know the worry behind it. Blank out in the beautiful sun! Meanwhile, think of me, chained to the drawing board, in the middle stages of 'designeritis', a mysterious malady composed of paint-stained fingernails and a peculiar assortment of ticks."

At the first dress rehearsal in New Haven, when Hal saw all my clothes together for the first time, he turned to me and said "In all my years as a producer, I have never seen this happen before. There is nothing, just nothing, that needs changing." He just kept looking at me, grinning from ear to ear. Was I now truly his designer for life?[20]

---

[20] She was not his designer for life. She continued to work with Hal Prince, either as director or producer, for three more productions, including *Fiddler on the Roof* (1964–72) and *Cabaret* (1966–9). After *Zorba* (1968–9), however, he did not use her again, a hurtful mystery to her. Prince began to use other costume designers, primarily Florence Klotz, the partner of Ruth Mitchell, Prince's main production associate. He did introduce her when she was inducted into the Theatre Hall of Fame in 1992, which smoothed any breach she may have felt.

She Loves Me, *Barbara Baxley as Miss Ritter*. Credit: Billy Rose Theatre Division, The New York Public Library for the Performing Arts; © Estate of Patricia Zipprodt.

My next project was *Fiddler on the Roof*, which brought me together again with Hal, this time as producer, and back with Jerry Robbins as a director. After my long lugubrious time working on Broadway, then a wonderful time working Off Broadway, these two men took me by the back of the neck and put me uptown where I belonged.

She Loves Me, *Jack Cassidy as Steven Kodaly, Daniel Massey as Georg Nowack*. Credit: Billy Rose Theatre Division, The New York Public Library for the Performing Arts; © Estate of Patricia Zipprodt.

She Loves Me, *Ralph Williams as Arpad Laszlo, Nathaniel Frey as Ladislav Sipos*. Credit: Billy Rose Theatre Division, The New York Public Library for the Performing Arts; © Estate of Patricia Zipprodt.

7

Fiddler on the Roof

In the early fall of 1963, Jerry Robbins sent me a script for a musical called *Tevye*, with music and lyrics by Jerry Bock and Sheldon Harnick, the composer and lyricist of *She Loves Me*. The book was by Joseph Stein, a veteran playwright and librettist, whose most recent play, *Enter Laughing*, based on Carl Reiner's autobiographical novel, was then running on Broadway.

Stein's book was based on stories by the Yiddish writer Sholem Aleichem about the dairyman Tevye and his tribulations trying to marry off his daughters in their shtetl in Russian-dominated Ukraine. The ancestors of Stein, Bock, and Harnick had all lived in this kind of Jewish village in Eastern Europe before the Russian Revolution. Jerry, with a similar Polish-Jewish background, felt deeply connected to these stories of Jews struggling, with humor and fortitude, to survive poverty, persecution, and exile from their homes.

I also found the material immensely powerful, even though that world was far removed from my own family heritage. I was particularly moved by the second act scene where one of Tevye's daughters defies him and Jewish tradition by marrying a man outside the faith. And I was beguiled by the relationship among the five daughters. My relationships with my two sisters had always been complex.

As I dug into this material, however, I found I had to put it aside, at least for a time. My sister Barbara had recently committed suicide after fifteen years of struggles with depression and a sizeable attempt on her life in the late 1940s. Over those years I'd provided her with much support, both in and out of hospitals. Her death absolutely broke my heart.

Sometime in October, I felt I could deal with real life again, so I called Jerry. He said, "Why don't you come by and talk about it?" I appeared at his little house on East Seventy-fourth Street at ten o'clock. His assistant offered me a seat on the couch in Jerry's very beige living room. Morning light was pouring in at the windows.

Jerry didn't show up and didn't show up and didn't show up. His assistant kept coming in and saying, "Oh, he'll be along." Finally he came down from upstairs wearing black from under his chin down to the end of his toes with a fierce look on his face. I thought, "Oh, god. What am I in for?"

He sat next to me and stared at me. The bright light behind him was in my eyes. Finally, he said, "Are you Jewish?"

They say when you drown, your whole life goes before you. Well, I was drowning. I thought, "If I say no, there goes my whole career out the door." I finally said, "Um . . . no . . . I'm not." And he said, "Well, what makes you think you can do this show?"

To myself I thought, "Well, you asked me, I didn't ask you." To him I said, "I did *Madame Butterfly* at the Opera Company of Boston last year, and I'm not Japanese." Silence. "Oh, well, never mind," he said. "We're going to show some films tomorrow. Why don't you come back at eleven o'clock."

So the shiksa left, and I came back the next morning feeling very, very insecure in this room full of non-gentiles. There was Joseph Stein. There was Jean Rosenthal, the lighting designer. There were Bill and Jean Eckart. Jean, born Levy in Chicago, was Jewish. There were Sheldon Harnick and Jerry Bock. And there was Jerry Robbins, born Jerome Rabinowitz.

Joe Stein, cigar going full blast, informed us we were about to see Sholem Aleichem films made in Russia. Jerry had gotten hold of them so we could see the atmosphere of those early twentieth-century Jewish villages.

I found myself a little hassock and crouched on it. Joe Stein announced, "No one should work on this show who isn't Jewish." Everyone gave a little cheer. Except me. I thought, "I've got to do something." Jerry was walking around as these films were going. I was at just the right height to jerk on Jerry's jacket edge as he'd go by. I whispered, "Jerry!" He'd go by again. "Jerry!" He said, "What!" "I called home last night, and guess what, I'm Jewish." Jean Eckart turned to me and said, "Are you really?" Everyone was looking at me now. Jerry said, "Pat will bring something special to it." So I became the token goy.

I began my research by going down to the *Jewish Daily Forward* on the Lower East Side, where I bought a book called *The Vanished World*, published right after the war, when people were realizing what a thriving culture among East European Jews had been destroyed by the Holocaust. I lived with this book for the next months, as it became my Bible.[21]

I also found valuable material at the YIVO Institute on Fifth Avenue at Eighty-sixth Street, a study center about European Jewish history, especially Yiddish culture. At that time YIVO had bins of pre-Holocaust photographs depicting Jewish life throughout Europe and Russia. It was a laborious process to copy these photos in the days before copying machines.

Jerry had as his choreography consultant Dvora Lapson, a classically trained Jewish dancer who had become an authority on Hebraic dance. He arranged for her to take me under her wing and instruct me in Jewish customs and ways. She was well connected in that world, and we took several trips to the Williamsburg section of Brooklyn, where there were large Jewish communities. I could watch women sewing in garment factories and talk to them during their work breaks. I would ask, "What did you grandmother wear?" "What did she put on her head?" I would get a multitude of answers, often contradictory, and these women often ended up arguing with one another.

---

[21]PZ is referring to *The Vanished World: Jewish Cities, Jewish People*, published in 1947 by the Forward Association, and edited by Raphael Abramovitch, Alexander Kahn, and Sol Rifkin. It included some of the first published photographs by Roman Vishniac, whose more famous book *A Vanished World* was published by Schocken Books, also in 1947. According to Alisa Solomon in *Wonder of Wonders: A Cultural History of Fiddler on the Roof* (2013), Robbins gave copies of the Vishniac book to all the designers.

Next we went to Friday Sabbath observances in Brooklyn. We would arrive for dinner at a home and then walk to synagogue services after sunset. I was able to sketch before sunset, but afterwards you were not allowed to draw or light a match. There I was, a three-pack-a-day smoker in those days, sitting through long hours among the Orthodox without a cigarette.

At the synagogue, I always sat with the women, who had to sit separately from the men. We peeked through little holes in the wall to watch the Hasidic men in their mink-trimmed hats praying while we all faced east.

Then I started going with Jerry and Dvora to orthodox Jewish weddings on the Upper West Side, from West Seventieth Street up to West Ninety-sixth Street. We would stand up in the balcony watching the klezmer players and the dancers and the bride and groom, absorbing all the details.

I began noticing that people were wearing predominantly blues and greens. These were particularly attractive shades when people moved outside. I thought, "That's nice under the moonlight." It was here that I first developed my color scheme for the wedding scene in *Fiddler*.

By now Boris Aronson had joined the production team, replacing the Eckarts, largely at Jerry's insistence and despite considerable resistance at first from Hal Prince, who was producing. Hal was afraid Boris might make *Fiddler* look like *The Lower Depths*.[22]

Looking back now, it is inconceivable to think of *Fiddler* not being designed by Boris, the son of the chief rabbi of Kiev and a personal friend of Marc Chagall, the Russian painter whose imagery and color palette became a major inspiration for the show's look.

Boris and I began trying things. He'd say, "Let's try it this way." "Let's try it that way." Some of the sketches looked like Hansel and Gretel. Some of them were definitely Chekhov. You could see the whole group playing in *The Three Sisters*.

Jerry came by one day and saw these drawings, together with some of Boris's early sketches, and immediately issued a decree that Boris and I would not be allowed to work together or even converse with each other. He seemed desperately afraid that Boris was influencing me too much. To collaborate with Boris, I had to sneak over to his apartment at night when no one was looking.

Jerry also came to the conclusion that the Chagall fantasy world should be expressed predominantly in the background of the design, while in the foreground, mainly in my costumes, we would deal with the homely realism of poverty. This was fine by me, since by now I had seen enough Chagall paintings and drawings to last me a lifetime.

I kept sketching in black and white. I did some beautiful drawings and sent them to Jerry, who was hard to find because he was in Philadelphia a lot trying to fix a troubled tryout of *Funny Girl* with Barbra Streisand. Finally I sent him a telegram saying, "Where are you? Where are you? Where are you? Where are you?" dozens of

---

[22] According to Andrew Harris in *The Performing Set: The Broadway Designs of William and Jean Eckart* (2005), it was the ballerina Nora Kaye, Jewish like Robbins, and at one time his fiancée, who persuaded the director to use Aronson. Aronson himself had campaigned to get the assignment. PZ believed she contributed to the director's decision to use Aronson.

times, all the way down to the end of the page. I got one back from him saying, "Color, Color, Color, Color" to the bottom of the page.

So I made two little palettes, summertime and wintertime, consisting of collages of people, and began my color work on *Fiddler*. The black and white illustrations were gradually transferred to full-color costume plates, but on very inexpensive paper. I lived in fear that Jerry would ruin me by wanting redos on good paper.

Why was I afraid of financial ruin? My fee for designing *Fiddler* was $5,000. We worked on the project for close to a year. I don't know what I lived on. I did design three plays for the Phoenix during that time, but those hardly brought in enough to cover my expenses. I must have borrowed money, but I can't remember from whom.

My palette for the entire production was inspired by watching Zero Mostel in *A Funny Thing Happened on the Way to the Forum* two years earlier. I sat very close and watched him pour sweat. Any makeup he had on was gone in four or five minutes. Now for *Fiddler*, I thought, "What color can I put on him that will complement his natural coloring?" He had a blue cast to his skin, so I decided to put him in blue instead of black, a midnight blue of the darkest shade. It became the main color of my palette. He was my central and key character; everyone stroked off of that. I rarely put any black on that stage, even though we think of Jewish men as always wearing black.

Fiddler on the Roof, *Men, Women, Family—quick sketches. Credit: Billy Rose Theatre Division, The New York Public Library for the Performing Arts; © Estate of Patricia Zipprodt.*

Fiddler on the Roof, *Men's group*. Credit: Billy Rose Theatre Division, The New York Public Library for the Performing Arts; © Estate of Patricia Zipprodt.

One of my tasks on *Fiddler* was to make poor people's clothes look realistically poor. That meant the tones of all their clothes had to be conservative and dark. Now, two-and-a-half hours of browns would just make your eyes give up. I had to develop a way to incorporate color in drabness, to find color that was hidden, so a brown vibrated rather than just being dull brown. And the clothes had to look old.

Take a pair of dancer's pants which have to look like worn-out work pants. I made them out of raw silk, which is soft, easy to move in, cool under stage lights, and breaks down very easily. The knees can be frayed and have nice patches on them.

Fiddler on the Roof, *Women's group*. Credit: Billy Rose Theatre Division, The New York Public Library for the Performing Arts; © Estate of Patricia Zipprodt.

Fiddler on the Roof, *Musicians—early study*. Credit: Billy Rose Theatre Division, The New York Public Library for the Performing Arts; © Estate of Patricia Zipprodt.

Fiddler on the Roof, *Tevye and family*. Credit: Billy Rose Theatre Division, The New York Public Library for the Performing Arts; © Estate of Patricia Zipprodt.

Fiddler on the Roof, *Tevye and family, Sabbath*. Credit: Billy Rose Theatre Division, The New York Public Library for the Performing Arts; © Estate of Patricia Zipprodt.

I started with the natural color of raw silk, which is a neutral creamy color. I wanted to end up with brown. I didn't know what I was doing when I started, but I used my painter's knowledge of color. I had done so much work in watercolor, I began to go at the aging process as if it were a watercolor problem. First I dyed the silk a reddish rust. Then I overdyed it with dark olive green and ended up with a kind of held-in brown.

Then I had to take the surface off. I had to wear the fabric down at key points. So we used vegetable graters or sandpaper or rubs of bleach as I had done with the prisoners' uniforms in *The Quare Fellow*. The reds and the greens would start to punch through.

Looking at the finished garment in the shop, you would say, "These are brown pants." But under stage lights, they had a lot of vitality. They were a painter's brown. They had red where the fabric has been worn on the seat or by hands going into pockets. Those reds were coming through the blends which made the browns. This was the way I worked with everything: pants, jackets, shirts, skirts, and shawls.

The English were doing aging in what I called the Motley School of Shakespeare: peasant costumes in heavy fabric, with the hems ripped and the folds sprayed with paint to make them look worn. And there were patches put on fabric that doesn't require patches. None of it said old to me; it just said theatre.

I invented my own particular techniques of aging that would be permanent, so when the clothes were dry cleaned, the color would hold and not vanish. With scenery, you can just paint and overpaint. Costumers have the practicalities of human beings wearing their garments. We have to deal with sweat and fading under lights and a weekly dry clean. Dry cleaning fluids are meant to remove things, and they can remove your color too. The fabrics had to be colorfast and durable, in addition to being vibrant. If I started painting the vibrancy on, it would be gone in a month.

I knew I was playing a long shot. But I was accomplishing two things at once. I was getting my color to buzz, and I was aging the fabric at the same time. So the pants were getting nice and limp before they went into their abrading and patching phase.

Tevye's pants were the darkest blue, with green tinges. His vest was a sort of gray-blue. His shirts, if they weren't blue, were red and yellow. And I gave him a rust-colored cap. The hat was again the double color effect. It was made out of a raw silk which was woven with green and orange threads. I blended those with a wash of beige just to hold it together. This was a rust-colored cap with a punch that you couldn't keep your eyes off.

Once Jerry approved my sketches, I spent hours at Grace Miceli's shop choosing fabrics from Grace's many, many sample books or from swatches my assistants, Connie Wexler and Albert Wolsky, brought in. Connie had worked with me on *Camino Real* at the Phoenix. Albert Wolsky was a top assistant to a number of leading Broadway designers before going out on his own and eventually landing in Hollywood, where he won an Oscar for Bob Fosse's *All That Jazz*.[23] After the

---

[23] Albert Wolsky located a rayon fabric for the Sabbath coats that was orange and blue on the front and black on the back. The coats were made with the black side out, but the weave was loose enough so there was a faint shimmer of color through the black. The fabric took the aging process beautifully. "Finding that fabric was a joyful moment," Wolsky recalled (email to AW, May 5, 2020).

assistants left for the day, I'd stay alone until all hours of the night, making choices until I almost turned into a piece of lint. A staggering number of fabrics had to be chosen before the shop could begin to cut.

Once the clothes were made, we began the aging process. We rented a large space at the back of a costume shop run by Kate Feller, the wife of Pete Feller, the technical theatre wizard who operated one of the best scenic studios in New York. We brought in ovens, huge vats, and tables. We put all these brand-new peasant clothes on racks at Grace Costumes on West Fifty-fourth Street and wheeled them through the pedestrians on Eighth Avenue to Katie's loft, which was on Fifty-third Street, hauled them up in the freight elevator, and went to work with our vegetable graters and sandpaper.[24]

I said to everybody, "If a jacket is hung over a chair, we should know who wore it." I wanted the clothes humanized, to look as if bodies had been in them for years. I invented things to hurry up the aging process. We put diluted Sobo Glue in elbows to give them wrinkles that would hold until the actors had put real wrinkles in them.

It's interesting how learning carries over. I'd had that disastrous experience with Sobo on *The Balcony*. That's how I knew this would work on the sleeves to hold them into shape. So *The Balcony* disaster wasn't a total loss.

Grace and Maria were Italian, and most of the makers in the shop were Sicilian and Calabrian women from very poor cultures who had come over to America to make beautiful ballet costumes for Karinska. They put such love into building these costumes.

Then we took them away and brought them back wrecked. When we put the first rack into the front hall of the shop, slowly the entire shop came to the front, and everyone looked absolutely struck. Two women crossed themselves. They thought I had lost my mind. I didn't have any reputation at the time; I was an untried designer. They were in tears that I had destroyed their handiwork. "Is this why we leave to come to America?" I heard one angry woman say.

Now I was telling them to fix these ragged garments. In the old country, their own clothes were heavily worn like these peasant clothes, and they know how to mend them. So after some grumbling, they went back to work and made the most beautiful patches and repairs. Each patch was picked purposely for where it went. Each thread patching color was picked and sometimes dyed to work just right. They looked wonderful.

---

[24]Brian Wolfe, general manager of Costume Armor, a leading maker of scenic properties in New York, reported a story told by the company's founder, Nino Novellino about PZ and Katie Feller. Feller's costume house, Costume Associates, was building one of PZ's shows. "Pat was constantly changing her mind and making them rebuild, all the while telling Katie it was her fault that she had gotten the instructions wrong. Katie had had enough and secretly recorded her in the shop. Pat and Katie were having a spaghetti lunch in Katie's office when Pat once again changed her mind after a dress was built and denied the previous choices. Katie pulled out the tape recorder and played the previous instructions. Pat threw the plate of spaghetti at Kate's head. Katie ducked, but the spaghetti and tomato sauce hit the wall, covered with a beautiful white silk moire, and smeared down to the floor. Nino was telling the story to illustrate that sometimes with designers it is just better to suck it up, make the changes, and stay in the designer's good graces" (Brian Wolfe, email to AW, February 27, 2024).

This was a completely new way of aging. I wanted to get into the absolute guts of the garment. We sometimes put linings into jackets that would shrink differently from the jacket itself so we got that funny look of a sleeve lining pulled out or the way a coat would buckle in the back if it's been hanging too long. It was a kind of aging that let you know a garment had really been worn and worn and worn.

Occasionally *Fiddler* had its own disasters in the aging process. The character of Lazar Wolf, the butcher, wore a long tent-like beige coat when he was going off to Chicago at the end of the show. It was an oatmeal color with a blue scarf and derby. The coat cost $400, which in 1964 was not an inconsiderable sum.

I wanted to dip it a bit lighter, so I filled up a huge bucket with water, poured in Clorox, sank the coat into it, and left for the night. The next morning, I said, "Let's see how the coat did." No coat. "Who took the coat out of here?" No one took the coat.

The water was very thick. Very thick. I could hear clicking at the bottom of the metal bucket. Buttons. Little machine-sewn cotton button holes were floating around. So that's how I learned that Clorox rots silk. I had to explain this to Grace and Maria and to the management. Those telephone calls were terrifying.

After much thought and guessing, the last dress I put into the works was the Bride's. Boris had done a beautiful Chagalesque wedding set with a dark blue sky

Fiddler on the Roof, *Stephen Wright as The Fiddler in the 25th anniversary production, showing costume patching and aging. Photograph by Martha Swope; Billy Rose Theatre Division, The New York Public Library for the Performing Arts; © NYPL.*

and very muted, wonderfully rich stained glass colors. Jean Rosenthal[25] was lighting it accordingly. I thought, "What color will read white?" After my experience with *The Gang's All Here* and *Period of Adjustment*, I knew it would have to be robin's-egg blue.

I was taking a gamble because I didn't have Jo's light booth to go into and play with fabric. I just had to make these deductions from my overall palette and my knowledge of value. I chose an Oxford weave silk that had a shine to it which would reduce the blue. So I had to balance these two things out, and finally, like going off the high dive, I said to the dyers, "Go. Go."

Back in those days, we had a dress parade. Nobody does dress parades anymore. No one has time. Grace's shop is not very big, and there is only one real fitting room. I was a little nervous because this was my first dress parade for this huge musical. I was getting the male chorus as a group ready to go out. Zero was nearby getting into his costume. For this occasion, I had chosen to wear a very pretty pale pink crepe dress which dropped straight down and had very little body to it. Zero adored this dress.

As I was checking one of the men, I suddenly saw nothing but pink in front of me. It took me a moment to realize what had happened. My crepe dress had been suddenly lifted from my hips over my head. There I was, just shoes, legs, no stockings, and a pair of very brief panties. There was a huge whoop from the male chorus, followed by loud laughter from Mr. Zero. He could be very bad.

I had saved the Bride for last. When she came out, Jerry said, "What's that!" "That's the bride." "That's not a bride. A bride wears white." "Well, it will look white." "It won't look white. It's blue." I said, "Jerry, it's going to be white in Detroit. It's going to be the lightest color on stage. If it were a real white, you wouldn't be able to see anything else on stage." Jean Rosenthal wasn't there to back me up. Jerry said, "Pat, I won't open this show if that dress is blue."

When we got to Detroit, where the show was to have its first tryout, I happened to walk into the Fisher Theatre one evening when it was empty except for Jerry and Jean working on the lighting. Jean was at her desk console, Jerry was in the back of the house, and my Bride's dress was on stage on a mannequin. I heard Jerry call down to Jean, "What color is that dress?" "It's white, Jerry," she said firmly. I thought, "I'll get out of this theatre as fast as I can and leave well enough alone." And that's the last I ever heard about the dress.

When the show opened in Detroit, there was a newspaper strike on. So the first review that came out was by a stringer for *Variety* named Fred Tew, who was a publicist for Chrysler. It began, "Everything is ordinary about *Fiddler on the Roof* except Zero Mostel. He's extraordinary." Everyone and everything were damned as mediocre; talented people but a mediocre display of talent. Boris's sets, he said, were

---

[25]Jean Rosenthal (1912–69) was the pioneering lighting designer who helped establish the field as a new position apart from the scenic designer or electrician. She worked on the Federal Theatre Project and the Mercury Theatre with Orson Welles and John Houseman and designed for Martha Graham, the New York City Ballet, and the Metropolitan Opera. Her Broadway musicals included *West Side Story* (1957), *The Sound of Music* (1959), *A Funny Thing Happened on the Way to the Forum* (1962), *Fiddler on the Roof* (1964), *Hello, Dolly!* (1964), and *Cabaret* (1966). She died of cancer in 1969 at age fifty-seven.

Fiddler on the Roof, *Wedding dress. Credit: Billy Rose Theatre Division, The New York Public Library for the Performing Arts; © Estate of Patricia Zipprodt.*

"serviceable, rather than spectacular. So, too, are the costumes by Patricia Zipprodt, and the lighting by Jean Rosenthal."

This was dispiriting, of course, as this was the review our friends in New York would read. Later, some of the newspaper reviews were read on radio, and they were more favorable. The show always sold tickets.

Everyone was frantically making changes in Detroit and in Washington, where we moved next before the Broadway opening. Astonishingly enough, I only made two changes. I redid the eldest daughters to make them more ordinary. On my first Broadway musical, *She Loves Me*, Hal had been amazed at the first dress rehearsal in New Haven that no costume changes were needed. Now I had almost done it again.

I think this is because I am such a slow designer. I agonize a lot. By the time the show is on stage, I have thought through so many different ways of doing it, so many different colors and textures and shapes, it has a very good chance of staying put.

Jerry really loved the costumes. One night in Washington, he turned to me and said, "The clothes are just wonderful. Every night I look at them I see something I haven't seen before, a patch here, or where a pocket was aged. It's absolutely fascinating."

Opening night of *Fiddler* was Tuesday, September 22, 1964, at the Imperial Theatre on West Forty-fifth Street. During the day, florists and messengers kept coming up to my little apartment then on Central Park South with boxes of roses

Fiddler on the Roof, *Hodel, Perchik, Tevye.* Credit: Billy Rose Theatre Division, The New York Public Library for the Performing Arts; © Estate of Patricia Zipprodt.

Fiddler on the Roof, *Motel, Tzietel, Fyedka, Chava.* Credit: Billy Rose Theatre Division, The New York Public Library for the Performing Arts; © Estate of Patricia Zipprodt.

Fiddler on the Roof, *The Nightmare*. Credit: Billy Rose Theatre Division, The New York Public Library for the Performing Arts; © Estate of Patricia Zipprodt.

and bouquets that stood four feet tall without a vase and enormous art books and glorious notes. Hal's note said that I'd done the best job he'd ever seen. Jerry's note said what an enormous contribution the costumes were.

The opening night party was very exciting. It was at the Rainbow Room on the sixty-fifth floor of the RCA Building in Rockefeller Center, the same building where I had that first frightening interview with Hal in his office many years ago. I danced and danced and danced.

Jerry came up to me and began to expand on what he'd said on the card, that the costumes were incredible, just perfect. Hal went out of his way to repeat and repeat what he'd written in his note which accompanied eight buckets of flowers.

Several of Hal and Jerry's good friends came up to me throughout the evening to tell me they had been hearing all day about Patricia Zipprodt's costumes from Hal and Jerry. Joe Masteroff, who wrote the script for *She Loves Me*, said Hal had mentioned the costumes to him at least five times in the last two days. "Now you can raise your price on him," Joe said, and we chuckled madly, because Hal was famous for being a tightwad.

As the night waned to a close—it really hadn't begun until after midnight, when people began arriving from the theatre—I went to say my farewells to the people sitting at the big table with Hal. Hal said to me again, "You are the best designer in the business. If I ever do a show without you, it will be because I can't help it or because I know you'd be bored to death with the kind of work required. But whenever possible, you will always do my shows. Every time I see that stage filled with those people in those costumes, I feel good. I feel satisfied, as I feel good when I look at a Chagall painting. You wrapped it up, baby, you just wrapped it up!"

By this time, I was ready to either faint or burst into tears. He finished me off completely by introducing me to the whole table as his number one designer.

I melted away to say goodbye to Jerry. He grabbed me by my upper arms and began speaking each word with emphasis. "I don't think I made it clear enough in my note. These are the best costumes I have ever seen, ever. Ever. Do you understand me? Do you understand me? They are the best I have ever seen. Is that clear?"

By this time, I was realizing that Hal and Jerry had probably had too much champagne. And probably so had I. "Jerry," I said, "you're crazy." He said, "What do you mean, I'm crazy? I've had to look at the show every night since July. And every night, I found something new, something I hadn't seen before, that you had done. Everyone here tonight says that this show will make a star out of you. And, Pat, it will. Do you hear? Is that clear?"

"Oh, no," I wailed, "it's the wrong kind of show! I don't want to do rags again. What do I do now?" "Now," he said, "you can say no to me." We both laughed, and I went home.**

The next morning the lines of ticket buyers for *Fiddler* seemed to wind all over New York City. We were all overwhelmed and thrilled. Everyone seemed to feel the show was good for a four-year run.

That Sunday night, I was in both a giddy and a reflective mood, and I sat down and started a long letter to my parents to capture some of the past week. I headed the letter: "A nice gentile girl makes good." "Here I type away," I said, "still on that Corona you gave me, Dad, in 1933. It and I have traveled a long way together."

At the end of the letter, I told them what I called "a deep dark secret." I said, "When I begged and begged the Fashion Institute of Technology for that scholarship in 1951, so that I could design for the theatre, I knew I could and would be at the very top if I wanted it enough, with the top people and without playing tricks and that's what I have gotten. And I still don't know where I got this notion of theatre designing in the first place."

The Tony Awards ceremony was held the following June 13, 1965, in the wonderfully rococo Grand Ballroom of the Astor Hotel on Broadway at Forty-fifth Street. (It would be demolished only two years later.) In those days the Tonys were like a family affair, with maybe 400 people seated at dinner tables. And it was seen only on local, rather than nationwide television.

**So what was the first thing I was offered next? A musical version of *How Green Was My Valley* called *A Time for Singing* that Gerald Freedman was directing from his own adaptation of the Richard Llewellyn novel and the 1941 film. It was set in a Welsh mining town, I dubbed it *Fiddler in the Pit*. I went to Wales, toured the valleys, and went down into the mines. I talked with young people about what their grandfathers wore and what they carried on their belts for lunch in 1885. And I got photographs. In the end, I turned all the research material over to Theoni Aldredge. I just couldn't do the project, because I thought If I did two rag shows in a row, I'd never be offered anything else. One of the ways I have survived in this business is by constantly changing and moving on, trying not to get caught in one pattern.

Fiddler won for Best Musical, Music and Lyrics, Book, Producer, Director, Choreographer, Leading Actor, Supporting Actress (Maria Karnilova), and finally Best Costume Design.*** I wore a dress of my own making: black crepe with a slit showing shocking pink fuchsia lining. It was cut so tightly that I hadn't worn any stockings or panties underneath. I panicked for a few second as I walked up the steps to the stage that the whole dress might split.

The room had a seating gallery along the sides, above the ballroom floor, with Corinthian columns dividing it into kind of theatre boxes. After I had thanked Jerry and Hal and Boris and Jean, I looked up and saw many of that wonderful cast sitting there: Austin Pendleton, Julia Migenes, Leonard Frey, Joanna Merlin, and Bea Arthur. I began to feel I was really talking to them. They all had been so remarkably patient in their many fittings, while the staff and I plotted and marked where their sit spots would be or a pocket rubbed or an elbow or a knee had worn, so we could concentrate our aging points. Of course what the audience saw was that this bunch of rags didn't fit a soul.

So I thanked them "from the bottom of my heart for just standing still." The ballroom erupted with laughter and applause. Somebody said afterwards, "Pat, I never knew you were so funny."****

Fiddler in Amsterdam

When *Fiddler* was done in Amsterdam, where it was called *Anatevka,* the producers were Paul Kijzer and Hans Boskamp. They were one of the few producers who contacted me for the costumes. Everybody all over the world was just ripping them off. My agreement with them was that I would send over the costume bible, the album documenting the entire wardrobe, with all the fabrics, directions, and photographs, so they could have them done. I would come over for dress rehearsals.

I'd never been to Amsterdam before. I flew over in December 1966 and walked into the theatre, where a dress rehearsal was going on. It looked like Hansel and Gretel-land. All the little sleeves were puffed, all the little collars were clean, the aprons were ironed, and the babushkas were tied in pretty knots. The whole thing looked ridiculous. I thought, "What happened to all the notes about aging and all the talk about dying colors over colors and all the instructions and all the photographs?"

What had happened was this. The contract for the costumes went of course to the lowest bidder, a funny little lady who ran a shop in The Hague. She just didn't read English. She had polyester blouses. I thought, "No one knows but me and maybe this producer, who was pretty smart, how the show really looks." And the wedding dress was scald-your-eyeballs white.

***Boris was deeply chagrined that he did not win for Scene Design, but in his eight further collaborations with Hal, he won five Tonys.

****On Saturday, June 17, 1972, *Fiddler on the Roof* became the longest-running show on Broadway. To celebrate the 3,225th performance, Hal flew in all the Tevyes from every national and international company around the world. They all stood on the stage at the end of the performance in their Tevye costumes, along with Bock, Harnick, Stein, Robbins, and Prince. The Mayor gave a proclamation. Everyone cheered. Boris, Jean, and I sat in the audience.

I thought, "I can either spend a few days riding around in the December canals or I can fix this thing." So I decided to roll up my sleeves, and I single-handedly re-dyed the whole show. Bit by bit, we laid out clothes on the workroom floor in the theatre, where there were great big tin work tubs. The only warm water was in the men's room. The two guys who were painting the sets, who later became dear friends, would fill these up at twelve o'clock at night. When the dress rehearsal was over, I would take a section of clothes, and I had my three vats—murk one, murk two, and murk three—and I would just throw these clothes in. When they got good and soft, I'd stir them around in the darkness of the theatre (there was no real light) and hang them up to dry on clothesline we had strung all around. And we finally got the show done. Paul Kijzer said, "Now that's the way the show's supposed to look." I didn't have the sense to put in a bill for my services.

The white wedding gown was still a problem, however. They did have an ager and dyer in Amsterdam. "Oh, yes, we have the best ager and painter in Europe," they said when I inquired. Whereupon I was taken up to an atelier and introduced to a man in a long, white, immaculately clean chemist's smock, down to mid-calf, white hair, clean hands. He had a palette and brushes with signs of taupe and gray that he was painting on some costumes to age them.

I said, "I need some help from you with the wedding dress." No one had even dipped the white satin. It just crinkling new and terrible. I asked him if he would work with me. The dress was all sewn together. What could we do about it? I suggested we get some dye, mix it with alcohol, paint the dress, and never dry clean it. He went crazy. He ran all over the theatre, saying I was going to ruin the dress, that he was not responsible, that I was this mad young woman from America who didn't know what she was doing, who was trying to tell him how to do his job, and he was the number one ager-painter in all of Europe. He walked off.

I thought, "Well, I've got to do it." So I sat down, and started mixing the dye. First I painted the puff sleeves. I was scared to dip, because I didn't know what was going to happen to the fabric. I didn't have any scraps to test, because they had long been discarded in The Hague.

For some reason or other, the ager-painter came back one time, saw the dress half-done, and got intrigued with it. So he stayed, and we painted it together. It was a long full skirt, and we had to paint, paint, paint, so it wouldn't be streaked, so it would look like it was dyed. And we finally did it.

It got up on the stage, and exactly what happened in Detroit happened again. There was a beautiful white dress in place. He saw every single preview. He brought his family. He said, "Look at the dress I had painted blue, it's white." This man was completely overwhelmed by this experience. He had everybody in Amsterdam from his group come to look at the blue dress that was white, that he had painted himself. He and Jean Rosenthal, may they rest in heaven, are probably still talking about it.

Fiddler on film

When Norman Jewison was getting ready to film *Fiddler* in 1970, he asked me to do the costumes. He came back from Paris one time and had the art director's drawings to show me and lure me into this trap. He kept saying, "Miss Zipprodt, I've found the most marvelous location in the mountains of Croatia." I thought, "That's all I need." By this time, I had done *The Graduate*, and I found it miserable enough living in Hollywood. I didn't want to be on a Communist mountaintop, speaking no Croatian, watching only government television for my evening companion. So I never got near it.

He hired two English designers, Joan Bridge and Elizabeth Haffenden, who designed together and were always referred to as "The Bookends." They went backstage at *Fiddler* in London and went through the entire wardrobe.

8

Cabaret

I loved the writer Christopher Isherwood, and I had adored *I Am a Camera*, John Van Druten's 1951 play based on Isherwood's *The Berlin Stories*. Julie Harris as Sally Bowles was one of the great theatre-going experiences of our time. So I was delighted in 1965 when Hal Prince asked me to do the costumes for *Cabaret*, the great big blown-up version written by Joe Masteroff, with music and lyrics by Kander and Ebb. Hal was producing and directing, and Ron Field was choreographing. And I would be working again with Boris Aronson, who had designed *I Am a Camera*, and Jean Rosenthal.

The research was fascinating. I had a German friend named Paul Falkenberg, a filmmaker who had edited Fritz Lang's 1931 film *M*, starring Peter Lorre as a psychopathic child killer. Paul and his wife, Alice, a portrait photographer in Berlin, had to get out of Germany when Hitler came to power, but they did manage to bring with them their albums of photographs of that era. I went to their apartment on West Fifty-fourth Street to look at images of street life of Berlin—people walking to the shops and the bakeries—in the early thirties.

Paul said, "Go look at the G. W. Pabst films, you'll find something that will be valuable to you." So I went over to the Museum of Modern Art and ran their Pabst films through one of those hand players, watching them go by frame by frame. Every now and then I would see something that would tell me what my parameters were. I would see a group of women in one of those honky-tonk entertainments: the stockings, the shapes. How does the hat really go on, how do all these people look?

Boris was friends with the caricaturist Al Hirschfeld and his wife, Dolly Haas, a German-born actress who had worked in theatre and films in Berlin during the early thirties. Dolly had scrapbooks from that time, and she and I would talk at length and go through the scrapbooks. She'd try to remember what she wore and how she felt about this and that.

Nothing was directly usable, but the fact that I saw this world as it was photographed gave me a kind of reassurance. The scrapbooks and the Pabst films gave me a base of knowledge a designer needs about what really happened. When I shot off from it, I knew that I could get back. I knew how far away I could go and still have the ring of the period.

I also went out to the Brooklyn Museum and went through the historic clothes and the fashion books of that time. Really getting the cut of the clothes, getting all that craftsmanlike information, made a whole big pie which ultimately came out as *Cabaret*.

The very first costume I designed is one of my favorite costumes of my whole life. How does one dive into a huge musical and such a complex one as *Cabaret*? The painter will say, "Oh, my god, look at all that white canvas." The writer says, "Oh, my god, look at all these white sheets of paper." I look at a script and say, "Where's the door? How do I find my way in? How do I get to know the people? Who's carrying the burden of the script?"

And for some reason or other I went right to Fräulein Schneider, the Lotte Lenya part. I hadn't met Lenya yet (she was still in Germany), but of course I had seen her as a performer. I listened over and over to the music of her first song with Herr Schultz, "It Couldn't Please Me More (A Pineapple)," and I began to put Lenya into position singing that song in this funny boardinghouse which Boris was still sketching.

Suddenly I began drawing what I called the Pineapple Dress. It just poured out of my little pencil onto the paper. I don't know where it came from. It did not come from research. I had never seen it before or since, but it landed right on the nose of the show for me, a dark, dark green satin jumper-style dress with circular-cut tiered ruffles. It had a peach-salmon chiffon blouse with puffed pleated sleeves and a Peter Pan collar with lace around it. It was absolutely German yucky—the worst of the Alps, you might say.

That dress became for me the logo of the show. For most people, the Kit Kat Girls were the logo, with their little hats and their legs, but for my heart of hearts the Pineapple Dress was the show. And that's how I began it. I came right in on that. I never changed a sketch since.

The dress still exists. I found it at Eaves in 1987, when I was going through their stock to find costumes for a show about my work called *Fashion is Theatre* that the Fashion Institute of Technology was producing at the Waldorf Astoria for a

Cabaret, *Lotte Lenya and Jack Gilford, "It Couldn't Please Me More (A Pineapple)." Photograph by Don Hunstein; © Sony Music Entertainment.*

scholarship benefit. I couldn't believe it: there was Lenya's dress, a historical treasure, twenty years later, hanging on a wire hanger.

I had to do all of Lenya's clothes without meeting with her because she was in Europe. So I just boldly plowed ahead and sketched what I thought Schneider should be wearing. I did pretty well on the whole. The wretched old kimono and the baggy stockings and the old bedroom slippers, she thought they were fine. The black velvet ribbon around her neck with the cameo, that was fine. The Pineapple Dress she adored, which is all I cared about. The rest of the whole show could go as long as I could have my Pineapple Dress.

The dress she was to wear in the fruit shop she didn't like at all. I adored it. My ego was still tightly bound to my work in those days, and I had to learn to be able to let it go and put my thoughts to the needs of the performer sometimes ahead of my own needs as a designer. I never really liked the fruit shop dress she asked for. It was too modern to my eye, almost classical. I felt it needed some garbage on it. She didn't want any garbage.

Cabaret, *The Fruit Shop dress*. Credit. Billy Rose Theatre Division, The New York Public Library for the Performing Arts; © Estate of Patricia Zipprodt.

The hat, she said, was too big. It was a wonderful velvet hat, like a Renaissance beret and tam cut into pie pieces. At the fitting, I put this enormous thing, like the sketch, on her little face. "Excuse me, Miss Lenya, you were right." So we made the same hat reduced in size so she could wear it almost like a pancake. It was wonderful on her. Ideas can be good but scale can be off. Someone else would need the big one. It's always a matter of tuning the item with the person for scale and color.

Hal was very instrumental in establishing the look of the Master of Ceremonies. He had seen many of these funny little guys at work during all his travels in Munich and Berlin. He had the image of the white face definitely from that. He and Joel had a great time experimenting with makeup and getting the wig right. We had wonderful fittings getting Joel into all the funny clothes at Eaves.

These images are the costume designer's ant's eye view of this great production. It opened on Broadway on November 20, 1966, and ran for three years. In the spring of 1967, it won eight Tony Awards, including my second Tony for costume design. After he had been overlooked for a Tony on *Fiddler*, Boris won for scenic design and began a winning streak with wonderful collaborations with Hal.

Cabaret, *Kit-Kat Girl with saxophone.* Credit: Billy Rose Theatre Division, The New York Public Library for the Performing Arts; © Estate of Patricia Zipprodt.

Cabaret, *Master of Ceremonies and gorilla.* Credit: Billy Rose Theatre Division, The New York Public Library for the Performing Arts; © Estate of Patricia Zipprodt.

Cabaret, *Sally Bowles*. Credit: Billy Rose Theatre Division, The New York Public Library for the Performing Arts; © Estate of Patricia Zipprodt.

Cabaret, *Sally Bowles*. Credit: *Billy Rose Theatre Division, The New York Public Library for the Performing Arts*; © Estate of Patricia Zipprodt.

9

Mike Nichols, *The Graduate*, and Why I Hate Hollywood

After *Fiddler on the Roof* opened on Broadway in September 1964, Jerry Robbins had said the show would make me a star. But that hadn't happened.

In fact, my next show, *Anya*, a musical based on Guy Bolton's *Anastasia*, closed after sixteen previews and sixteen performances in December 1965. My next show after that, *Pousse-Café*, was a musical adaptation of the 1930 film *The Blue Angel*, set in the French Quarter of New Orleans in the 1920s. Although it was directed by my wonderful José Quintero and had a score by Duke Ellington, it closed in March 1966 after just three performances.

But with the opening of *Cabaret* in November 1966, I was suddenly very popular with the world. I was the new hot ticket.

Among those who wanted to hire me were Ray Stark and Mike Nichols. Stark, a successful independent film producer, wanted me for the film version of *Funny Girl*, which he had produced on Broadway with Barbra Streisand. She was to star in the movie as well.

Nichols wanted me for *The Graduate*, a film to be based on a 1963 comic novel by Charles Webb. It was about an aimless 22-year-old East Coast college graduate who comes home to his family in Southern California, has an affair with the wife of his father's law partner, and then falls in love with her daughter.

Funny Girl and *The Graduate* were scheduled to shoot at the same time, so I had to make a choice. I found myself in a very interesting position because I had never done a film.

I met first with Stark and his wife at their apartment on East Fifty-seventh Street in Sutton Place. Fran Stark was the daughter of Fanny Brice, whose life was portrayed in *Funny Girl*. They really wanted me to do the film. I wasn't too sure I wanted to lock horns with Streisand because I had heard a lot about her. There was a lot of blood around already. "She designs her own clothes," I thought, "why does she need me?"

We talked at length. Because it was a huge film, their idea was to break it into sections—musical numbers and periods of her life—and use two designers. They had spoken to Dorothy Jeakins about being the other designer, and she was agreeable to this. I had a great respect for Dorothy, who had shared Oscar nominations with both Karinska and Edith Head, Paramount's longtime head of costume design. I thought between the two of us we could it get it delivered in time.

Curiously, what Stark absolutely didn't want to do, he said, was to use Irene Sharaff, who had designed the Broadway production. Ultimately, she did the film and did it brilliantly.

Stark started explaining to me that *Funny Girl* would be my big break into film and that he was prepared to offer me $750 a week. I said, "Does that include expenses?" He said, "No, no, that's it." I considered this for a moment and then said, "That's really not enough. I'd need a car, and I'd need housing. I have to keep an apartment in New York, and there will be taxes taken out and social security."

"But Miss Zipprodt," he said, "you don't understand, I'm offering you twenty-six weeks." All I could think was, "Oh, my god, I'll be away from New York for half a year. No, no. I can't do that." He said, "Miss Zipprodt, you must realize I'm offering you security." What I said to Mr. Stark was, "I'll have to think about it." What I thought to myself was, "If I had wanted security, Mr. Stark, I would have married a dentist."

Then it came time to talk to Mr. Nichols. He had started out as part of the improvisational comedy duo Nichols and May, which led to a Broadway engagement called *An Evening with Mike Nichols and Elaine May* in 1960. Then he had turned to directing with Neil Simon's *Barefoot in the Park* in 1963 and won his first Tony Award. He went to Hollywood to direct the film of Edward Albee's *Who's Afraid of Virginia Woolf*, which was the third-highest grossing film of 1966 and earned him his first Oscar nomination. He was *the* director of the moment.

There was no script yet. Buck Henry, a young actor, improvisational comedian, and friend of Mike Nichols's, was still writing it. (His script for *The Graduate*, which won an Academy Award, launched him on a major career as a movie and television writer.) So I read the book. I was living then in a loft on University Place. The building had no elevator, and my loft could only be reached by five flights of stairs. I had one huge white wall in the living room on which I had never hung any pictures. I decided to use that wall as a kind of blank screen to run imaginary films of *Funny Girl* and *The Graduate*.

I had seen the stage production of *Funny Girl* twice, so I had a pretty good idea of its flow and structure. It looked terrific in my mind. I knew exactly where it was going. The big numbers were gorgeous. I enjoyed the whole thing.

Then I put my version of *The Graduate* in my little imaginary projector and flashed it up on my white wall, and I couldn't see a thing. I could *not* see a thing. And I thought, "That's the one to do!" And that's how I ended up doing *The Graduate*.

Nichols and his co-producer Lawrence Turman also agreed to pay me a little more than Stark, $1,000 a week, although I still had to cover all of my expenses. Ten percent went to my agent right off the top, there was my hotel and car rental, and the rest was lunch money. I discovered when I arrived that my agent did not think to negotiate a parking space on the Paramount lot, so I had to pay for parking six or seven days a week for the next several months. That was the last time I ever used an agent. Afterwards, I just used a lawyer to negotiate my contracts.

About a month after *Cabaret* opened and before I was to begin work on *The Graduate*, I was diagnosed with cervical cancer. I was forty-one. You read about how a cancer diagnosis changes your life, how it takes a quick turn and you can never go back to where you were. It is true that once you have that, you are cut off and into another space. You've crossed a little barrier.

My doctor advised me to discuss my condition with as few people as possible. "Just don't talk about it," he said, "or your economic life may be affected and prospective employers may avoid hiring you." The attitude toward cancer was so uninformed, he told me, that some people still think the disease is contagious. So I confided the knowledge to just two close friends, Gjon Mili and Leonora Hays, David's wife. I didn't say a word to my parents or my sister.*****

I briefly toyed with the notion of calling Mike Nichols to say I had an ovarian cyst and he should find someone else to do *The Graduate*, but I was determined to go ahead with the film. The surgery took place in the winter of 1967. I got an infection in the hospital, which delayed my recovery and my flying out to California. What was to be six weeks of pre-production work before filming began was reduced to three.

So I was still in Manhattan when the Tony Awards were held on Sunday, March 26, at the Shubert Theatre. They were presented for the first time to a nationwide television audience. Boris Aronson and I were the first two recipients, for scenic design and costume design in a musical for *Cabaret*. We accepted our Tonys off camera, before the national broadcast started at nine o'clock. Alexander Cohen, the Broadway producer who had persuaded CBS to broadcast the Tony Awards, was not particularly interested in designers and he didn't think the American public would be interested either. After our awards, we were marched out of the theatre and across Forty-fourth Street to Sardi's, where some members of press were waiting to interview us. So Boris and I sat in the restaurant and missed the entire show, including awards to Hal, Kander and Ebb, and Joel Grey.

The next morning I boarded a plane to the coast, and by that afternoon, their time, I was sitting in Mike Nichols's office at Paramount. I was absolutely off balance. I was still getting over the fact that I had had cancer surgery and was alive and didn't get bumped off by those pesky streptococci. I was getting over the fact that I had won my second Tony and my mother hadn't seen it and no one out there knew. I was starting into jet lag. And I was trying to figure out how to do a film. It was a lot to deal with at one time.

*****I was under a very fine medical watch after my cervical cancer, having X-rays and a Pap smear every year. Two years after the cervical cancer, a small lump was found in my left breast. The extraordinary thing was that because of the constant observation, the lump was so small that even after they located it by X-ray, they couldn't feel it. I wasn't in the mood to lose a breast, so my doctor performed a lumpectomy. He was a brilliant surgeon. He used to do strippers, so he was very conservative in the way he cut me. Fortunately it was benign. But in 1985, when I started work on *Sweet Charity*, the revival that Bob Fosse was doing with Debbie Allen, another tumor was found. This time I had a lumpectomy followed by radiation. The difference with the two cancers was the openness with which I could talk about it in 1985 as opposed to 1967. I'd have design meetings while I was in the radiation waiting room at Cabrini Medical Center on East Nineteenth Street, near Gramercy Park.

The production company, Joseph E. Levine's Avco Embassy Pictures, was renting space from Paramount as an independent company, and Paramount was only required to provide minimal services to those working on the film. Here I was, a New York designer who had never done a film, and the Paramount staff designers did not appreciate my being there when they were sitting around without a film to do.

I was given a terrible office on the first floor of a building that practically abutted up to another building. The windows had a grille over them, and what little light that filtered through seemed gray. And the room was painted elephant gray.

The desk was a regular old businessman's desk with a chair with crisscrossed legs that you could swivel and lean back in. It had swiveled and leaned so many times it had worn through the carpeting down to the concrete floor, with shreds of carpeting around it, immobilized by the thousand of pieces of yarn in its wheels.

For a light, there was a fluorescent desk lamp which wobbled, and there were fluorescent lights overhead, which made the room even grayer. The entire building was unheated in the California style, and California was having a cold snap. I was freezing to death.

I had not brought any winter clothes with me, so I layered on all the clothes I could. Dustin Hoffman, the little-known thirty-year-old New York actor who was playing the lead, had to go back to New York for something. I said to him, "Please, please, help me out. I don't have any winter clothes with me." So he went by my loft and got what I needed from my sublessee, Miguel Ferreras, the fashion designer who had executed Ethel Merman's clothes for *Happy Hunting*.

I didn't have the sense to walk out to wherever Nichols was and say, "Come look at this rat hole they've got me in, number one, and number two, I can't work in it, and I'm leaving, and number three, I can't park my car, and I'm leaving." Instead, I tried to accommodate myself to this situation.

I found an old electric heater, the kind that lets off sparks the moment you plug it in, and I was trying desperately to figure out how to break down my first movie script. There was no shooting schedule. And there was never one until the weekend before we started shooting. So I was trying to get the whole film ready at once.

I was sitting there, feeling very sorry for myself and not knowing what to do, when there was a knock at my door. I had gloves on and my coat pinned up to my throat. "Yes, come in," I said, and in walks this little woman with dark hair and bangs and big brown glasses.

"Are you Patricia Zipprodt?" she said. "Yes, I am." "I admire your work so much and just wanted to come and say hello. My name is Edith Head." She looked around. "What in god's name are you doing in this hellhole of an office?" she said. I said, "This is where the Paramount people put me, Miss Head. I'm desperate for a drawing board and a light and a chair." "This is ridiculous," she said. "I'm leaving today. Why don't you take mine?"

After forty-four years at Paramount, with some thirty Oscar nominations and seven wins, Miss Head was being dumped by the studio's new owners and was moving over to Universal Pictures. She said, "Come with me right now." So I followed her to her office." You work here," she said, and handed me the keys.

It was a beautiful office, with wall-to-wall carpeting and a beautiful fitting area clearly built to make important people comfortable. She showed me an attached office which had a drawing board, good light, and a bathroom with a sink, so you could use running water, which artists do. With the other office, I didn't have any running water, let alone a bathroom.

I will never forget that act of kindness. Her own frame of mind might well have been to detach herself from Paramount without caring what happened next. There was none of that. She just said, "Here, use this." And that's how I got to use Edith Head's office. With this now settled, I could catch my breath and start to work properly on the film.

There were three weeks of rehearsal before we began shooting, and it seemed we were moving faster and faster toward to that first day. The film was what in the theatre I would have called a shopping show, with only some of the clothes to be made.

One of the first things I said to Nichols was, "Mike, how do you want the clothes to look? Do you want them to be how we think the world might look when the film is released in a year and a half? Or do you want it to look like now? You might end up with a period look." He said, "I want this to look right now, this very instant of life in Southern California."

Nichols wanted to shoot *The Graduate* in black and white, as he had done with *Virginia Woolf*. But Levine insisted that he do this one in color, since that was already an important factor for a potential television sale in 1967. But Nichols still had the vision in his head of black and white, so he told Richard Sylbert, the art director, and me to plan all of our designs as close to monochrome as possible.

No one ever notices this until I mention it to them, but most all of the Beverly Hills houses are white with black shutters, while for the crowd scenes at Berkeley, all bright objects were hosed down to grays and beiges and middle colors. The only real color notes are Dustin Hoffman's red Alfa Romeo, the blue sky shining onto the water of the swimming pool, the grass, and the plants. In the Braddock kitchen, which is all white with black accents, there's a big carton of orange juice sitting on the counter. When some of it is poured into a glass, it's absolutely bright orange, and it's lined up so we see an orange tree out the window. So not only was I designing and making or shopping for Anne Bancroft and all the principals, I had to make sure that all the extras in the crowd scenes had color control.

For the scene when Benjamin comes back home, and his parents give him a cocktail party at which he meets Mrs. Robinson, I asked all the extras to arrive with three or four choices of black, white, soft gray, pale beige or muted blue items from their own wardrobes. In Southern California at the time, everyone dressed in lime green and bright yellow. So I had to shop most all of the crowd scenes. All the women's dresses were shopped at Saks to stay within a very tight color range.

Anne Bancroft as Mrs. Robinson was wonderful to work with. She's a fabulous actress, and because she knows her character so well, she's very, very helpful. She's in marvelous physical shape at all times, so you never have any physical problems of any crunchy sort when you're working with her. She wears clothes like a million dollars.

As the world knows, the motif for Mrs. Robinson's clothes was feline animal and jungle. Her first outfit was a tiger-print lamé sheath gauzed over with a black chiffon cage dress, which was very big in the sixties.

As I was shopping for Dustin, I began to realize that there was no way in hell I could buy clothes for him, because he was possessed of a 17.5-inch neck set into a 5-foot 6.5-inch body with a 29-inch sleeve. Because he was so pear-shaped—this broad neck, set into shoulders which tapered off immediately—I couldn't get a blazer that looked right.

So about a week and a half before the shooting was to start, I realized I was going to have to have everything for him made: shirts, jackets, pants, the whole megillah. I started running all over Beverly Hills trying to get tailors to put everything aside to crank out wonderful things for this unknown designer with this unknown actor, a not very well-known director, and a not very big studio behind me. "Dustin Who?" "Mike Who?" "And where did you say you were from, miss?"

I would bring flowers. "You gotta help me." I would be there at eight in the morning, crying, "Please help me." And I finally talked enough people into it. Paramount's workroom took on the blue blazer that Benjamin wears in the first party sequence and through the rest of the initial evening with Mrs. Robinson.

The Graduate, *Mrs. Robinson—tiger-print sheath dress*. Credit: Billy Rose Theatre Division, The New York Public Library for the Performing Arts; © Estate of Patricia Zipprodt.

For each shirt we had to have four duplicates. There were twelve different shirts times four, so that's forty-eight shirts. I still had no shooting schedule, so they all had to be ready at the same time. I was running all over the place going crazy, going back to fittings, trying to keep my eye on the Paramount workroom, which was an almost impossible task.

This is how the Paramount workroom operated. I had a suit for Mrs. Robinson in work there. It was a Chanel suit, black with leopard trim, with a little leopard hat, a little shell of a jacket that hit the hip, no more, with sleeves to the wrist, a little standing collar, and a gentle A-line skirt which stopped just at the knee on Anne Bancroft, who was a very small woman.

About this time, Larry Turman, the producer, said, "Pat, check the price on the clothes that are in work at Paramount." I didn't know what he meant, because I had gotten prices. They priced the fabric and the labor, totaled it up, and said, "This is what it's going to cost." In New York, that would be the price. In California, that was not the price. That was what they tell you they think the price will be. Each item they make has a number. Everybody who works on a garment punches a time clock. Someone has one hour on that piece, fifteen minutes on this piece. At the end of the day, they total it all up, and that's the labor cost for each item for that day.

They were at the point where I was ready for a fitting, but Anne wasn't feeling well, so we had to wait. Then came this request to get all the figures. The original estimate for the suit was about $500, which was quite a lot at the time, and that was without the fur. When I called in for what we had spent so far on this suit, without one fitting, we were up to $800. How was that possible? On fittings you can lose hours.

The Graduate, Mrs. Robinson—Chanel suit. Credit: Billy Rose Theatre Division, The New York Public Library for the Performing Arts; © Estate of Patricia Zipprodt.

What I found in looking into it was this. I asked for a dark brown fabric for the lining for the little black jacket. They showed me four or five swatches. There were no prices on these. I picked one which looked good with the black fabric, a two-ply crepe which would give the suit the right feeling. I knew it should cost about $50 a yard, and they would probably need three-quarters of a yard, a yard at most.

They bought four yards. This was a jacket lining that would never be seen, unless Mike had Mrs. Robinson take it off, which was not in the shooting script. So they had bought an extra three yards of gorgeous brown crepe that was charged to my budget, which they would have for their own use.

Mike was very clear that he wanted diamonds for Mrs. Robinson and for Benjamin's mother, played by Elizabeth Wilson. I found some top-drawer imitation diamonds at XIV Karats, had them sized for the women, and brought them in to show Mike on the Friday before we were to start shooting on Monday with the cocktail party scene.

"These won't do," he said. "Mrs. Robinson has to have real diamonds." I thought, "What for? When light hits them, you're not seeing the ring anyway, and these aren't dime store junk." I didn't know where to go. The Paramount wardrobe people didn't know where to go. So Saturday morning, I started frantically going up and down Rodeo Drive looking for jewelers. I finally found one on South Beverly and told them my story. "We can do whatever you want, lady. What do you want?" They got out all their marquise cuts. "No problem. When do we see Miss Bancroft? We can size them for her over the weekend." "Oh, my god, you're saving my life."

This gentleman opened up his shop on Sunday, and Anne arrived with her retinue. Mike arrived with his retinue and his big dogs. They invaded this shop and picked out what they wanted. The man kindly said everything would be there Monday morning, eight o'clock, Studio 18, the back Paramount lot, and all would be well. Indeed it was. The jewelry was there, and Brink's was there with it.

When Larry Turman found out it was rental, he said, "We can't afford to rent jewelry. We have to get it for nothing." I said, "From where? Where do we get it for free? I don't know anybody out here." He said, "Harry Winston in New York." "Free, from Harry Winston?" He said, "Yeah, call Mr. So and So."

We had already shot the cocktail party scene by then, so I had to duplicate the West Coast jewelry with the East Coast jewelry for the other scenes in which Anne and Liz Wilson appeared. I was on the phone at six in the morning California time to call Winston's when they opened at nine, work out screen credit, and describe to them meticulously the exact shapes and sizes we needed. They flew it out the second or third week we were shooting, more Brink's arrived, and the rental stuff went back to South Beverly Drive.

Liz Wilson was allowed to keep her imitation stones. During a party scene set-up, I heard her say, "Look! My diamonds are fake, and Annie's are real, and you can't tell the difference!" "Into the swimming pool with her," I thought.

I went to every single one of Dustin's fittings throughout the preceding three weeks except the one for his blue blazer, which was being made in the Paramount workroom. I was in Pasadena when that happened, taking care of fitting Katharine Ross's wedding dress, and nobody bothered to tell me the fitting was taking place. My assistant, a barely competent man from the wardrobe union, had been the only one present.

We all appeared on the set early Monday morning. Everyone was nervous. Nichols was nervous. Dustin was nervous. He had on his penny loafers and his chinos and his navy blue blazer for the fishbowl scene. Suddenly Mike said, "Where's his waterproof wristwatch?"

I didn't know he was supposed to wear one, because in New York prop people do watches. People had to run out and get ten underwater watches for Mike to look at. He didn't like any of them. So they ran out and got ten more.

Now Nichols came up to look at Dustin's blue blazer. By this time, I was a nervous wreck, and I had no one to talk to, no assistant, no friends. Mike said, "Who did this?" I said, "It's the navy blue blazer you wanted." "But it's wrinkled."

So he stopped the shoot until the Paramount tailoring department was summoned, ripped the jacket apart, and put it back together again, with the entire crew standing there and watching. I was dying a thousand deaths.

Lunch hour came, and the blazer still wasn't ready. Mike took another look when everyone reassembled and declared that the collar was too low and must be raised an eighth of an inch.

That was my first day on the set of my first movie. I still shake when I think about it.

And there were more incidents like these to come. I did several versions of the leopard coat for Mrs. Robinson in Southern California and none of them suited Mike. Then I went to Maximilian Furs in New York. There were phone calls made at dawn. I would sketch a coat, and Mike would say, "Oh, yeah, that might work." I would phone Anna Maximilian Potok: "We need double-breasted with leather buttons, cuffs that turn back, and a notch collar piped in black calf."

Two or three days later would come by airmail a leopard coat done to our specifications. "Too heavy looking," Mike said. "All right, let's try single-breasted." "Hello, Mrs. Potok? Do you think we could have the same thing but single-breasted?"

The Graduate, *Dustin Hoffman in the blue blazer*; © *Shutterstock*.

Larry Turman seemed to take it all in stride. He was basically a very decent man. Near the end of my time on the film he said, "You know, you could really have a nice career out here." "I don't think so," I said. "If this is the way it's done out here, I don't think I'd live another year." It was without doubt the most miserable eighteen weeks of my life.

Mike Nichols was scheduled to go back to New York to direct a production of Lillian Hellman's *The Little Foxes* at the Vivian Beaumont Theatre at Lincoln Center almost immediately after *The Graduate* finished shooting at the end of August. Anne

The Graduate, *Mrs. Robinson—leopard coat. Credit: Billy Rose Theatre Division, The New York Public Library for the Performing Arts; © Estate of Patricia Zipprodt.*

The Graduate, *Mrs. Robinson—leopard coat*. Credit: *Billy Rose Theatre Division, The New York Public Library for the Performing Arts; © Estate of Patricia Zipprodt.*

Bancroft was to star as the icy Southern matriarch Regina Giddens, a role originated on Broadway by Tallulah Bankhead in 1939 and then played by Bette Davis in the 1941 film.

To my surprise, Nichols asked me to do the costumes. Rehearsals were to begin on September 20. *The Graduate* was moving up to San Francisco for shooting in early August. There were delays, with shots canceled and Annie being sick. Days seemed to be drifting by. I wrote Nichols a note: "If you want me to do *Little Foxes*, I've got to go home." He said, "Oh, go home." So that's how I got off *The Graduate* four weeks before final shooting.

Little Foxes was a horse of another color because I was on my own ground. I had my backup. I had an assistant I knew, Patricia Quinn Stuart.[26] I knew where to go to get the shoes. I knew what shops to go to and what shops to stay out of. I knew how to design for the stage.

Mike walked into the Beaumont and saw all those long, long rows of banked red seats and decided to do another monochrome show. The light bounces off the audience sitting there in color in these bright seats. There was no way to compete with those seats.

I put Bancroft mostly in black, with Margaret Leighton as Birdie in silver and pale lavender. It was a lovely palette to work with. George C. Scott, E. G. Marshall, Richard Dysart, and Austin Pendleton were also in the cast. For a time Dustin seriously considered understudying Austin as Leo to have some income until *The Graduate* was released in December. I remember Mike working on editing the movie simultaneously with rehearsals for *The Little Foxes*, which opened in October.

I did one more show with Nichols, Neil Simon's *Plaza Suite*, with Maureen Stapleton and George C. Scott playing three different couples who visit the Plaza Hotel. Rehearsals started while *The Little Foxes* was still running and just as *The Graduate* was opening in New York and Los Angeles to qualify for Oscar consideration.

The Little Foxes. *Credit: Billy Rose Theatre Division, The New York Public Library for the Performing Arts;* © *Estate of Patricia Zipprodt.*

---

[26]Patricia Quinn Stuart (1939–2010) was a theatrical costume designer, whose Broadway credits included *A Cry of Players*, *The Me Nobody Knows*, and *Lost in the Stars*. She also taught costume design and history of fashion at the Fashion Institute of Technology, 1981–2006.

Plaza Suite, *Maureen Stapleton as Karen, Act I. Credit: Billy Rose Theatre Division, The New York Public Library for the Performing Arts;* © *Estate of Patricia Zipprodt.*

Plaza Suite, *Maureen Stapleton as Karen, Act II. Credit: Billy Rose Theatre Division, The New York Public Library for the Performing Arts;* © *Estate of Patricia Zipprodt.*

Once again there were some strange demands. George C. Scott's blazer had to have real gold buttons from Dunhill's. His shoes had to be custom made by John Lobb in London, so when he put his feet up on a table, we would see a certain kind of sole. I called Lobb's and was told it takes six months to order. Mike wanted to know why I hadn't called six months earlier. Well, six months ago I was in Hollywood. I could never do things right for him. It was worse than Jerry. There was something perverse about the choices he was making. You don't need real diamonds. You may need a real fur coat, but you certainly don't need real gold blazer buttons or shoes from Lobb's. What is that all about? It doesn't read on film or on stage.

Mike has a wonderful sense of humor. He is a marvelous director, and I have nothing but admiration for the way he works with actors. But I simply could not ever connect with him as a designer.

Yet he continued to ask for me. I was down in Louisiana in March 1969 working with Sidney Lumet on a film called *Last of the Mobile Hot Shots* when they called me. Would I go with Ernest Adler, the hairdresser, to Rome to costume the whorehouse scene in *Catch-22*? I was glad Sidney wouldn't let me off. I did not want to go to Rome to hire and dress whores.

Then he sent me Jules Feiffer's screenplay for *Carnal Knowledge*, about the sexual pursuits of two men, played by Jack Nicholson and Art Garfunkel, over twenty-five years from college onward. The male characters reminded me of just the sort of men I grew up with in Chicago, the kind of men I had spent a lot of time trying to get out of my life. I hated the script completely. The thought of spending time with people impersonating these characters was almost more than I could bear. And they were going to film in Vancouver. I could barely make it in Los Angeles. How would I survive Vancouver?

I had just finished the script when the phone rang, and it was the unit manager. Could I fly out immediately to find a special bra for Ann-Margret, so she could have super-breasts that could expand and contract on cue? That did it. I said no to Mike, and he never asked me to work for him again.[27]

The Graduate has, of course, become a movie classic, and it still holds up for its wonderful screenplay, performances, direction, editing, cinematography, and musical score.[28] I will always be glad I chose it over *Funny Girl*. But I never recovered from

---

[27] Gordon Davidson, the original director of Neil Simon's 1981 *Fools*, asked PZ to design the costumes. When Davidson was replaced by Mike Nichols, the costumes were already constructed, and she and Nichols had little interaction.

[28] In *Decades: A Century of Fashion* (London: Bloomsbury, 2012, p. 130), Cameron Silver and Rebecca DiLiberto write, "Mrs. Robinson was the original cougar in part, at least, because of her chic, seductive wardrobe. Costume designer Patricia Zipprodt dressed Anne Bancroft in sheer, silky blacks and tactile leopard prints in order to prove that a woman's animal instincts are ageless. The first time we see her, Bancroft wears a gunmetal metallic shift that seems poured onto her waspy frame like quicksilver frozen in time. Over this armor floats a diaphanous layer of black silk chiffon, which makes Bancroft seem like a Sicilian widow traveling through outer space ... When Mrs. Robinson disrobes, much to Benjamin's horror and fascination, we see she is wearing a leopard-print lingerie ensemble. Later in the film, she appears in a twenty-five-thousand-dollar Somalian leopard-skin wrap. One wonders whether some of the recent affinity for comparing older women to exotic cats found its genesis in Mrs. Robinson's wardrobe. With her skins and streaks, pencil-skirts and lace, Mrs. Robinson might as well have been dressed by Dolce and Gabbana."

that first day on the set. I did do the film version of *1776*, but that was a redesign of my clothes from the stage version I had done for Peter Hunt, who was also directing the film.

My experience with *The Graduate* is why I did not go into the movies and why I turned down *Cabaret* and *Fiddler*.

10

Fosse

Pippin

In early 1972, the producer Stuart Ostrow asked me to read a script for a musical called *Pippin*, a highly fictionalized story about the youngest son of the Emperor Charlemagne and his quest to find the meaning of life. It had music and lyrics by Stephen Schwartz, himself a young man just out of Carnegie Mellon University, where an earlier version had been produced.

I had worked for Stuart on the musical *1776*, which opened in 1969 and was still running in 1972. Then in 1971 I worked for him on *Scratch*, a play by the poet Archibald MacLeish based on Stephen Vincent Benét's short story "The Devil and Daniel Webster." It was one of those shows which seems to open and close in one night, although it did manage four performances.

Now Stuart was looking to produce a musical that would bring a new youthful audience to Broadway. His director was Bob Fosse, who was just back from filming *Cabaret* in Germany. Fosse had asked me to do that film. I had a brief interview with him in his office above the Carnegie Deli, two blocks down and across the street from Carnegie Hall. I told him, "Mr. Fosse, I just can't do that; it's too difficult."

The idea of doing a musical in Germany, where suddenly they say, "Okay, tomorrow morning we're having seventy-five extras," and I'd think, "Where am I going to get the shoes?" was too daunting. I learned such painful lessons with *The Graduate*, I couldn't face a huge project in a foreign country with a director I didn't know. As it turned out, I think I made the right move.

Fosse hadn't directed on Broadway since *Sweet Charity* in 1966, with Gwen Verdon, his wife, in the lead. He did not have a good experience with Irene Sharaff as his costume designer. He was still so shell-shocked he didn't know how to deal with a designer he didn't know.

For Gwen's costumes, Irene had shown him sketches where there were a few little sequins on them. When the real things arrived and were on stage, they were ablaze. He couldn't see anything but sequins. He was ripping them off and tearing them up and spraying them down. The little black dress which Charity wore and which became the logo for the show was from Gwen's own wardrobe, constructed, I think, out of a black slip she had worn in rehearsal.

I met Fosse at ten o'clock in the morning at the Carnegie Deli, not a good hour for him, nor a particularly good hour for me. We sat opposite each other at his regular table with cups of coffee.

The script for *Pippin* said the time of the play was "780 A.D. or thereabouts," and the first stage direction was "Enter the strolling players of an indeterminate period." Now the minute you put a pair of shoes on someone, the period is not indeterminate. So I opened the conversation with, "Mr. Fosse, how do you see this musical being done? What are its characteristics?"

It turned out that Fosse is shy, and I'm shy, so here were these two perilously balanced people trying to talk.

He thought for a while, stirring his coffee. I stirred my coffee. I kept thinking of Wendy Hiller as Eliza Doolittle in the film of *Pygmalion*, having her first afternoon tea with Henry Higgins's mother and the Eynsford-Hills after she's just learned to talk properly. They all sit there awkwardly stirring their tea. Clinkity, clinkity, clinkity, clinkity.

He finally said, "Uh, it should be magical." "Oh," I said, "that's great." And I thought, "Magical. That's really good. Yeah." We both stirred some more. Then I said, "Well, you know, in addition to its being magical, Mr. Fosse, is there anything else that might give me some insight?" Stir, stir, stir, stir. He said, "It should be very anachronistic." "Oh, great," I said, "terrific. Magical and anachronistic. I sort of get a feeling of how to go about it now." I actually thought I did. I thought I had enough to get the sketches going, so we could work from that point.

Pippin, *Pippin as warrior.* Credit: Billy Rose Theatre Division, The New York Public Library for the Performing Arts; © Estate of Patricia Zipprodt.

Then I got home and sat at my drawing board for about two hours thinking, "Gee, magical and anachronistic. I know what I mean when I use the word anachronistic, but I have no idea what this total stranger means when he uses the word anachronistic. What's the style?"

I called him up. "Hello, Mr. Fosse, this is me again. What do you mean by anachronistic?" There was another long, long pause. Then he said, "I mean, like Jesus Christ in tennis shoes." And there it was, a visual image. It gave me the whole show. "Oh, I got it now, goodbye." That served me. It became my guide.

Fosse never felt that he was making himself clear with designers. But he really was. He could give you a bold motif, Jesus Christ in tennis shoes, that you could work constantly.

Pippin's costume fairly flew off my sketch pad. It helped that John Rubinstein wore every article of clothing in a very dashing way, from sleeveless Greek Island net shirts to ermine capes.

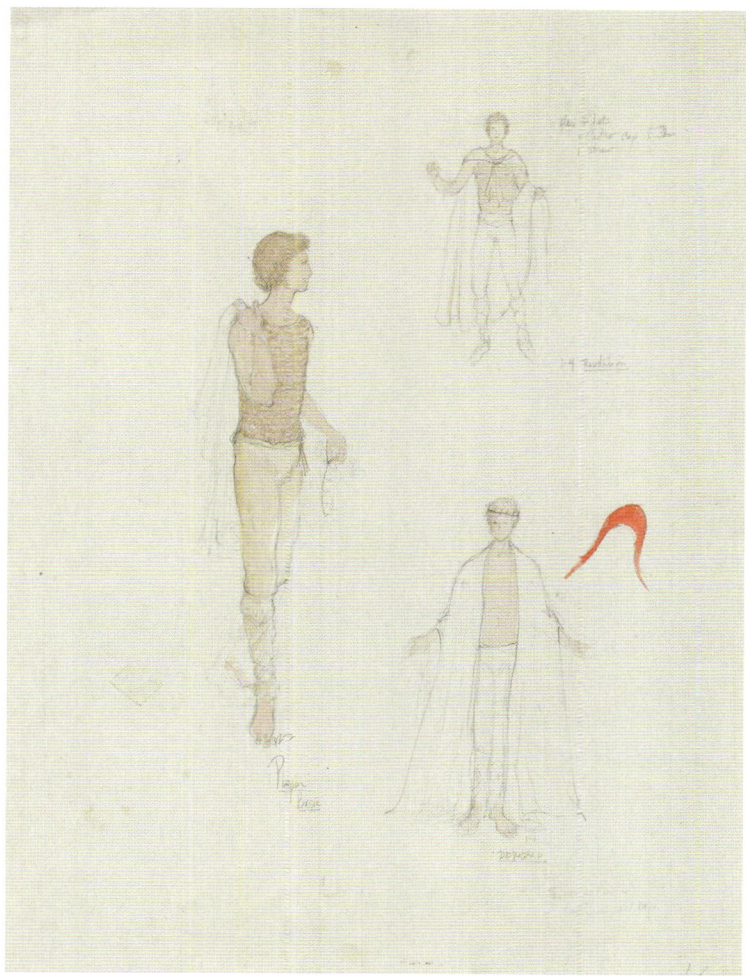

Pippin, *Pippin in Greek net shirt.* Credit: Billy Rose Theatre Division, The New York Public Library for the Performing Arts; © Estate of Patricia Zipprodt.

I did a lot of work for that show on weekends at my house on Martha's Vineyard. One weekend, when I was planning to work on the strolling players, the house had plumbing problems, and getting those attended to took a lot of time that I meant to devote to drawing. I was due back on Monday morning for a meeting with Bob, Stuart, and Tony Walton, who was designing the scenery. We had talked at length about the palette for this show, and it was finally agreed that it would be what is known as the Zipprodt palette: muted, murky, offbeat colors.

I design in sketches. I do the physical design for a show and the color scheme separately, and then I put them together. I don't do them both at once, because that's not the way my head works. I had the strolling players all done in off-whites, with little beige shadows, like the wash over the drawing on Rembrandt's early sketches, to dimensionalize it.

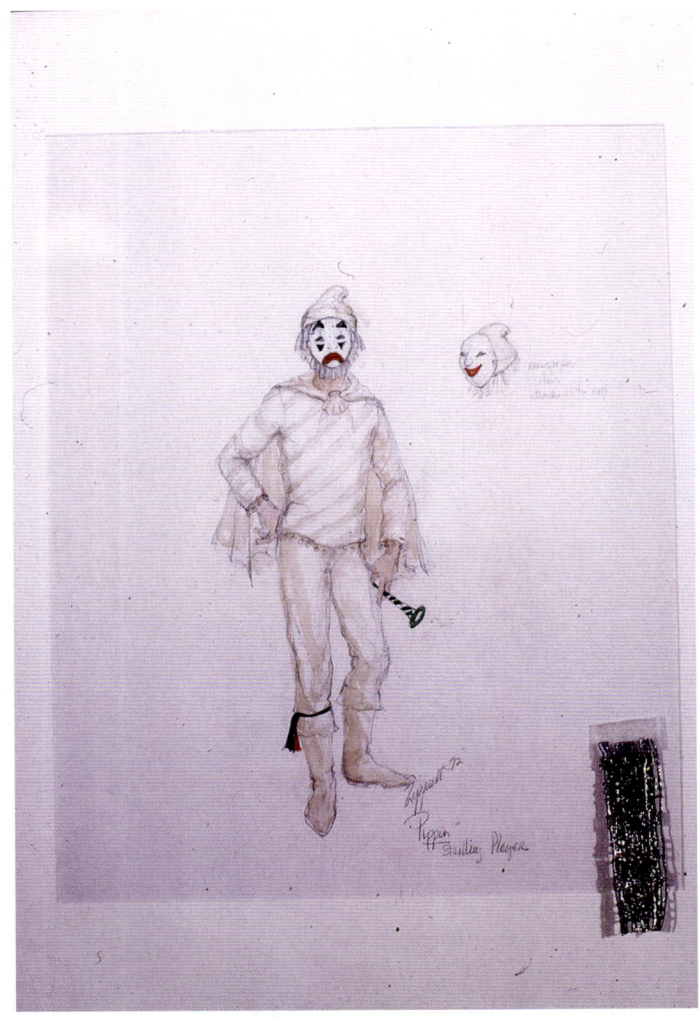

Pippin, *Strolling Player*. Credit: Billy Rose Theatre Division, The New York Public Library for the Performing Arts; © Estate of Patricia Zipprodt.

Suddenly, it was Sunday night, and I had to close up the house. I thought, "Oh, I'll finish these later." Then early Monday morning, when I got to the airport, I phoned Tony Walton in a panic. "I haven't had time to color the sketches. I don't know what to do. Bob's expecting them to be finished." He said, "Don't worry, come over anyway."

I went straight to the meeting at Tony's apartment and studio on the Upper West Side and pulled out these drawings from my portfolio. I was just about to say, "Now, I didn't have time to color these properly," when Tony said, "Oh, brilliant, Patricia! Of course, off-white! These look wonderful. I just recently designed a nearly all-white production of *The Love for Three Oranges* in London for Sadler's Wells Opera, and it works like gangbusters. Just vary this tight palette a little: mushroom white, silver white, warm white, all these different shades."

Pippin, *Strolling players*. Credit: Billy Rose Theatre Division, The New York Public Library for the Performing Arts; © Estate of Patricia Zipprodt.

Pippin, *Strolling players*. Credit: Billy Rose Theatre Division, The New York Public Library for the Performing Arts; © Estate of Patricia Zipprodt.

Later, when I showed them to Bob, he said, "This just might work. But let's have the principals in strong colors." I said, "Uh, well, of course." There they were, and there they stayed, different whites with different textures. It was very much like the palette you think of from the Jacques Callot commedia dell'arte etchings. Maybe instinctively I didn't hurry because they looked so good to me, I didn't want to mess them up with color. That's how serendipity serves us.

I had the strolling players in hand, and then Charlemagne, played wonderfully by Eric Berry, quickly came together. His costume was a juxtaposition of two forces. I realized that I could bounce one element off another: a basic Tannhauser tunic from the twelfth century—skirt above the knees, wide belt, sword, beaded collar with big stones—juxtaposed with a fourteenth-century cape taken from French illuminated manuscripts, with ermine tails painted on the inside and golden fleurs-de-lis on the outside against a purple background.

For his legs I wanted leg wraps, so I took two sleeves off an Aran Island sweater and added tic-tac-toes to give it extra texture. One of them was complete with a line through the O's. If Jesus Christ can have tennis shoes, Irish sleeves with tic-tac-toes on them can be leggings for a medieval king.

But I had a terrible problem with Fastrada, the wicked stepmother, played by Leland Palmer. She really had me stumped. Bobby had no idea what he wanted, so I just started sketching. I tried a sketch of her as the Eastern Roman Empress Theodora, the wife of Justinian, who ruled with him in Constantinople in the sixth century.

Pippin, *Charlemagne*. Credit: Billy Rose Theatre Division, The New York Public Library for the Performing Arts; © Estate of Patricia Zipprodt.

Pippin, Eric Berry as Charlemagne. Photograph by Martha Swope; Billy Rose Theatre Division, The New York Public Library for the Performing Arts; © NYPL.

Then I tried her as a medieval lady from the year 800. He didn't like either of them. I moved up to the Renaissance. I was clumping my way through history.

I kept showing these plates to Bobby. "I know this is not Fastrada," I said, "but I've got to show you something so you can tell me how wrong they are." He said, "They're not Fastrada at all." I said, "Well, do you have any ideas?" He said, "No, no, I do not. I do not understand Fastrada myself."

I then did a lady in a spider web cape, the kind that shouts to the audience, "I am a spider, and I will catch you in my net!" You know you're in deep trouble when you start doing spider webs on wicked stepmothers. Bobby said, "Uggghhhh!"

One night I was at one of those cocktail parties you don't like to go to very much because it's so noisy. I began to think, "What if Fastrada walked into this room? What if Fastrada were here?" Then I suddenly saw her. She was in a silver lamé dress, with lots of red hair piled up, a choker of fake jewels that would knock your eyes out, lots of ass, lots of tits, lots of leg. Stay away from her, Pat, because this is a lady who has to have her end of the room. She's totally lethal.

I went home and drew her up and took her to show Bobby. "I don't know what you're going to do with this," I said, "but here she is." He looked at it. He looked at me. He looked at Fastrada again. "That's it! That's it! You're the first person who's understood what I'm doing with this show."

When you first saw Fastrada on stage, she was in a pillar of light, without any narrative buildup, a totally contemporary woman in the middle of all the medievalism

Pippin, Leland Palmer as Fastrada. Photograph by Martha Swope; Billy Rose Theatre Division, The New York Public Library for the Performing Arts; © NYPL.

Pippin, Fastrada. Credit: Billy Rose Theatre Division, The New York Public Library for the Performing Arts; © Estate of Patricia Zipprodt.

and mixture of period. It was no contest. No one ever commented on it. It was Jesus Christ in tennis shoes. But what a long trip to get there.

There was a section of the show we called the War Ballet that came into being by the skin of its teeth. Bobby had originally conceived it as a mixture of minstrel show, burlesque, and vaudeville. I spit out a bunch of really outrageous sketches: three girls who were supposed to be the Andrews Sisters in oversize Elizabethan armor; hula skirts with Roman tunics; long baggy coats with armor over them. The tennis shoes theme was going full blast. We had a divine time, and they all went into work quickly.

Bobby always choreographed very privately. After he got a piece to a certain point, he would ask me to watch so I could adjust my costumes to work with the body movements. After about two weeks into rehearsal, the stage manager, Phil Friedman, called and said, "Bobby would like you to come in now and look at the War Ballet."

As soon as they began, I thought, "Oh, my god!" They were bending forward, and they were bending backward. They were bending to one side and bending to the other. They were gyrating their hips. They were like wet spaghetti. My heart went right down to my shoes. Bobby had been clear that he wanted metal armor. Armor does not bend. Bobby, metal armor does not bend.

I said, "Does anybody have a dime?" I ran to the nearest pay phone and called Fred Nidha, whose shop was doing the armor. "Stop!" I said. "I don't care what you're doing, just stop. We have to rethink the whole thing." Fred came to rehearsal and was appalled. He said, "There's no way." I said, "Fred, we've got to find a way."

I said to Bobby, "Forget these sketches. Just forget the whole thing. Everything you're doing here has nothing to do with what I've got being made. I've just called it to a halt." Almost overnight I eliminated the minstrel stuff, the big funny coats, the Andrews Sisters, the hula skirts, and the Roman togas, everything with rigid armor over it. We had to get everything stripped way down so that people could move.

Fred and I began to talk. I said, "What is armor made of now?" It's made of either Celastic, a fabric impregnated with a plastic which is moldable after it's immersed in a solvent and dries rigid. Or it's vacuum formed out of a thin plastic that also becomes rigid. I said, "Can't we just do them in latex?" He said, "We could, but to keep the rubber from rotting, we have to put in sawdust filling to hold its form and to keep it from pulverizing very quickly. So it becomes rigid too."

Then we began to talk about a kind of a lamination process, the way plywood is made. We ended up with a new way of making armor out of latex by pouring a very thin layer of latex, about one-eighth of an inch, into a mold made from each dancer's body, then putting a layer of cheesecloth over it. We let that dry, and then we poured another layer of latex, another layer of cheesecloth, and so on, until we finally built up a shell of about seven layers of latex and six layers of cheesecloth into forms we had cast which looked like armor. The finished product retained the flexibility of the latex, but it was bonded by the cheesecloth, which is also flexible.

I redesigned everything with bellies and breasts instead of more formal forms of armor. We put cording around the edges of those little shells and sewed them right onto the leotards.

I was scared to death they wouldn't dry-clean or that the dry-cleaning process would be such a nightmare that the wardrobe people would have to take each shell piece off. Then they wouldn't get them back on in the right places. We had tracing lines around everything so when they took it off, they could reattach them correctly.

Pippin, *Leading Player*. Credit: Billy Rose Theatre Division, The New York Public Library for the Performing Arts; © Estate of Patricia Zipprodt.

But they turned out to be so functional that the wardrobe people were able to just wash the leotards with the laminated shells on them in cold water wash Woolite once a week and hang them up to dry. No rotting at all; the cheesecloth really bonded it. They lasted up to two years. Cloth won't last that long, getting that kind of beating every night. Once every six months someone would come in to touch up the enamel glaze on the shell because it would be banged around.

The design for Ben Vereen's costume as the Leading Player took some time to find. I made sketch after sketch, sometimes with capes, because he had "magic to do," sometime with vests, sometimes headgear, sometimes boots, sometimes tennis shoes. But nothing was really right. The costume for Ben was something we all just kept thinking about.

We finally decided just to get him a tuxedo for rehearsal and let him start working in it. Stuart Ostrow pushed for a white tux because I had done some sketches for the Devil in *Scratch* in white. So we did the Leading Player in white. No. We went right back to black. Then I thought about a black satin shirt. So it all evolved, and he ended up in exactly what he belonged in. Who would go for that black tuxedo right away?

Ben's performance, is, of course, legendary now. He was a lovely human being to work with. I would put his performance alongside Joel Grey's Master of Ceremonies in *Cabaret* as the role of a lifetime.

Our out-of-town shakedown was at the Opera House of the Kennedy Center in Washington during a very turbulent August 1972. Protests against the Vietnam War were going on in Washington and at the Republican National Convention in Miami, where President Nixon was to be nominated for a second term. What the White House described as a "third-rate burglary" had taken place in June at the Watergate complex right across from the Kennedy Center.

There were frequent bomb threats to both the Watergate and the Kennedy Center. One afternoon people were being mustered out as fast as the cops could get them out. They ran up four flights of stairs to where Bobby was rehearsing the dancers. "Clear the room," they said, "there's been a bomb threat." "Just a minute," said Fosse, who was right in the middle of working out a complicated dance step, "we just need to do this one more time."

When *Pippin* opened on Broadway on October 23, 1972, the critics generally disdained the book and sometimes the score, but they loved what Fosse had done with it. The designers, usually ignored, even got their share of praise. Clive Barnes in the *New York Times* called the story "trite and uninteresting . . . with aspirations to a seriousness it never for one moment fulfills." However, he said Fosse's staging, "takes a painfully ordinary little show and launches it into space." His dances "swing with life. Mind you, Mr. Fosse has two master collaborators in Tony Walton and Patricia Zipprodt." Walton's scenery, he said, "manages an almost impossible combination of Holy Roman Empire and Fifth Avenue chic . . . Miss Zipprodt has accomplished her task with equal adroitness and elegance—her clowns look Italian and Fellini and her girls look French and naked. It is probably just right for the Holy Roman Empire."

The following Sunday, Walter Kerr wrote in the *Times*, "Patricia Zipprodt's costumes leap centuries with wit and grace." Fosse captured something of the spirit of the unsettled times we were living in, and the show ran until June 1977.

Chicago

My next collaboration with Fosse was *Chicago* two years later, while *Pippin* was still running at the Imperial Theatre. He was making the show for Gwen, from whom he had separated in 1971. They had purchased the rights to a 1942 Ginger Rogers film called *Roxie Hart* and the original 1927 play *Chicago* by Maurine Dallas Watkins about two vaudeville dancers, Roxie Hart and Velma Kelly, who become celebrities after they murder their lovers and are acquitted.

Fosse took the project to Kander and Ebb, composer and lyricist for *Cabaret*. All three of them envisioned an acerbic musical reflecting the tone of corruption in the Watergate era. For his costume and scenic designers, Fosse brought back me and Tony Walton.

Tony showed me a set model that was all black vinyl and chrome. It perfectly set the Art Deco look of the 1920s and the sinister world that Bobby was trying to create. Although he and the lighting designer Jules Fisher, who had also done *Pippin*, used some brilliant splashes of neon tubing, Tony's essentially monochrome design allowed me a free hand with color.

Bobby wanted to have his Greek chorus of dancers surrounding Roxie and Velma just put things on and take things off of sophisticated leotards, an extension of the little hat-and-cane way of life that was so vital to him.

For my research I looked at clothes of the 1920s, but I really found my goodies in the small artifacts of the period: buckles, cigarette lighters, compacts—museum-

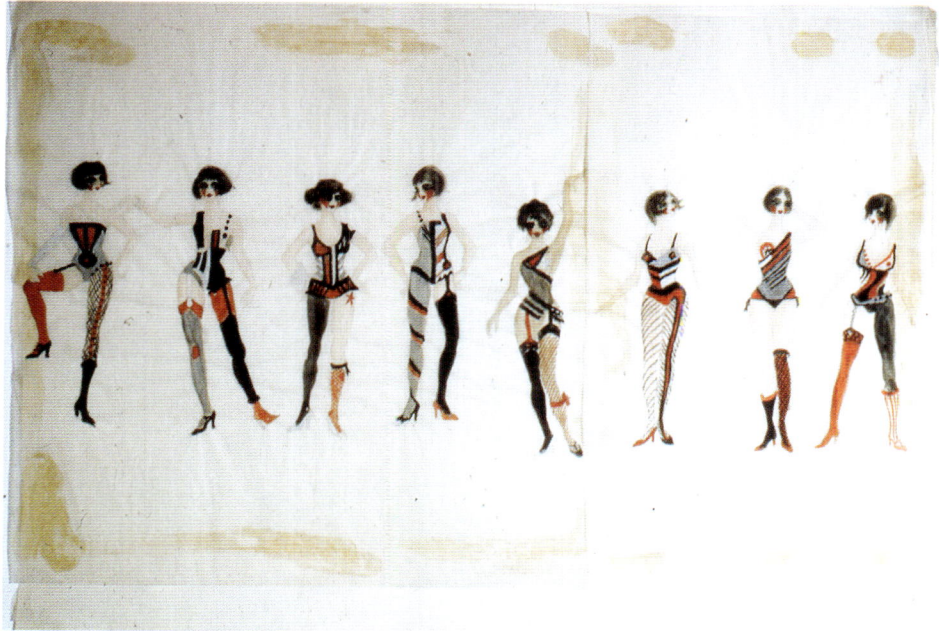

Chicago, *Chorus.* Credit: Billy Rose Theatre Division, The New York Public Library for the Performing Arts; © Estate of Patricia Zipprodt.

Chicago, *Chorus*. Credit: Billy Rose Theatre Division, The New York Public Library for the Performing Arts; © Estate of Patricia Zipprodt.

Chicago, *Chorus*. Credit: Billy Rose Theatre Division, The New York Public Library for the Performing Arts; © Estate of Patricia Zipprodt.

Chicago, *Chorus*. Credit: Billy Rose Theatre Division, The New York Public Library for the Performing Arts; © Estate of Patricia Zipprodt.

quality pieces of exquisite design. From those small pieces and from wallpapers and furniture of the period, I developed a look which was one of my favorite things I'd done in a long time.

When I first did the chorus, I wanted to make a prototypical statement for Bobby to explain how the hats and the gloves would go over the body garment and how we could change the character looks of everyone as the evening progressed without changing their underlook. I sketched him a set of girls with their little skirts, little hats, little feather boas, all very rough and watery, just a thought-sketch, and he was really quite taken by it.

Later, as I began to solidify the chorus look, I had to do front views and back views, because it was very three-dimensional designing. These drawings were very detailed, painted to the edge, because they had to serve for patternmakers and painters.

Bobby would look at these sketches and say, "Well, they're very nice. But where's the one I like?" He meant that funny, rough, watery thought-sketch. I'd explain that these new drawings were what the shop needed to get the feeling he liked. "Are you sure?" "Yes, I promise you," although I knew better than to promise. I couldn't go to a meeting without that first drawing because that was his security sketch.

He was very nervous about the visuals. Bobby had to have control in an area he was not comfortable in. He wasn't like George Abbott, who would say, "Draw me some sketches. I'll see the sets and costumes in New Haven." Fosse just bled over every line drawing. He had to monkey around with models. He was very demanding of his designers in that sense, which is good. Once he felt secure enough, he would use us collaboratively.

For Velma and Roxie's finale costumes, I originally did some marvelous hoochie-coochie-looking things out of silver glittery fabric and rhinestones, with stars for bras, hearts on their pubic bones, and big headpieces with cutout letters in rhinestones that spelled out "Velma" and "Roxie." They played in these for quite a while during dress rehearsals, tryouts in Philadelphia, and previews in New York. Then Bobby decided the ending wasn't upbeat enough, so I redesigned them in white tail coats with beaded lapels and white leotards trimmed with rhinestones. They had white top hats with sparkles on them saying "Velma" and "Roxie" with big angora balls in green and purple.

Everyone thought these were very pretty and a lot of fun, but the raunchy ones had been photographed so much that when all the reviews came out, those were the ones that were printed: Velma and Roxie in these hearts and shiny stars on their tits, instead of the grand showbusiness ending. I love to compare the photographs.

In my endless quest to integrate the costumes with Tony and Jules's black vinyl, chrome pipe, and neon tubing scenery and lights, I decided to put the girls in the "Cell Block Tango"—Bobby's jailhouse rock number—in robes made of a cotton fishnet dyed what I call jail khaki with black vinyl stripes an inch wide sewn on. The seamstresses sat for hours stitching these on a dozen robes, but they looked absolutely smashing over their Art Deco leotards. You could see the image of show working through all the time.

For Jerry Orbach's look when Billy Flynn went to court with Roxie, I used Clarence Darrow's outfit as my image: blue suit, red tie, white shirt, and suspenders, so he would be red-white-and-blue.

The production was halted two weeks into rehearsal in November 1974 by Fosse's near-fatal heart attack, which he later dramatized so brilliantly in his film *All That Jazz*. We were just starting to get into the heavy work in the shop, with fabrics coming in and things being put up on the dress forms in muslin. We were going full blast.

The management worked very hard to keep the cast together and help them stay solvent with temporary work in television commercials and industrials. I don't think we lost anyone. For the designers, however, it just meant that the little money we got in the first place had to cover a longer period of time. I don't remember that they ran out and got us any television commercials.

I visited Bobby several times in the hospital, as did everybody who knew him. It was possibly the busiest hospital room in the entire history of New York Hospital. The nurses were absolutely transfixed by all these gorgeous women floating around the bed of this bypass surgery patient.

When *Chicago* finally opened on June 1, 1975, *A Chorus Line* had been captivating theatregoers at the Public Theatre since April and would move to Broadway in July. Both were dance shows about showbiz, and the comparisons were inevitable. Critics and audiences found *A Chorus Line* uplifting and hopeful. They saw *Chicago* as dark and cynical. Indeed, cynical became the critics' word of choice.

Chicago, *Finale*—the hoochie-coochie version. Credit: Billy Rose Theatre Division, The New York Public Library for the Performing Arts; © Estate of Patricia Zipprodt.

Chicago, *Finale.* Credit: Billy Rose Theatre Division, The New York Public Library for the Performing Arts; © Estate of Patricia Zipprodt.

The following spring, when it was award time, *Chicago* received eleven Tony nominations, including design nominations for costumes, scenery, and lighting; *A Chorus Line* received twelve nominations. *A Chorus Line* won nine awards that year; *Chicago* took home zero.

Sweet Charity

Joseph Harris, a veteran Broadway general manager and producer, had a long association with Bobby and Gwen. He was the company manager for one of Gwen's earliest shows, Cole Porter's *Can-Can* in 1953; he was general manager for *Pippin*; and he was one of the producers for *Chicago*. He was organizing a revival of *Sweet Charity* for the Los Angeles Civic Light Opera's summer season in 1985, and he asked Fosse to direct. Bobby didn't like to revisit old work, and he was already planning his next musical, *Big Deal on Madonna Street*, so most of the heavy work for the *Sweet Charity* revival went to Gwen.

Bobby asked me to design the costumes. He had hated Irene Sharaff's costumes for the original production in 1966, and he wouldn't work with her again. Robert Randolph, who had designed sets and lights for the original, was recreating what he had already done.

Bobby didn't want to spend any time talking to me about the costumes. He kept telling me, "Look at the movie, look at the movie," which he had directed in 1969 with Shirley MacLaine doing Gwen's role. He sent me a copy, and I looked at it and looked at it. I thought, "First Irene Sharaff did it, then Edith Head did it, and now I get to do it." He was really not in the mood to go through this whole thing of explaining a show he had already done. So I had to stir my own soup.

I realized that what Sharaff had done in the mid-sixties and Head did a year or two later was totally different from what I saw looking back from the mid-eighties. Now I had the freedom to tackle *Sweet Charity* as an actual period piece. I researched the sixties until I was silly. Even though I had lived there in my Little Orphan Annie high hair and my little skirts up to my crotch, I still had to research it. As you look back on it, it gets even more exaggerated, so you know exactly what things to pull out that spell the essence of the sixties, not just 1964, '65, '66.

Gwen was recreating the choreography, with Debbie Allen taking on Gwen's role. Debbie was well known from her television appearances on the CBS sitcom *Good Times* in 1976 and her role as Alex Haley's first wife in the 1979 miniseries *Roots: The Next Generations*. She was Tony-nominated for playing Anita in a 1980 revival of *West Side Story*, and she was currently starring in the television series *Fame*.

Gwen is long and thin in the thighs; Debbie is shorter, with weight in her thighs. This immediately created a problem for the black slip that was the logo dress. Not only had the original photo been reproduced countless times, but Gwen and Bobby wanted it copied exactly. So the reproduction became Dress A.

Then I developed Dress B as an alternative, with little gores in the skirt to give it fullness and so it would dance well on Debbie. She still opened the show with the classic slip, but then switched to Dress B as the scenes progressed.

When I designed the costumes for the eight girls and eight guys in "The Rich Man's Frug," I went for full-out sixties with the most outrageous black dresses and

Sweet Charity, *Debbie Allen. Courtesy of Arnold Levine; © Estate of Patricia Zipprodt.*

wild hairdos. I sat up nights trying to think what specific dress would be right for each girl. I photographed them all and tacked the pictures of their bodies to my drawing board as I worked. I was very proud of the results, because it was hard work.

I put them all out before Bobby one at a time. "Gee, Pat," he said, "these are the best I've ever seen. These are really terrific." Then he paused. "But what we really need is just one good dress that they all wear. See, the dance is based on repetition, and it strengthens the repetition of the action." I thought to myself, "You could have told me that a week ago."

Rehearsals moved out to Los Angeles, where Debbie Allen was still filming *Fame*. Meanwhile, we were making the costumes at Matera's in New York, and we had to pack everything, fly to Los Angeles, take over a big room, fit everybody, and get back on the plane, all practically within a twelve-hour span. Since the cast was out there, I decided I would have the tuxedos for the Frug number made out there. I found a very good tailor.

The cut of pants for Fosse was unlike anybody else. No other choreographer makes the kind of demands on the physical body and the clothes that Fosse did. He

Sweet Charity, *Dana Moore, Michelle O'Steen, "The Rich Man's Frug."* Credit: Billy Rose Theatre Division, The New York Public Library for the Performing Arts; © Estate of Patricia Zipprodt.

liked them very tight and very high in the crotch. He pointed to his own, which he had worn every day for twelve years, and said, "I want them like this." I said, "No one can move in those stovepipes but you." "Fred Astaire did," he'd yell. "I need it higher in the crotch so I can kick." I'd yell back, "Fred Astaire didn't wear his pants up in his crotch and he danced very well. Mr. Balanchine said so." "Well, I want them."

The West Coast tailor was doing the tuxedos and the pants. The Matera tailor was doing the costumes for "I'm a Brass Band" with black pants and red jackets. At the first fittings, when we all flew to LA, we had the two tailors there, each in his own corner, each fitting, each looking at the other. I had the guys do everything they do, splits, midair flips, the whole thing, because these pants really had to hold up.

The West Coast tailor said, "Oh, the fabric couldn't be stronger; this is the strongest fabric there is." They all went away and sewed up all the clothes. We all came to Los Angeles again. The West Coast tailor had gone to Italy for his summer vacation, and his head of shop was supervising.

The men got into their pants, and the head of shop, who had done a lot of dance clothes for films, checked them again. The men in their tuxes were doing the Frug. After a while they stopped. "What's the matter?" "Our pants are breaking." "Your pants are what!" "Our pants are breaking." The seams didn't pop, the seams were fine, the seams were so good that they held. But the fabric itself was giving way, in funny little red-cross-shaped rips. The New York tailor was sitting in the house, chuckling wickedly. I knew he was thinking, "You went to the West Coast, you didn't stick with us, you were disloyal, and you deserve this."

Then we got to the parade number and out came the men wearing their uniforms from Matera's, beautiful red jackets with swag shoulders, and all of sudden, the same thing happened. Twenty-four pairs of pants were now shot to hell. These were unfixable pants.

The fabric I had used on these sets of pants had always worked for other choreographers.[29] I used it for Gower Champion, I'd used it for Jerry Robbins. This was the fabric you used for dance pants in those days. Not for Bob Fosse.

It was a moment of horror. We had thirty-six hours until opening. We ended up getting heavyweight suiting Spandex and using it on the dull side. We only had time to make twelve pairs, so the same pants were worn in both numbers. They were tight enough for Fosse's wishes, long and lean in the leg, and they didn't tear.[30]

Before we moved out to Los Angeles, Gwen and Bobby worked days and days recreating the dances in his favorite place, the room with all the mirrors at the Broadway Arts Building at 1755 Broadway, near Fifty-fourth Street, upstairs over a car dealer. I would be up there a lot with my sketches, so I would be privy to these sessions.

---

[29] Arnold S. Levine, PZ's assistant on the production, recalled that she specified silk barathea fabric, a soft fabric, with a hopsack twill weave giving a surface that is lightly pebbled or ribbed. It moved well on the dancers and looked like real pants, not dance wear. (Email to AW, July 2020)

[30] Arnold Levine also recalled that PZ insisted that the men's shirts for the "Frug" should be made of silk, although the wardrobe supervisor pleaded for them to be made in a polyester blend for easier maintenance. PZ said silk would move better when the men took off their jackets during the dance. But it became clear that by that point in the dance, the men had sweated heavily, so the silk sleeves stuck to their arms and did not move at all. Eventually the shirts were remade with a poly blend.

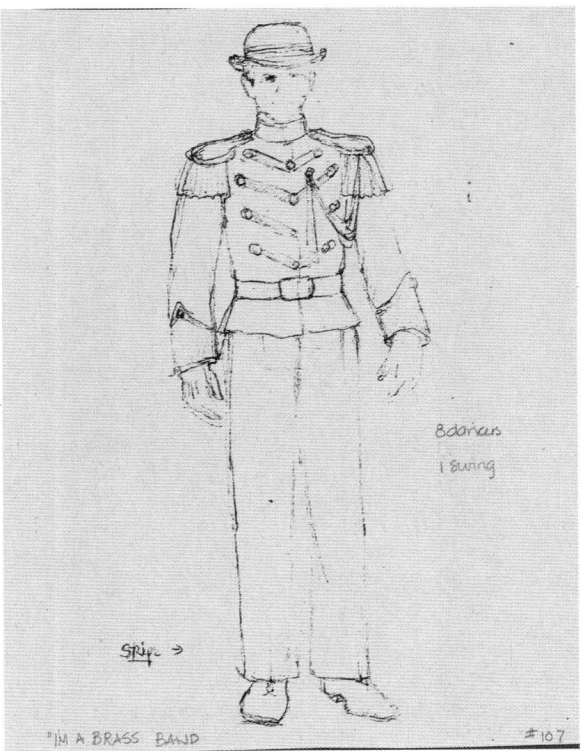

Sweet Charity, *"I'm a Brass Band." Credit: Billy Rose Theatre Division, The New York Public Library for the Performing Arts; © Estate of Patricia Zipprodt.*

Gwen could remember kinaesthetically when Bobby couldn't remember. The movie hadn't exploited enough of the dancing, so it wasn't the best reference. Gwen would start to move. "I think it went . . ." she'd say. You could see it coming back and working its way through her body memory. Bobby would say, "No, Gwen, it wasn't like that . . ." She'd say, "Yes, it was." He'd say, "But before that, didn't we do . . ." "Yes, but we struck that in New Haven." This aching, painful reconstruction was fascinating to watch.

Gwen, as everybody knows, was utterly loyal to Bobby and represented him whenever he wasn't there. She patrolled wardrobe. She drove a lot of us totally nuts. "It wasn't that way, Pat; they played football in that scene." "How could they play football in the spring, Gwen, in the Central Park scene?" "Well, they did." "Do they have to now?" She really rode hard, and I found it a little tough to deal with. She'd just tell you to do it the way it was done before.

Bobby could be sweet. We were walking around backstage at the Chandler Pavilion in Los Angeles after the show opened, when he said, "You know the applause that the girls get at the rail for 'Big Spender' is for the costumes. You know that, don't you?" I laughed. "Well, thank you very much," I said, "but I think it also might have

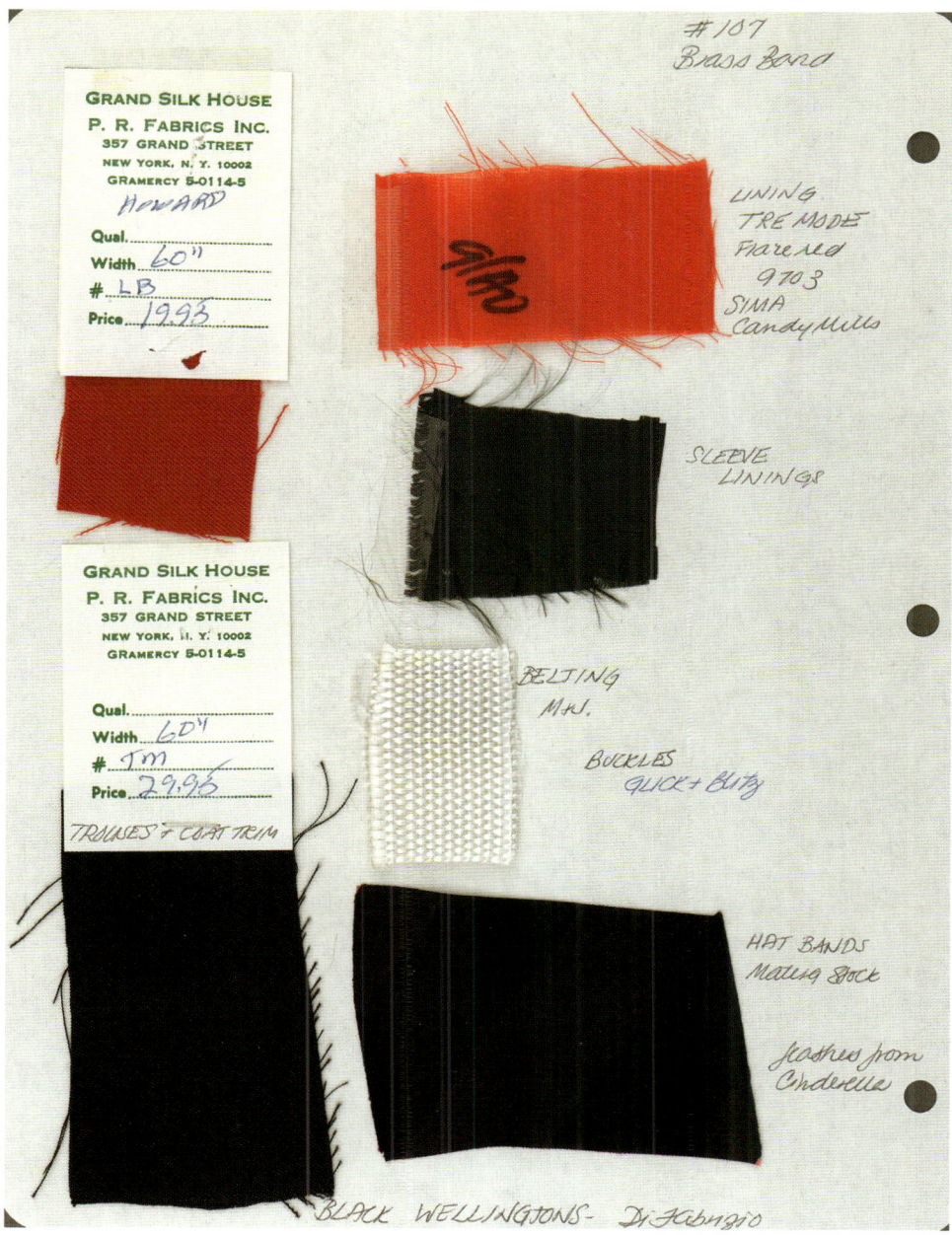

Sweet Charity, "I'm a Brass Band." Credit: Billy Rose Theatre Division, The New York Public Library for the Performing Arts; © Estate of Patricia Zipprodt.

Sweet Charity, "*Big Spender.*" *Photograph by Martha Swope; Billy Rose Theatre Division, The New York Public Library for the Performing Arts;* © *NYPL.*

a little to do with the way it's staged so we don't miss the costumes." It was a wonderful moment: the girls coming downstage as the rail is coming up, and finally as they all got there, draping themselves over it, and socko!

As soon as we had opened in Los Angeles in August, I was back in New York working with Bobby on his next project, *Big Deal*. It opened in April 1986, as the *Sweet Charity* revival was making its way back to New York. In June *Charity* won me my third Tony.

Big Deal

In 1960 Bobby optioned the rights to an Italian film called *Big Deal on Madonna Street,* starring Marcello Mastroianni and Vittorio Gassman as bumbling small-time thieves trying to rob a pawnshop. He had been thinking about it as a stage or movie musical ever since. It was now to be his return to Broadway after eight years. Sadly, it would be his last show.

Big Deal was a misery to work on. Bobby wore all the hats there were to wear. He directed, he choreographed, and he was sole book writer. He even chose the songs from a catalog of standards: "Life Is Just a Bowl of Cherries," "Happy Days Are Here Again," "I'm Just Wild About Harry," "Isn't She Sweet," "Button Up Your Overcoat." He had Ralph Burns, the jazz pianist and composer who had orchestrated

Chicago and *Sweet Charity* and won an Academy Award for supervising the music for *Cabaret*, come in and orchestrate them to fit his choreography. They were Fosse-ized almost beyond recognition.

Bobby transposed the Italian story to the Black community on the South Side of Chicago. It was just not appealing to our theatre-going public. I think he was just so deeply uncertain in his heart of hearts and so isolated by taking on all those jobs that there was no one around who could say, "You need to do something about the second act," "Hey, the orchestration is too loud here." Gwen, who was working on *Sweet Charity*, wasn't around.

I've never had the kind of trouble with him with costumes as I did on *Big Deal*. I did them over and over. If we were doing a set of chorus girls, which is where we were doing most of our hard work, I would just Xerox a whole set of bodies, five or six times, and I would do one version after another. "Do you like this, Bobby?" "Do you like this?" "You like this? There are eighty ways to design *Hamlet*, Bobby. Just let us know what you have in mind."

Peter Larkin, who was designing the sets, sank from sight in Boston, where we were trying out. He was reducing and enlarging and reducing and enlarging bits of scenery in the basement of the Colonial Theatre. Bobby was never sure whether he liked it or not.

And he was very harsh on everybody. Nobody escaped, except the cast. He loved his actors. The rest of us, it was all we could do to just get through each day.

When it opened on Broadway on April 10, 1986, just two weeks before *Sweet Charity*, it fared badly with press and public and closed after eight previews and sixty-nine performances.

Bobby died in Washington, DC, on September 23, 1987, just as the *Sweet Charity* revival was about to open its national tour. Gwen was with him when he collapsed on the sidewalk with a massive heart attack.

Big Deal isn't the way I want to remember Bob Fosse. I'd rather recall peeking in through the half-open doorway of the studio on the second floor of Broadway Arts, watching him—alone, with top hat, cane, and gloves—meticulously working out all those great dance steps over and over in front of all those mirrors while occasionally checking over his shoulder for my reaction.

11

Dealing with Addictions, Buying God's Pocket

About ten years after my first cancer surgery, I began to think seriously about dealing with two heavy addictions in my life: smoking and alcohol. I tackled the smoking first because I thought it would be the more difficult habit to break.

By 1977 I was going through three or four packs a day and smoked almost as much as Jerry Robbins did in those days. On a day when I managed to get eight hours sleep, I'd smoke three packs. When I was having a late day because of a design assignment, I'd go further. Smoking had me really terrified because I was so totally controlled by it.

I was living in my top-floor loft with skylights on University Place in a building without an elevator. It was technically only five flights up, but because some of the ceilings were fifteen feet high, it was more like a six-flight walk-up. When it got to be midnight and I found myself down to two cigarettes, they'd look up at me and say, "Oh, we're getting very lonely. Would you mind just running down and picking up some more of us?" I'd walk down six flights to the corner deli and pick up a pack so I'd have cigarettes for the next morning. Or they would be there if I woke up in the middle of the night. It was as if these cigarettes told me when to smoke, what to smoke, how to go and get smokes, how to carry them, and how always to have matches.

It all started back in high school in Winnetka when we'd sit around and smoke at White's Drug Store. We'd drive around in our convertibles and smoke. We'd meet boys and smoke. Smoking was fine because people in the movies smoked. Surgeons general didn't have anything to say on the topic, nor did anybody else. Our mothers smoked. Our fathers smoked. Smoking was the normal part of growing up. That's what you did.

I'm convinced smoking is a much more devastating addiction than alcohol. It is much deeper and harder to get rid of. From my experience, smoking is much more frightening as a possibility of going back to it. It only takes the smell of a Gauloise to turn me on. For many years I'd follow people down the street so I could experience their second-hand smoke, particularly if they were smoking European cigarettes.

When the Metropolitan Opera canceled a production of Tchaikovsky's *Queen of Spades* I'd been scheduled to design with Ming Cho Lee, to be directed by Liviu Ciulei, they paid off our contracts. (The Met did produce a set of playing cards I had designed in the style of the costumes.) So I had money in my pocket and a gap of time

Queen of Spades, *playing cards designed for the Metropolitan Opera. Credit: Billy Rose Theatre Division, The New York Public Library for the Performing Arts;* © *Estate of Patricia Zipprodt.*

when there was no other design work for me. I joined Smokenders and for eight weeks all I did was not smoke.

I went through all the steps Smokenders recommend, most particularly disassociating smoking from all my other habits. If you had a cup of coffee, you couldn't have a cigarette. If you had a glass of wine, you couldn't have a cigarette. When you ate, you had to wait for an hour before you had a cigarette. Even before I completed the course I found it easier to walk up my six flights. I could tell the difference in my lungs.

I came to this glorious knowledge that I could really stop smoking and take back control of my life. I discovered that I was capable of change. This was very important to me, because I seriously thought I was doomed to those traits I was burdened with from my family. The fact that I ultimately learned I didn't have to either smoke or drink proved to be one of the most empowering experiences I've had. It changed my life from a thing of depression to a thing of optimism. It was the beginning of my turnaround.

At this point, I realized clearly I was getting into trouble with alcohol. It was no longer something I just did. It was taking me over the same way the cigarettes had. It was taking control of my life. I was terrified that I found myself sounding more and more like my mother in her moments of horror. I was getting caught up in a downward spiral. It has been said over and over again that you don't have to end up in the gutter to qualify as an alcoholic. Some people are merely heavy drinkers, but my experience indicates that the true alcoholic goes through a change of soul and spirit and personality. I always thought my mother was Dr. Jekyll and Mr. Hyde. That is a true alcoholic nature.

My own particular alcoholic nature came to a head one evening when I attended a spring party at the Guggenheim Museum. Everyone was in black tie and evening dresses. The dinner was incredibly late, and I just kept drinking cocktails and glass after glass of wine until the meal finally arrived around 9:30 p.m. It was served on tables along those spiral ramps. I ended up getting absolutely blotto. Of course, everyone could see me as I attempted to stagger down the spiral to street level.

Fortunately for me, I was escorted by a friend who happened to be a member of AA. He got me home safely and the following day phoned to say he thought I had a drinking problem. I was relieved for him to tell me this. I started attending meetings with him, but it wasn't until a good six months later that I really stopped drinking totally. Why? Well, I had a business trip planned to Spoleto, Italy, for design conferences over the summer, and I just couldn't imagine having real Italian food without wine.

But come fall I did finally stop completely. I found the AA meetings initially very difficult. My friend from the Guggenheim event was gay, so at first I attended mostly gay men's meetings. It took me a long time to accept it, because I hated those stories. It seemed like everyone was dying of something or had murdered somebody. Nothing as middle-class as my problems. Doesn't anyone grow up in the suburbs? Whatever happened to the upper-middle-class drunk? Nowadays I realize the problems are all identical, but I didn't then.

I think Alcoholics Anonymous is one of the most amazing phenomena of the twentieth century, along with Igor Stravinsky and George Balanchine. It continues and grows without any sort of a power structure or governing body. It perpetuates itself and regulates itself, and everyone carries responsibility for themselves and their particular group. I wish we could transfer these characteristics directly into the political structure of our country. Our world would certainly be better off.

Two years after my cancer surgery, three years before the five-year statute of limitations then established by the medical profession regarding the illness, I realized I not only felt strong enough to work a full schedule but to take another major step.

In March 1969, I was in Louisiana working on Sidney Lumet's film *Last of the Mobile Hot Shots*, based on Tennessee Williams's play *The Seven Descents of Myrtle*. We were shooting on location in swamp territory around St. Francisville, about thirty miles outside of Baton Rouge. We worked out of a little house in the midst of live oaks and Spanish moss and the ants that go with Spanish moss. A special telephone line had been run out to this house for the one phone in it.

I was wearing my snake boots and working alone in the house when the phone rang and rang and rang. When no one came, I thought I'd better answer it. I picked up and said "Swamp City," or something like that. It turned out the call was for me.

It was my friend Arthur Hadley, a journalist, author, and editor who won several prizes for his magazine reporting from Vietnam. "Where are you?" Arthur said. "I've been looking everywhere for you." I said, "How did you find me here? How did you find this number? I don't even know this number myself." He said, "Lena Horne's daughter, Gail, who's now married to Sidney Lumet, used to live with a friend of mine, so I called him, and he called her, and she gave me the number to the swamp."

Arthur and his wife Jane had a house on Martha's Vineyard, and about a year before, I had said to him, "If an old house ever turns up on the Vineyard, I would surely like to think about buying it." I just loved it there because it reminded me of my one and only trip to Ireland. Now Arthur was frantically calling to say, "Patricia, I think your house is on the market." "What are you talking about? What house?" "Don't you remember saying . . ." "Oh, yes, I do. Tell me about the house." "Well, I never thought they'd sell because it's a historic little house; everyone's lived there. It just feels right for you." "Does it have fireplaces?" "Yes. It's also got beach privileges." That was very important on the Vineyard, because the beaches are all private.

I said, "Do you think I should get it?" He said, "I don't know, but it's an awfully nice house." "What's the price?" It was in the twenties. I said, "Why don't you put in a bid for me." He said he would.

Two days later I came back from the swamps to the motel on the edge of Baton Rouge where we stayed so we could get to work without going through the city. There was a telegram in my mailbox. I thought, "Oh, god, who died?" It said, "Your bid has been accepted," and it was signed by the owners of the house, Barbara and John Scannell. It turned out that Barbara was a writer and the niece of the celebrity drama critic Alexander Woollcott.

So that's how I bought my house on Martha's Vineyard. After cancer, it was strange saying to myself, "I'm alive, I feel fine, and it hasn't come back." Purchasing the house gave me a renewed sense of my own future.

I finally got up to the Vineyard two months later, because Sidney wouldn't let me go while we were still filming. "No, no, you can't fly, "he said, "you're not insured." The two women brokers met me at the airport in their pick-up truck, which held two large black dogs, brooms, and hay. I was in my brown suede sixties miniskirt, high Orphan Annie hair, and lots of chains and beads and feathers. I'm sure I was a shock to these ladies who hailed from a long line of Vineyard generations and couldn't believe I'd purchased something I was only now about to see for the first time.

The house, in West Tisbury, was typical Vineyard Greek Revival, sixty feet long and twenty-five feet wide. It had been built in 1835. There were two stories with three bedrooms upstairs, three fireplaces, and very ancient flooring. As I walked up the brick walk, still deep in early spring mud, I saw brass letters on the white door. The name of the house was God's Pocket. I thought, "How did I end up buying a house on the phone named God's Pocket?" It seemed very mysterious, very predestined.

One of my first tasks was to strip the white paint off the door and restore its beautiful maple luster. I put the letters back on, because the house had borne that name since the turn of the century, and I was smart enough not to even think of fighting that.

The door had been in place for 150 years and never had a lock because you didn't need a lock on a door in the Vineyard. Then life there changed in the seventies. People took it upon themselves to help themselves to anything, on the theory that there is no such thing as ownership. So we began to lock our doors.

I found a carpenter named Danny and said, "I've got to do something about getting this door locked, and I don't know how to do it." "I don't think we can simply add a lock," he said, "I'll have to insert a whole new section with a lock and handle in it." As he did this, I saw the whole original shape of the door change. Suddenly there was this very new raw piece of wood with a sparkling new handle and lock inside it. It looked like a piece of plastic on this beautiful mellow maple door. It made me miserable every time I opened and closed it. Danny would say, "Oh, it will be all right. It will age. It will mellow." But I could only feel that we had damaged this beautiful old door.

An architect friend came to visit me, and I showed him this horror. He looked at the door for a long time and then turned to me and said, "No, no, that lock is now part of the history of the door." I looked again and saw what he meant. The door would heal, and the lock would indeed become a part of its history. And suddenly everything was all right.

Last of the Mobile Hot Shots ended up shooting the interiors in New York. It was finally released in January 1970. When it opened I was in New Haven for three weeks getting *1776* ready, so I missed that whole period. When I finally got back to

God's Pocket. *Photograph courtesy of John Siffert.*

New York, I went to see the film for an eight o'clock showing, and it was gone. I said to the person in the box office, "But it says here in the paper . . ." "Well, we ran it at five o'clock to an empty house, so we just pulled it." In her review in *New York* magazine, Judith Crist said, "Tennessee Williams' 1968 play (*The Seven Descents of Myrtle*) was a disaster and that's a polite word for this visual expansion, gross miscasting and ludicrous pretension of the film written therefrom by Gore Vidal and produced and directed by Sidney Lumet."

So that's what happened to *Last of the Mobile Hot Shots*. It took me years to find that film.

12

In Sum

My life took on another major change in 1992, when Colonel Robert Emmett O'Brien re-entered it after an absence of over four decades. I had last seen him in Chicago in 1949 when I had politely declined his offer of marriage because I was hellbent on having a career.

O'Brien married and had a most happy forty-four-year marriage living on a horse farm in Upperville, Virginia, outside of Washington. When his wife fell ill, she was confined to her bed for a number of months. One day she spotted my name in an ad for *Fiddler on the Roof* at the National Theatre in 1991. When she died the following year, O'Brien, after a period of mourning, contacted the theatre's manager personally to find out how to reach me. The program said I taught at Brandeis, so he tried to contact me there. They refused to reveal my whereabouts, so he phoned Wellesley's alumnae office. They also refused. It never occurred to him I might live in Manhattan and all he had to do was try NYNEX Directory Assistance.

So O'Brien called Brandeis several more times and finally told the secretary it was absolutely essential he be able to contact me. "Why do you need to speak with her?" she asked, bemused at his persistence. "Because I'm going to marry her," said O'Brien defiantly. "Oh," was her stunned response. And she phoned me up in New York.

I guess you could say the rest is history. I presently live on a simple and lovely farm called Happy Hill Farm in the hills of Virginia, in a modest but charming house about ninety minutes from our nation's capital. There are a number of horses grazing here, and the atmosphere is tranquil and conducive to a delightful sort of quiet living that I never ever experienced in the hubbub of Manhattan, where I still maintain my apartment on King Street with a roof garden.

So now that I am a septuagenarian, is my career in design over? Oh, don't you believe it. After all, Boris Aronson did some of his most creative work in his eighties. So look for my name on many, many projects to come all over the country, in theatre, opera, dance, and television. Should I include film in that mix? Don't count on it after what I told you of my experiences on *The Graduate*. But since everything else about my life has been so unpredictable, you never know.

Patricia and O'Brien at Happy Hill Farm. Credit: Estate of Patricia Zipprodt.

Epilogue

Patricia ends her memoir reunited with her long-ago prince. And they did live happily, just not forever after.

In the summer of 1992 O'Brien began laying siege to the Brandeis Theatre Arts Department to get in touch with Patricia. At the time she was designing a revival of *My Fair Lady* for the British director Howard Davies and was often in London for meetings with him. After she gave permission to give out her address, O'Brien mailed a handwritten note on July 29 with a photograph of one of his horses. "Dear Patricia," he wrote, "this is 'Button' waiting to go up for his race. I have others and some hunters, but no more polo ponies. I would be truly happy to show them off to you if I could just locate you and if you would call me or write." He signed, "Yours, Bob."

Patricia called. The next day he boarded a train from Washington to take her out for Sunday afternoon tea. For all his assurance on the telephone with the Brandeis secretary, however, he later confessed to Phyllis Meras, a journalist friend of Patricia's on Martha's Vineyard, that he was murmuring to himself as the train started down the tracks, "But what if she *won't* marry me?"[31]

Meanwhile, Patricia too was having jitters. She called her friend Anstice Carroll, a professional caterer and cookbook author. They had met through Robert L. Green, a fashion historian and critic and the one-time fashion director of *Playboy* magazine.[32]

"He's arriving on the one o'clock train," Patricia said, "and I don't know what to wear. What should I wear?" "For god's sakes, Patricia," Anstice replied, "you're a costume designer." "But I don't look good in this," Patricia wailed. "And I don't know about that. I'm a nervous wreck." She was, Carroll remembered, like a girl in high school.

Whatever worries they both may have had, a year later, Patricia and O'Brien were married in Upperville on Saturday afternoon, June 5, 1993, at Trinity Episcopal Church, a stone chapel built in the twelfth-century French style by Paul Mellon.

Prior to the wedding there was a week of nuptial events in New York and Virginia. Robert L., as Green was known, hosted a dinner for the couple at Carroll's large loft

---

[31] Phyllis Meras, "At Long Last, Love: Couple Is Wed 43 Years After Proposal," *Vineyard Gazette*, Martha's Vineyard, MA; June 11, 1993.
[32] Green had taken extensive oral histories with Patricia for the Fashion Institute of Technology. He had been friends with Carroll's former in-laws, the screenwriter Sydney Carroll and the Broadway lyricist and actress June Sillman Carroll.

Patricia and O'Brien, wedding photo. Credit: Estate of Patricia Zipprodt.

on Greenwich Street, near Patricia's King Street penthouse apartment. Originally planned as an intimate sit-down affair, Patricia kept adding names to the guest list until it ballooned to an enormous gathering. Green was annoyed, but he was famous for his large parties at his Bucks County farm, so he made his signature big crowd dishes: fried chicken, baked beans, and Toll Gate meatballs, named for his farm.

Patricia and O'Brien arrived late. She brought along a hairdresser and her party clothes and immediately disappeared into the bedroom to get dressed. O'Brien mingled with the guests as they waited for Patricia to make an entrance.

For her wedding gown, Patricia based her design on one she had created for Eliza in *My Fair Lady*. It was a long, loose, off-white chiffon sheath over an underskirt of pale gold chiffon. Both were scallop-edged. She incorporated sleeves from her mother's wedding dress into it. It was cinched at the waist with a wide belt, also pale gold, embellished with red and white daisies. The skirt and the sleeves were bordered with red, pink, and gold flowers and light blue vine motifs. The dress was made by Barbara Matera, one of Patricia's favorite costume makers. Martin Izquierdo, another favorite costume maker, painted the flowers from Patricia's designs, and Matera embroidered and appliquéd them. For a head covering, the preeminent Broadway milliner Woody Shelp created a wide tulle wrap, open at the top to show off her bright red curly bobbed hair.[33]

---

[33] Shelp and Patricia had first met when they both were working for Irene Sharaff on *Happy Hunting* in 1957.

Ann Hould-Ward was a young costume designer who had arrived in New York in 1978 after writing to Patricia to ask for a job. She became her principal assistant and then her co-designer on *Sunday in the Park with George* in 1984 before moving into her own career. Hould-Ward attended fittings for the wedding dress at the Matera studio and was detailed to fly the completed dress to Virginia via Washington the Friday night before the wedding. It was packed in tissue in a long garment bag that could fit in the overhead compartment. They did not want to risk packing it in a suitcase and checking it.

As Hould-Ward recalled the story, the flight was filling up with businessmen trying to get home for the weekend. She was seated after carefully laying out the garment bag in the overhead bin when a man came on and tried to put his briefcase on top of it. She got up and asked him not to. "It's the wedding dress of a 68-year-old woman," she said, "let us please be careful." The man huffily went on down the aisle. As the next man came on and tried to do the same thing, two men in the row behind Hould-Ward jumped up. "You can't put anything in there," they said, "that is the wedding dress of a 68-year-old-woman!"

At Happy Hill Farm, before the ceremony, Hould-Ward helped Patricia into the dress. "There were a thousand hooks," she recalled. Patricia, in her wedding dress, drove them to the church with a hay bale in the back seat.

For the ceremony O'Brien was dressed in a white suit. They exited the chapel under crossed swords held by O'Brien's military buddies. The reception was at Happy Hill Farm.

Patricia and O'Brien went back to New York for a reception at the Century Club on the following Wednesday and then departed for a European grand tour to visit

Wedding reception at the Century Club. Credit: Estate of Patricia Zipprodt.

places he had been during the war. After their return, Patricia divided her time between King Street and Happy Hill Farm.

But mostly Patricia settled contentedly into the life of a devoted wife of a Virginia country gentleman and horse farmer. She was delighted to be part of this small Southern community. It was so different from her life before. She became a stalwart at Trinity Episcopal Church. The architect Hugh Hardy, a friend since their early days assisting Jo Mielziner, noted her glee at being accepted into the Upperville Garden Club, "a social accomplishment both so unexpected and so awesome her pride was contagious."[34] She developed a huge following because she was a member of the Motion Picture Academy and got videos of all the nominated films. She would take them to Virginia and lend them out.

O'Brien had a glass-enclosed room built onto the farmhouse as her studio. It was eight feet wide and fourteen feet long, with tables all around the edges for her to stack her books and paperwork. She completed *My Fair Lady* for previews at the end of November 1993 and then designed a November 1994 production of *The School for Scandal* for the Shakespeare Theatre Company in Washington.

She accepted an assignment to design Steve Martin's *Picasso at the Lapin Agile* for its New York premiere in October 1995 at the Off Broadway Promenade Theatre. About that time she hired as her assistant Susan Ruddie, an experienced designer, costume maker, and costume shop manager who had worked with Hould-Ward. Ruddie became the factotum who oversaw the King Street apartment and studio and kept Patricia's New York life organized. She made trips to Virginia to organize her life there as well.

Anstice Carroll kept an extra set of keys to King Street at her nearby loft. Patricia would come back from Virginia on a late flight. "Inevitably," Carroll recalled, "I would get a call." "Woohoo, woohoo," Patricia would say, "guess what!" "I bet you forgot your keys." "I did. Can I just come and spend the night?" "Of course you can."

Because of her busy catering work, Carroll was often still at her desk at eleven o'clock when Patricia arrived. She would stick her head in Carroll's office and say, "Woohoo, woohoo, what does a girl have to do around here to get a little something sweet?" Carroll would give her ice cream and frozen cookies. In the morning, after a pot of tea, she took her keys and was off.

O'Brien's health began to fail in 1996, and he was diagnosed with Parkinson's Disease and early stage dementia. Because Patricia still had to commute to New York, she moved him into a small nursing home in Marshall, Virginia, a twenty-minute drive from Upperville. When she was in Virginia, she drove down every day to make sure that he was up and dressed in nice slacks and a good shirt with a neckerchief. She would bring cookies for the staff.

She also brought along costumes to work on while she sat with him. (She was designing a production of *You Can't Take It With You* for Arena Stage in Washington.) She was greatly amused, she told Phyllis Meras, when a hospital official announced firmly one afternoon that they could not allow her to make and sell clothes on the

---

[34]Hugh Hardy, "Patricia Zipprodt," Memorial Tribute to Patricia Zipprodt, Booth Theatre, New York, October 6, 1999.

premises. She had brought a clothes rack into O'Brien's room to hang her finished costumes.[35]

While Patricia was caring for O'Brien she developed a serious cough. Her doctors in New York diagnosed aggressive small cell lung cancer. Still traveling back and forth between Virginia and New York, she began radiation and chemotherapy. There were two courses of treatment, with intervals of remission.

Her friends were astonished at her insouciance. Having survived two bouts of cancer, she thought she was going to beat this one. "She'd come from Virginia to have either chemo or radiation," Carroll recalled, "and we'd go out to dinner that evening. I was gobsmacked."

O'Brien died on August 24, 1998. General William Westmoreland, his 1936 West Point graduating classmate, delivered the eulogy at Trinity Episcopal Church where he and Patricia had been married. Some of his ashes were scattered at Happy Hill Farm. When Patricia sold the farm, she had the contract written so some of her ashes could be scattered there with his. She also had two trees planted near the paddock at the racetrack at Glenwood Park in Middleburg, Virginia, where O'Brien had raced his horses. Some of his ashes were scattered there.

Patricia's cancer had returned by the end of 1998, and she began a third course of treatments. In December, a friend of Anstice Carroll's, Jonathan Dudley, an opera and symphony conductor and the music director of Middle Collegiate Church in Greenwich Village, was enlisted for several months to drive her to her weekly appointments. He sat in the car reading books while she went in. Afterwards, they went to lunch together. "I was not a churchgoer," Dudley said, "and neither was Patricia. We laughed a lot about that."

In March 1999, after a stay in the hospital, she was told that no further treatment was possible. It was time to arrange home hospice care.

Jane Ashe, an experienced hospice nurse working for the Jacob Perlow Hospice at Beth Israel Hospital on the Lower East Side, had recently asked her manager to switch her to home care. Her manager knew she loved the theatre so he assigned her to what he called "a VIP patient with a very interesting history." She was told her patient would probably be having celebrities visiting.

At the same time, a group of close women friends whom Patricia called her Mafia began organizing for her to come home. They included Lucia Evans Moffett, a friend from Martha's Vineyard, Anstice Carroll, Whitney Blausen, a longtime design assistant, and Bella Linden, her lawyer. The Mafia decided that Susan Ruddie would become full-time, working five days a week to handle all clerical matters. Moffett, who had a home in Ireland, engaged three home health aides referred to as "Irish nurses" from Kearney Home Care. They would attend day and night.

The chief organizer was Moffett, the former owner of the popular Helios restaurant on the Vineyard. She had an apartment on Patchin Place, a short walk from King Street. She bought groceries and came every day to cook. She also oversaw what became for a time a surprisingly busy social life for Patricia. As Ruddie recalled, "Lucia made sure there was someone there every day to visit, that there

---

[35]Phyllis Meras, "Patricia Zipprodt, 74, Was Celebrated Costume Designer," *Vineyard Gazette*, Martha's Vineyard, MA, July 20, 1999.

Patricia and Lucia Moffett. Credit: Estate of Patricia Zipprodt.

were delicious looking meals, that there were always flowers, and that everything was pretty."

Along the length of the King Street penthouse was a long garden terrace that Patricia loved. It opened into her bedroom as well as the living area. Because she had only lived there off and on since 1993, the plantings were in poor condition.

While she was in the hospital, she told Hould-Ward she wanted a new garden to see from her bed. Hould-Ward bought hardy plants that could withstand the rooftop wind, and she enlisted helpers, including Martin Izquierdo and another costume designer friend, John Glaser, to install them in time for Patricia's homecoming on March 11. "For some remarkable reason," Hould-Ward recalled, "God saw to it that we never had another frost and she got to enjoy it for the rest of her time."

Jane Ashe came for her first assessment visit the following week. Patricia was now spending most of her days in bed. The room was large—Patricia referred to it as a "bedsitter"—and she used it as a social space as well as a bedroom.

A four-poster bed draped top and sides with gauzy white fabric sat low to the floor near the doors to the terrace. On the other side of the room a Moroccan brass tray table was positioned with a love seat and two Louis XV fauteuil chairs upholstered in white. Large pots held dracaena and philodendron. Framed costume sketches, her own and those of friends, hung on the white walls. Behind the sitting area stood a tall wooden screen shaped and painted like the New York street scene and skyline to mark off her dressing area.

Patricia's bedroom, King Street. Credit: Estate of Patricia Zipprodt.

Patricia's bedroom, King Street. Credit: Estate of Patricia Zipprodt.

Patricia's bedroom, King Street. Credit: Estate of Patricia Zipprodt.

For Jane Ashe, walking into Patricia's bedroom was like walking onto a stage set. "She was surrounded by the most gorgeous pillows and sheets and duvet covers," Ashe recalled. For friends who visited in June from Virginia, the scene reminded them of the French painter David. Patricia had twisted "a Roman striped scarf about her head which fell onto her pillow in negligent folds. The effect with her very pale and drawn face was devastating, but exquisitely painterly."[36]

By the fourth week in March, Moffett was scheduling three or four social visits a day in addition to the hospice care providers who came weekly. There were weekly visits from a massage therapist and a yoga instructor. Peggy Gould, a movement specialist and dancer, came to give Alexander Technique lessons, which provided some relief from the increasing immobility and discomfort Patricia was experiencing.

Her sister Connie came from Chicago for several days each week. Joel Grey came regularly and called often when he was away working. Other regulars were Leonora and David Hays; Arthur and Jane Hadley; the choreographer Tina Ramirez, the director of Ballet Hispanico; T. Edward Hambleton; Hugh Hardy; and the lighting designer Jules Fisher and his wife, the choreographer Graciela Daniele.

Patricia went out for afternoon and evening excursions. On one afternoon jaunt with Grey, they had exited the building when Patricia realized she didn't have her keys. It was pouring rain. Grey called Anstice Carroll, who was preparing dinner for friends. She turned off her stove, found a cab, and delivered the keys.

On April 12, Patricia attended the afternoon Broadway memorial for Jerome Robbins, who had died the previous July. Moffett ordered a car that could

---

[36] Unidentified tribute, Memorial Service for Patricia Zipprodt O'Brien, Trinity Episcopal Church, Upperville, VA, July 24, 1999.

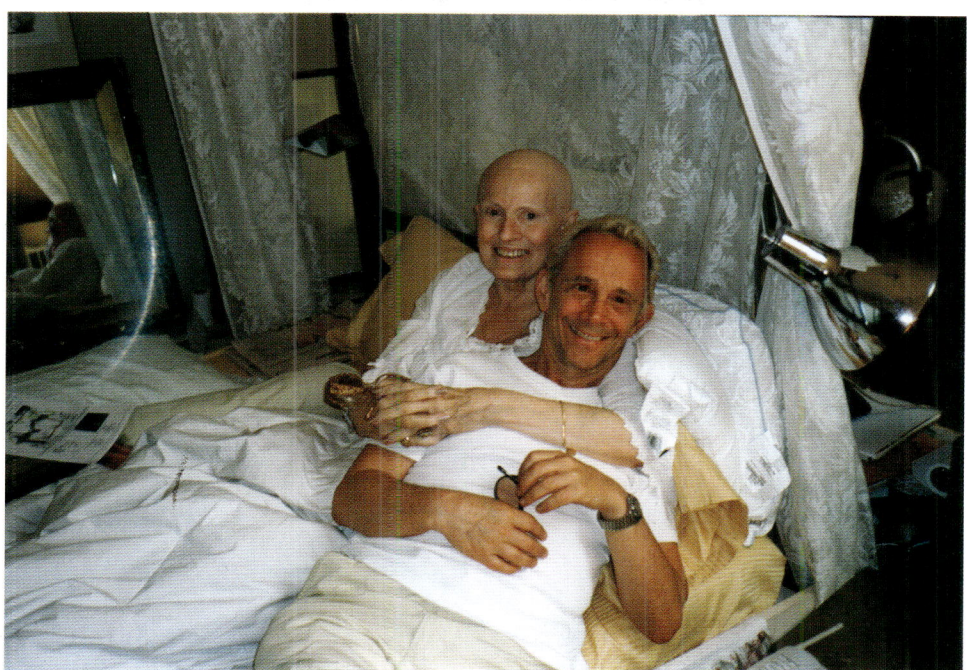

Patricia and Joel Grey. Photograph by Lucia Moffett.

accommodate Patricia's wheelchair to take them to the Majestic Theatre. She wore the baseball cap with gold sequins that she had adopted rather than a wig. Carroll accompanied her. "On the way up," Carroll recalled, "she laid her head in my lap. She was not feeling well."

She was seated at the end of the front row, with her wheelchair beside her. Austin Pendleton was on stage with the other memorial speakers waiting for the program to begin. Patricia called out to him, and he came down to speak to her.

He had not known she was ill. "She was very up," he recalled, "very funny. I said, 'What's the matter? What is this?'" "Oh," Patricia said lightly, "it's the cancer thing." He thought she was trying to communicate that she would be all right. "There was no sense of holding any feeling back," he recalled. "To her it was just 'the cancer thing.'"

Hould-Ward took her to a matinee of the Frank Wildhorn musical *The Civil War* at the St. James Theatre and an evening performance of the New York City Ballet. She attended performances of American Ballet Theatre and Ballet Hispanico.

During Jane Ashe's visits, Patricia did not talk about her life in the theatre. She told and retold the story of her love affair with O'Brien: how they met, his dramatic call to locate her, the wedding, O'Brien's demeanor, their farm and house, the horses, their life in Virginia. She kept a wedding photograph tucked in a nearby mirror.

In April she had what Ashe perceived was "a call" to go back to Virginia. She began to orchestrate a trip from her bed. She enlisted Tim Lynch, a young man who

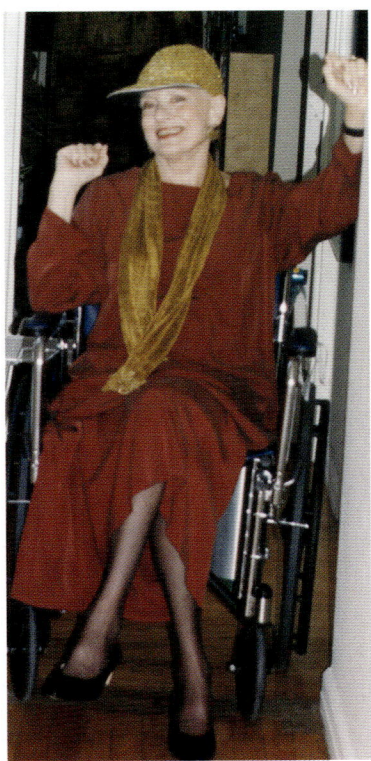

Patricia in her gold sequined baseball cap. Photograph by Lucia Moffett.

had assisted on the farm, to drive up for her in his van. The hospice team got the doctor's approval and arranged for oxygen and pain medication to travel with her. One of the Irish nurses would accompany them.

She left on a Thursday in mid-April and returned on Monday. Although there is no record of what she did in Virginia, the trip seems to have given her a jolt of energy and determination. She kept a busy schedule of visitors and outings through the last full week in June.

Douglas Colby, a collector of theatrical designs, hosted a festive tea party in her honor at his apartment near Carnegie Hall on May 5. It was attended by the designers Miles White[37] and Tony Walton, the film director Anthony Harvey, and Lisa Aronson, Boris Aronson's widow.

The following week, Carroll took her to a matinee of *Wit* at the Union Square Theatre. Kathleen Chalfant, a friend of Carroll's, was playing a university professor

---

[37]The seven-decade Broadway career of Miles White (1914–2000) included *Oklahoma!* (1943), the first Rodgers and Hammerstein musical, as well as ballet, circus, and film. At an American Ballet Theatre performance of Agnes De Mille's *Fall River Legend*, with White's costumes, PZ went up to greet him and introduced him to her friends as "God." PZ designed costumes for Anthony Harvey's (1930–2017) 1973 television production of *The Glass Menagerie* with Katharine Hepburn.

Patricia kept a wedding photograph tacked in a nearby mirror. Photograph by Lucia Moffett.

dying of ovarian cancer, and she had shaved her head for the role. After the performance, Patricia and Chalfant had their picture taken together, first with their baseball caps on and then with no caps.

Also in May, a woman named Sarah Morgan who had been a young protégée of Patricia's reappeared in her life. They had met when Sarah was twelve and living with her mother in Greensburg, Pennsylvania. Her father, Jim Morgan, an architect and associate editor at *Architectural Record* magazine, was dating Patricia at the time, and they came to visit at Christmas. Sarah and Patricia became close.

In 1975, when Sarah was fifteen, Patricia arranged for her to work for the summer at Lucia Moffett's Vineyard restaurant (she was Lucia Evans then). Sarah sometimes stayed with Patricia at God's Pocket. On outings together, people would ask if Sarah were her niece.

In 1999, Sarah Morgan was a sales representative for textile manufacturers and had an office near King Street. She could see Patricia's terrace from her office. When Lucia let her know that Patricia was in home hospice, she began visiting weekly.

"The thing that struck me," Sarah Morgan recalled, "was that when you went to the apartment, there was not a somber air around. Patricia seemed to be herself. She still had her sense of humor. Lucia was the most loving soul. When she was there, when the caregivers were there, it was a lovely, peaceful, comforting environment."

Sarah Morgan called her father and said, "You've got to get over and see Patricia; she's very ill."

Like her other boyfriends, Patricia called Morgan by his last name. They first met at a fortieth birthday party for Hugh Hardy that his firm had given on a chartered Circle Line boat. All the editors of *Architectural Record* were invited. "I was walking toward a bulkhead door," Morgan recalled, "when on the other side coming in my direction was this dramatically attractive woman."

She was wearing Phi Beta Kappa keys dangling from each ear. "Wow," he said, "where did you get two of those?" She gave him a dazzling smile as she brushed past. "Them what has, gets," she said.[38]

The next day, he went into the office of the editor he had seen with her and asked, "Who was that woman you were talking to?" "Her name's Patricia Zipprodt," was the reply, "she's in the theatre, and she's too old for you."

She was forty-seven to his thirty-eight. About a month or two later, he saw her name on a poster for the Mike Nichols production of *The Little Foxes* at Lincoln Center. He looked her up in the telephone directory and saw that she lived on University Place, near his apartment. "I had enough gumption to call the number," he said. A lunch date followed. And then another. "I think she was quite charmed that I was interested in her when I had no idea of who she was," he said.

One Tuesday in late October 1972, Patricia called his office at Rockefeller Center. "Would you be able to get a tux and come to the theatre with me this evening?" It was the opening night of *Pippin*. He asked his assistant to go out and rent him a tux. After work, he changed and walked through Central Park to meet Patricia for a reception at David and Leonora Hays's home on East Sixty-fourth Street.

When the curtain went up at the Music Box Theatre, Morgan was astonished at the dramatic opening number, "Magic to Do." "There were all these people wearing all these amazing clothes," he recalled. He looked over at Patricia who was snapping her fingers to the rhythm. "My god, this woman is a genius." he thought. He suddenly understood that he was about to embark on something remarkable.

For the next four years, Patricia and Morgan were a couple. He accompanied her to the theatre and theatrical parties, stayed with her in Los Angeles for a month while she worked on *Mack & Mabel*, the Michael Stewart/Jerry Herman musical directed by Gower Champion, and spent two weeks cruising the Adriatic and Aegean seas on a yacht owned by the husband of her friend the Greek conservationist Lily Venizelos.

Eventually, however, Patricia's intense dedication to her career—and Morgan's lack of direction for his—as well as the age difference, caused them to drift apart.

After Sarah's call, Morgan arranged with Lucia Moffett to see Patricia on May 1. When he went into her bedroom, she was wearing her baseball cap. She took it off. "There she was, all of her hair gone," Morgan recalled. "And her hair had been one of her glories." He visited over the next six weeks. "We ended up as friends in a different way than we had been before," he said. "My relationship with her was deep and transformative for me."

Toward the end of June, Patricia had what she told Jane Ashe was "a vision." "For my last trip," she said, "I have to go Colorado and be in the mountains and see the

---

[38] It was her standard rejoinder to this frequent comment.

sunset. I know where I want to go. I know the hotel." Her caregivers tried to dissuade her. "No, no, I'm doing it! The vision was too strong. I can't get it out of my mind."

From her bed she began stage-managing the expedition. She called her veteran travel agent Marvin Rapp to make the arrangements. She wanted to stay at El Tovar, the historic 1905 chalet located on the rim of the canyon. Lucia Moffett and Susan Ruddie researched airline regulations about oxygen. Moffett would accompany Patricia, along with one of the Irish nurses, Noelle Clancy. Her friends thought Patricia wanted an apotheosis of dying at the Grand Canyon.

She was scheduled to fly on Sunday, June 27, 1999. Jane Ashe went over to King Street that morning to assess her and get her ready. Patricia was flustered and keyed up. Ashe said, "Let me take you into the bathroom and help you get dressed." Patricia could barely put her arms through the dress. She looked at Ashe. "I can't go," she said. "Call it off. I can't go." Moffett called Rapp to cancel with the airlines and the hotel.

As she had with everything in her life, Patricia orchestrated her final arrangements with great determination. She signed her will on March 24, two weeks after she came home from the hospital. She made bequests to the School of American Ballet and Ballet Hispanico. She left funds to Trinity Episcopal Church of Upperville to renovate the parish hall for Christian education and to create a children's playground.

Now, in July, she instructed Bella Linden, her lawyer, and Josh Rednor, her accountant, to make immediate gifts to a number of people she felt gratitude to. Among them were Whitney Blausen, Anstice Carroll, Susan Ruddie, and Michele Elliman, a young dancer and choreographer who had assisted her for several years before the move to Virginia.

Moffett called the beneficiaries and told them to come for their checks right away. For tax reasons, they had to be deposited before Patricia died.

Carroll's daughter and two-year-old grandson were visiting in New York when she got the call. They left for King Street. "She was lying in her bed, with all these lace draperies around her. I held her hand. I knew I would never see her again. She nodded and squeezed my hand. I asked her if she would like to meet my grandson. 'Oh, yes,' she said."

Carroll wasn't sure how this would go. "She looked a little scary," she recalled. She wheeled his stroller next to the bed. She looked at him, reached out her hand, and smiled. He sat, mesmerized. 'He got her aura," Carroll said, "like there was some magical person in front of him."

Afterwards, when Carroll opened the envelope with the check, she was startled. "I had thought maybe she'd left me $100 or $500, that it would just be a token." It was $10,000.

Michele Elliman and her husband had adopted a son from South Korea in 1998. They brought the baby to a party Patricia hosted at King Street. Elliman dressed him in a beautiful traditional Korean hanbok, knowing that Patricia would delight in the colors and fabric. He napped in her four-poster bed, a resplendent sleeping prince, as Broadway luminaries chatted and sipped their drinks in her bedroom, kitchen, and studio.

In June 1999 the Ellimans had gotten word that there was the opportunity to have his sister placed with them as well. When she heard from Moffett that Patricia would make her a gift, she knew it would be a meaningful and welcome contribution to the adoption costs. She sent Patricia a picture of the child and then called. "She wasn't able to vocalize, but she was able to listen. I wanted to let her know that this little being was coming our way."

She told Patricia that they would include a Z in their daughter's name to honor her. They called her Isabel, and her nickname from early days was Zazi. After Patricia's death, "Whitney and Lucia had me come to the studio," she said. "They had very quietly set aside for our daughter a pink marble Z which had sat on Patricia's shelf." Elliman put it in Zazi's room, next to a photograph of Patricia. "My daughter referred to Patricia as her fairy godmother."

After the disappointment of the Grand Canyon trip, Patricia became listless. In July, her friends began to make what they knew were their final visits. Those who couldn't visit called. Those who visited more than once called between visits.

Patricia's sister Connie arrived Friday, July 9, for the weekend. Morgan visited on Saturday and again the following Tuesday and Wednesday.

Joel Grey called on Sunday morning, July 11, to say he was leaving for Copenhagen. He called in the afternoon on the way to the airport. He called before his plane departed in the evening. "Everything is as it's supposed to be," he said to tell Patricia. The next day he called from his hotel in Copenhagen.

Among the callers was Lawrence Van Gelder, who would write Patricia's obituary for the *New York Times*. He was told to speak with Phyllis Meras, who had been faxed thirteen pages of information for her obituary for the *Vineyard Gazette*. The massage therapist came on Monday. She came again on Wednesday. Noelle Clancy painted Patricia's nails gold, because she loved gold.

On Saturday morning, July 17, Moffett and Clancy were sitting by her bed when Patricia suddenly sat up and stared ahead. "Are you seeing something beautiful?" Moffett asked. "No," Patricia said sharply. Then she lay back and drifted into unconsciousness. Around noon, the two women went out of the room for a few minutes. When they came back in, Patricia was gone. Clancy came over to her and sang the hymn "Be Not Afraid":

Be not afraid
I go before you always
Come follow me
And I will give you rest.

Jonathan Dudley, who had chauffeured Patricia to appointments, was scheduled to take Moffett to lunch. When he arrived at King Street a little before one o'clock, she opened the door. "Thank god, you're here," she said, "we need a church person. Patricia has just died. We need someone to pray over her."

They went into the bedroom. Dudley was at a loss. "Suddenly I remembered the musical settings of the Twenty-Third Psalm I had been involved in since I was a child," he recalled. "I realized that if I thought musically, I could get through the whole thing. And I did. I was so proud of the fact that I was able to do that."

He left and Moffett began her phone calls. She notified Robert Davenport, the rector of Trinity Episcopal Church in Upperville, who had married Patricia and O'Brien and officiated at O'Brien's funeral. She spoke with Sally Irish, the head of the Flower Guild, to arrange sunflowers and calla lilies for the service which was to take place the following Saturday.

EPILOGUE

After Ann Hould-Ward received the call, she went immediately to King Street with Maria Brizzi, one of Patricia's favorite costume makers. They stayed with Patricia until attendants came from the Frank E. Campbell Funeral Chapel, known for its celebrity services. "I removed all her jewelry," Hould-Ward recalled, "save the evil eye bracelet I had brought her back from Turkey to ward away spirits. That went with her to the beyond."

Sunday morning, Moffett, Anstice Carroll, Fran Kessler,[39] and Betsy and Ming Cho Lee met at Campbell's to arrange the cremation. For the wake and the viewing, Patricia was dressed in a yellow silk Chanel blouse. Her head was wrapped in a turban. "What I remember most," Hould-Ward said, "is seeing those beautiful hands for the last times—so long and elegant—so much of an artist."

The funeral took place at Trinity Episcopal in Upperville on Saturday, July 24. The ashes were in a tall olive green French porcelain urn on a pedestal surrounded by sunflowers and calla lilies.

Hould-Ward gave one of the tributes:

My dearest mentor, the greatest lessons you taught me in this last year as I watched you find courage to pursue the time to enjoy the last moments with good friends and family. You skillfully, ingeniously, and artfully arranged your bedside world and yet still found the energy to point out a picture of beauty, an exquisite color, or an inspiring garden flower to those around you on each visit. And I learned until the very last day, when there on your desk was written this remarkable quote from you, "There are no decisions, only points in time."

The day after the service, Patricia's sister Connie and her nieces and nephews took the urn to Happy Hill Farm, renamed Runaway Farm by the new owners. Under the watchful eye of a horse, they scattered her ashes near where O'Brien's had been scattered. Later, Robert Davenport scattered both their ashes under the memorial trees Patricia had had planted near the paddock at the Glenwood Park racetrack in Middleburg.[40]

---

[39] Frances Kaufman Kessler (1926–2022) was a model for Charles James when she and Patricia met and became friends. She worked on the political campaigns of Democrats, including Ramsey Clark, and as assistant to the editors of both *New York* and *Esquire* magazines.

[40] Lucia Moffett and Phyllis Meras scattered ashes at God's Pocket on Martha's Vineyard. For many years, Moffett would bring the remaining ashes in a red velvet bag to a gathering of friends who shared recollections on or near the anniversary of Patricia's death. A memorial tribute was held at the Booth Theatre in New York on October 5, 1999; among the speakers were Harold Prince, Barbara Cook, Jules Fisher, Joel Grey, Hugh Hardy, David Hays, T. Edward Hambleton, Ann Hould-Ward, and Bernadette Peters.

Memorial trees for Patricia and O'Brien at Glenwood Park racetrack. Photograph by Middleburg Photo LLC.

Afterword

Cat on a Hot Tin Roof

Patricia did not include Cat on a Hot Tin Roof *in* If The Song Doesn't Work, Change the Dress, *but she left a lively account of meeting with the production's star, Kathleen Turner.*

In 1990, the producers Barry and Fran Weissler were putting together a starry revival of Tennessee Williams's *Cat on a Hot Tin Roof* and asked me to design the costumes. The Weisslers had done revivals of *Fiddler* and *Cabaret* using my designs, and we had worked together in 1988 on a *Macbeth* revival with Glenda Jackson and Christopher Plummer. That troubled production went through three directors and two scene designers before it reached Broadway, where it lasted only seventy-seven performances.

Barry and Fran had seen a very successful 1988 production of *Cat* at the National Theatre in London, directed by Howard Davies with Lindsay Duncan, and they had the idea for Davies to direct it here with Kathleen Turner as Maggie. Turner had made a sensational movie debut in *Body Heat* nine years earlier and was now a top star after a string of hits that included *Prizzi's Honor*, *Peggy Sue Got Married*, *Romancing the Stone*, *The Jewel of the Nile*, and *The War of the Roses*.

To up the show's star power, they cast the well-known movie and television actor Charles Durning as Big Daddy and Polly Holliday, popular in the television sitcom *Alice*, as Big Mama. Playing Brick was Daniel Hugh Kelly, who had just appeared in a Broadway revival of *Born Yesterday*.

Kathleen had in her contract that she had approval of the costume designer. Now, I don't know if that was her idea or her agent's, but it was not a good idea, because it was badly handled. I said to the Weisslers, "Do I have to go interview her? Is she interviewing me? Doesn't she know what I've done?" "No," they said, "this is just a formality."

Where would this occur? At first it was supposed to be at the Weisslers' office, which was fine. But something didn't work about that. It ended up at the office of Miss Turner's agent. Not neutral territory.

It felt weird when I got there. Her agent was wearing agent's clothes and had the kind of long sticky hair that gets mangled in his collar. His office was a very West

Coast agent's office, with lots of black leather. I would have thought I was in the lower seams of Hollywood.

And where the hell was Kathleen? He ushered me into his office and indicated that I could sit on this very low black leather couch. I had on a black leather skirt and a black leather jacket with big shoulders. I ended up scrunched into a cavity of the couch.

He brought in Miss Turner, who was tall and in heels up to here. We looked at each other. I couldn't get up. She pulled up a straight-backed chair—an important chair, the kind you find in old furniture shop, reupholster, and have in your apartment as The Chair for the King.

He then said, "I'll just leave you two girls alone." Kathleen and I were now girls. Neither one of us knew how to conduct this. I didn't know what she knew about my work. Did I have to explain that I worked my way through FIT by waitressing at Schrafts?

She was playing a role, and it put me into playing a role, but I didn't know what role I was playing. And I was in the wrong chair.

She said, "Well, here we are."

"Yes, here we are."

"I guess I should ask you a few questions."

"Feel free."

She had these mannerisms with her head, where she throws her head around. I'm surprised she doesn't have whiplash. I was beginning to feel like a turtle, in my leather jacket on this leather couch.

She said, "Why do you want to do this play?" I have an hyperactive mind, and about eighty-five answers surfaced all at once. I thought, "What a dumb question."

"Well, this is what I do."

That brought the conversation to a halt.

Then I said, "To tell you as best I can, I'm really a director junkie. If there's an interesting director and he wants to do the phone book, I'm for that. I really like the challenge of a director."

Then she began to explain to me her physical problems. She's extremely long-legged, and she's square. She's not waisted. She's bony and lean. She'd been looking fat in movies lately, and it had her very distressed.

I looked at her and said, "You have wonderful coloring." It was not unlike my sister Connie's coloring, tanned skin, with blonde streaked hair. Kathleen's eyes weren't as blue as Connie's; they're more green-gray, mysterious, cat-like. That's when I began to think about putting her in a lavender slip, instead of the traditional white. I could see that color being beautiful on her.

We finally decided to end the interview and get us both out of our misery. I managed to climb out of the couch and stand up. And there we were at eye level together. It was the first time she found out who I really was. I said, "Excuse me, do you know what I've done? Would you like me to tell you?" If only one of the producers had been there. It started us off on a most uncomfortable basis.

She looked me and said, "That's a very nice outfit you're in." So I went away, and that's how I started to design the show.

It's such an example of how not to put a star and a designer together. Everything was done wrong. We should have met in Central Park on a nice day.

This routine having been gone through, it was evidently satisfactory that I design Kathleen's clothes and the rest of the show. Then it got postponed because she was doing another film. Everyone's plans had to be changed. Howard Davies, who had had his whole schedule at the National Theatre in London changed so he could come over and do this, had to go back and rechange it.

During this time, I went cross-country riding in the Berkshires in the early fall, when all the trees were yellow. I took a fall, the horse left, and I managed to walk three miles home with three broken ribs.

When we into rehearsal, Howard Davies's set designer, William Dudley, who had done it in London, came over. The set was shipped over. I was the only new element in the design.

I went about my way with my broken ribs. I couldn't move too fast for a long time because I couldn't get enough breath. This seemed to irritate Kathleen, who has a lot of nervous energy and is constantly on the move.

I showed her my designs. I showed them to the director. I showed them to the producers. I did all the showing and telling that you do and then put them into the shop at Barbara Matera's, who was extremely busy at the time.

We went for first fittings. Kathleen didn't like what I put her in. The first dress was a party dress of the period, the fifties, in red-violet with a huge full skirt. Underneath she wore the lavender slip. The slip was very carefully made to balance out her natural build and to exploit the length of her legs, which are extraordinary. I nipped it in slightly under the bust, because she has no waist. She went straight up from her hips to her rib cage. And she's not a big woman, so we amplified her in the bust to do a Kathleen Turner version of what the world thinks Maggie looks like. The world has been imprinted with the image of Elizabeth Taylor in a white slip.

I added just enough so you'd never realize anything had been added, and you'd just think this is the way Kathleen Turner is endowed. Over this slip, we fitted two dresses. She didn't like herself in them. I had the feeling that most of her time in Hollywood she was dealing with West Coast designers who go shopping and get modern clothes, so she had never had things really designed for both her and the character.

Fitting was very long and very difficult because of Kathleen's restlessness. You can't meditate too much in a fitting with her. When it was all over, when we got through the two dresses and the slip, Barbara and I both felt that she understood what we were doing and that we were on the way to a wardrobe that she could feel physically and psychologically comfortable in and that would enforce the character.

Meanwhile, an underground rumbling was starting that I didn't know anything about because I wasn't at rehearsal very much. I needed to guard my energy level and not take any unnecessary trips anywhere, so I was mostly in the shops.

We had fifteen costumes, we were in five shops, and we also had a lot of shopping to do. This was over Christmas, during a winter that was bitterly cold. We were shopping in this weather, with the short days coming dark early. Getting to all these shops for fittings, I must have spent two hours a day in transit, all with my broken ribs, out of the eight hours available to work in the shops,.

I had a fitting booked for Kathleen on a Friday. Friday morning the phone rang, and it was Fran Weissler. "I understand you have a fitting with Kathleen today." "That's right." "You don't mind if I join you, do you?" I said, "No, of course not.

What's up?" Fran didn't usually come to fittings. She said, "Kathleen has a lot of complaints about her clothes, and I just think I'd better come to the fitting and hear them and see what you've got her in." I said, "No problem."

I was trying to think, "Why didn't someone say something to me?" When I asked my assistant, Marcia McDonald, why she hadn't said anything about complaints from Miss Turner, she said, "I didn't want to hurt your feelings."

Kathleen and Fran arrived at the shop in a limo. Kathleen, who's very direct, walked in and said, "Well, I just have to say what I have to say." She looked fat, she said. I was trying to make her look like Elizabeth Taylor. She couldn't bear the idea of any kind of padding. If her clothes didn't feel close to her body, how could she act? How could she perform sensitively?

There was a knock on the door, and the director arrived. "I thought I'd better come too," he said. So here we had the classic scene of the director, the producer, the star, and the designer.

We put the clothes back on her. She said, "Please, I feel like I'm over-padded. I can't stand it." She went behind the screen and Barbara took the padding out. She came out, and Howard and Fran said, "Oh, it looked much better the other way." "Oh," said Kathleen. So Barbara put the padding back, which also helped with the way the dresses fit over the slip.

Now she came out in the red-purple dress with the big full skirt. I explained that this was my version of a Ceil Chapman Original, the glamorous cocktail and evening dresses worn by celebrities and by women who wanted to look like them. This is what I thought Maggie would wear to this party, trying to look like she was member of this disjointed family.

"It doesn't represent you at all," I said, "so in a page and a half, when you drop the dress and step out of it, we never see it again on you. Then, bang, when we see you in the slip and in the coral dress, it's all about body, body, body, body."

Everyone agreed that was not a bad idea. So we stayed with all the original wardrobe and everyone was very happy.

Everyone else was fine. For Daniel Hugh Kelly as Brick, I found an absolutely smashing pair of white pajamas at Bergdorf's, but the management had a stroke because they cost $350. They said, "Couldn't you find pajamas for $125?" I said, "Yes, with purple piping and acetate in it. You'll just love it." We had lucked on the perfect pair or otherwise they would have to be made at a lot higher cost

I showed them to Howard Davies. He said, "They're perfect." They had a fabric that picked up the light so Brick could glow. The pajamas gave him an aura.

I transformed Polly Holliday into the role of Big Mama. We built a whole big body with flabby arms, and we gave her funny hair. Then we put the dress over all of it. She was totally different on stage from what she was off.

She was something of a nitpicker. I was down in the basement checking on things, when we heard this loud voice calling, "I want to talk to you!" Here came Polly, not in civilian clothes, but in full costume. It was like my creation had come to life from my little sketch, jumped off from stage captivity, and was coming to get me. Be careful what you sketch, she'll find you in the basement.

I think I designed *Cat on a Hot Tin Roof* very well. Kathleen looked very good. She knew how to use the clothes. She used them and used them well. Everyone kept telling her she looked very good: her friends, her agent, her husband, her daughter.

I like what Michael Kuchwara, the theatre reporter for the Associated Press, said in his review: "Turner controls the play's first and third acts. The woman is a star, and it's not easy to take your eyes off her as she sashays around the stage in designer Patricia Zipprodt's lavender lace slip."

But I don't think she ever liked me. Maybe I didn't like her. Maybe we were oil and vinegar. The whole thing between us, as I read it, just got so off by the way that we were set up to meet. I never got rid of the taint of it.

Cat had opened in March. A few days before it closed on August 1, one of the two versions of the slip made for the production was offered at a charity auction to benefit Easter Seals. It sold for $1,200.

The Designs of Patricia Zipprodt

The scope of Patricia Zipprodt's career can be seen most vividly in her archive of papers and designs at the New York Public Library and Museum of the Performing Arts (https://archives.nypl.org/the/21733) and in their digital collections (https://digitalcollections.nypl.org/collections/patricia-zipprodt-papers-and-designs).

1957

The Potting Shed by Graham Greene
Directed by Carmen Capalbo
Broadway

A Visit to a Small Planet by Gore Vidal
Directed by Cyril Ritchard
Broadway

The Virtuous Island/The Apollo of Bellac by Jean Giraudoux
Directed by Sherwood Arthur
Off Broadway

Miss Lonelyhearts by Howard Teichmann
Directed by Alan Schneider
Broadway

The Rope Dancers by Morton Wishengrad
Directed by Peter Hall
Broadway

1958

The Quare Fellow by Brendan Behan
Directed by José Quintero
Off Broadway

Back to Methuselah by George Bernard Shaw
Directed by Margaret Webster
Broadway

The Crucible by Arthur Miller
Directed by Word Baker
Off Broadway

1959

The Night Circus by Michael V. Gazzo
Directed by Frank Corsaro
Broadway

The Gang's All Here by Jerome Lawrence and Robert E. Lee
Directed by George Roy Hill
Broadway

1960

The Balcony by Jean Genet
Directed by José Quintero
Off Broadway

Camino Real by Tennessee Williams
Directed by José Quintero
Off Broadway

Period of Adjustment by Tennessee Williams
Directed by George Roy Hill
Broadway

Laurette (pre-Broadway tryout) by Stanley Young
Directed by José Quintero
Broadway

1961

The Blacks: A Clown Show by Jean Genet
Directed by Gene Frankel
Off Broadway

Sunday in New York by Norman Krasna
Directed by Garson Kanin
Broadway

Madame Aphrodite by Tad Mosel, Jerry Herman
Directed by Robert Turoff
Off Broadway

The Garden of Sweets by Howard Teichmann
Directed by Milton Katselas
Broadway

1962

Oh Dad, Poor Dad, Mamma's Hung You in the Closet and I'm Feelin' So Sad by Arthur Kopit
Directed by Jerome Robbins
Off Broadway

Step on a Crack by Bernard Evslin
Directed by Herbert Swope, Jr.
Broadway

A Man's a Man by Bertolt Brecht
Directed by John Hancock
Off Broadway

La Bohème by Giacomo Puccini
Directed by Sarah Caldwell
Opera

Madame Butterfly by Giacomo Puccini
Directed by Sarah Caldwell
Opera

1963

She Loves Me by Joe Masteroff, Jerry Bock, Sheldon Harnick
Directed by Hal Prince
Broadway

Oh Dad, Poor Dad, Mamma's Hung You in the Closet and I'm Feelin' So Sad by Arthur Kopit
Directed by Jerome Robbins
Broadway

Next Time I'll Sing to You by James Saunders
Directed by Peter Coe
Off Broadway

The Dragon by Eugene Schwarz
Directed by Joseph Anthony
Off Broadway

Calvary by William Butler Yeats
Directed by Brooks Jones
Regional

1964

Too Much Johnson by William Gillette
Directed by Burt Shevelove
Off Broadway

The Love of Don Perlimplin by Federico García Lorca
Directed by Brooks Jones
Regional

Fiddler on the Roof by Joseph Stein, Jerry Bock, Sheldon Harnick
Directed by Jerome Robbins
Broadway

The Tragical Historie of Doctor Faustus by Christopher Marlowe
Directed by Word Baker
Off Broadway

1965

Anya by George Abbott, Guy Bolton, Robert Wright, George Forrest
Directed by George Abbott
Broadway

Sign of Affection (pre-Broadway tryout)
Directed by Carolyn Green, Ron Winston
Broadway

Les Noces by Igor Stravinsky
Choreographed by Jerome Robbins
Ballet

1966

Pousse-Café by Jerome Weidman, Duke Ellington, Marshall Barer, Frederick K. Tobias
Directed by José Quintero
Broadway

Cabaret by Joe Masteroff, John Kander, Fred Ebb
Directed by Hal Prince
Broadway

Hippolyte et Aricie by Jean-Philippe Rameau
Directed by Sarah Caldwell
Opera

1967

The Little Foxes by Lillian Hellman
Directed by Mike Nichols
Broadway

Katerina Izmailova by Dimitri Shostakovich
Directed by Frank Corsaro
Opera

The Graduate by Calder Willingham, Buck Henry
Directed by Mike Nichols
Film

L'Histoire du soldat by Igor Stravinsky
Choreographed by Anna Sokolow/Jerome Robbins
Ballet

La Sonnambula by Vittorio Rieti
Choreographed by George Balanchine
Ballet

1968

Plaza Suite by Neil Simon
Directed by Mike Nichols
Broadway

Zorba by Joseph Stein, John Kander, Fred Ebb
Directed by Hal Prince
Broadway

The Flaming Angel by Sergei Prokofiev
Directed by Frank Corsaro
Opera

1969

1776 by Peter Stone, Sherman Edwards
Directed by Peter Hunt
Broadway

The Tale of Kasane by Tsurya Namboku
Directed by Yoshio Aoyama
Broadway, Regional

The Poppet by Hans Werner Henze
Choreographed by Gerald Arpino
Ballet

1970

Georgy by Tom Mankiewicz, Carole Bayer, George Fischoff
Directed by Peter Hunt
Broadway

Annie, the Women in the Life of a Man (Anne Bancroft special) by Gary Belkin, Peter Bellwood, Mel Brooks
Directed by Walter C. Miller
Television

Last of the Mobile Hot Shots by Tennessee Williams, Gore Vidal
Directed by Sidney Lumet
Film

1971

Scratch by Archibald MacLeish
Directed by Peter Hunt
Broadway

1972

Pippin by Roger O. Hirson, Stephen Schwartz
Directed by Bob Fosse
Broadway

1776 by Peter Stone, Sherman Edwards
Directed by Peter Hunt
Film

The Rise and Fall of the City of Mahagonny by Bertolt Brecht, Kurt Weill
Directed by Sarah Caldwell
Opera

The Mother of Us All by Gertrude Stein, Virgil Thompson
Directed by Virgil Thompson
Opera

Lord Byron by Virgil Thompson
Directed by John Houseman
Opera

Watermill—Religious and theatrical music of Asia
Choreographed by Jerome Robbins
Ballet

Dumbarton Oaks by Igor Stravinsky
Choreographed by Jerome Robbins
Ballet

1973

Bette Midler's First Annual Farewell Tour
Regional

The Glass Menagerie by Tennessee Williams, Stewart Stern
Directed by Anthony Harvey
Television

Waiting for Godot by Samuel Beckett
Directed by Eugene Lion
Regional

1974

Dear Nobody by Terry Belanger, Jane Marla Robbins
Directed by Leon Russom
Off Broadway

Mack & Mabel by Michael Stewart, Jerry Herman
Directed by Gower Champion
Broadway

June Moon (Great Performances) by George S. Kaufman, Ring Lardner, Burt Shevelove
Directed by Kirk Browning, Burt Shevelove
Television

Don Giovanni (canceled) by Wolfgang Amadeus Mozart
Directed by Gunther Rennert
Opera

Dybbuk Variations by Leonard Bernstein
Choreographed by Jerome Robbins
Ballet

1975

All God's Chillun' Got Wings by Eugene O'Neill
Directed by George C. Scott
Broadway

Chicago by Bob Fosse, John Kander, Fred Ebb
Directed by Bob Fosse
Broadway

The Leaves are Fading by Antonín Dvořák
Choreographed by Antony Tudor
Ballet

Tres Cantos by Carlos Chavez, Lorenzo Fernandez, Silvestre Revueltas
Choreographed by Talley Beatty
Ballet

1976

Poor Murderer by Pavel Kohout
Directed by Herbert Berghof
Broadway

Caprichios by Enrique Granados
Choreographed by Anna Sokolow
Ballet

Four Saints in Three Acts by Gertrude Stein, Virgil Thompson
Directed by Virgil Thompson
Opera

1977

Tannhäuser by Richard Wagner
Directed by Otto Schenk
Opera

1978

Naughty Marietta by Victor Herbert
Directed by Dennis Rosa
Opera

King of Hearts by Joseph Stein, Peter Link, Jacob Brackman
Directed by Ron Field
Broadway

Stages by Stuart Ostrow
Directed by Richard Foreman
Broadway

1979

Charlotte by Peter Hacks
Directed by Herbert Berghof
Broadway

1980

One Night Stand by Herb Gardner, Jule Styne
Directed by John Dexter
Broadway

Queen of Spades (Pique Dame) (canceled) by Pyotr Ilyich Tchaikovsky
Directed by Liviu Ciulei
Opera

1981

Kingdoms by Edward Sheehan
Directed by Paul Giovanni
Broadway

Pippin: His Life and Times by Robert O. Hirson, Stephen Schwartz
Directed by David Sheehan
Television

Fools by Neil Simon
Directed by Gordon Davidson/Mike Nichols
Broadway

1982

Don Juan by Jean-Baptiste Molière
Directed by Richard Foreman
Off Broadway

Whodunnit by Anthony Shaffer
Directed by Michael Kahn
Broadway

The Barber of Seville by Giacomo Rossini
Directed by John Cox
Opera

Alice in Wonderland by Eva Le Gallienne, Florida Friebus
Directed by Eva Le Gallienne, John Strasberg
Broadway

1983

Sunday in the Park with George (designed with Ann Hould-Ward) by James Lapine, Stephen Sondheim
Directed by James Lapine
Off Broadway

Alice in Wonderland (Great Performances) by Eva Le Gallienne, Florida Friebus
Directed by Kirk Browning
Television

Brighton Beach Memoirs by Neil Simon
Directed by Gene Saks
Broadway

The Glass Menagerie by Tennessee Williams
Directed by John Dexter
Broadway

Sunset by Will Holt, Gary William Friedman
Directed by André Ernotte
Off Broadway

Llamada by Federico Torroba, Pepe Romero, Fernando Sor
Choreographed by William Whitener
Ballet

Estuary by Ralph Vaughan Williams
Choreographed by Lynn Taylor-Corbett
Ballet

1984

Accidental Death of an Anarchist by Dario Fo
Directed by Douglas C. Wager
Broadway

Tito on Tambales by Tito Puente
Choreographed by William Whitener
Ballet

The Love of Don Perlimplin by Federico García Lorca, Conrad Sousa
Directed by David Alden
Opera

Sunday in the Park with George (designed with Ann Hould-Ward) by James Lapine, Stephen Sondheim
Directed by James Lapine
Broadway

1985

Beads of Memory by Pyotr Ilyich Tchaikovsky
Choreographed by Helgi Tómasson
Ballet

1986

Sweet Charity (revival) by Neil Simon, Cy Coleman, Dorothy Fields
Directed by Bob Fosse
Broadway

Sunday in the Park with George (American Playhouse) (designed with Ann Hould-Ward) by James Lapine, Stephen Sondheim
Directed by Terry Hughes
Television

Big Deal by Bob Fosse
Directed by Bob Fosse
Broadway

1987

Into the Woods (costume design by Ann Hould-Ward, based on original concepts by Patricia Zipprodt) by James Lapine, Stephen Sondheim
Directed by James Lapine
Broadway

Cabaret (revival) by Joe Masteroff, John Kander, Fred Ebb
Directed by Harold Prince
Broadway

The Bacchae by Euripides
Directed by Liviu Ciulei
Regional

1988

Macbeth by William Shakespeare
Directed by Kenneth Frankel, Zoe Caldwell
Broadway

Brighton Beach Memoirs by Neil Simon
Directed by Gene Saks
Broadway

The Fall of the House of Usher by Philip Glass
Directed by Richard Foreman
Opera

Cada Noche . . . Tango by Astor Piazzolla
Choreographed by Graciela Daniele
Ballet

Inéz de Castro by Sergio Cervetti
Choreographed by Vicente Nebrada
Ballet

1989

Cat on a Hot Tin Roof by Tennessee Williams
Directed by Howard Davies
Broadway

Sondheim Suite by Stephen Sondheim
Choreographed by Ann Reinking, William Whitener
Ballet

1990

James Clavell's Shogun, The Musical by John Driver, Paul Chihara
Directed by Michael Smuin
Broadway

Fiddler on the Roof (revival) by Joseph Stein, Jerry Bock, Sheldon Harnick
Directed by Jerome Robbins, Ruth Mitchell
Broadway

1991

Coppélia by Léo Delibes
Choreographed by Arthur Saint-Léon, Enrique Martinez
Ballet

The Crucible by Arthur Miller
Directed by Yossi Yzraely
Broadway

The Sleeping Beauty by Pyotr Ilyich Tchaikovsky
Choreographed by Peter Martins
Ballet

1992

Little Hotel on the Side by Georges Feydeau
Directed by Tom Moore
Broadway

The Master Builder by Henrik Ibsen
Directed by Tony Randall
Broadway

My Favorite Year by Joseph Dougherty, Stephen Flaherty, Lynn Ahrens
Directed by Ron Lagomarsino
Broadway

Who Cares by George Gershwin
Choreographed by George Balanchine
Ballet

Chrysler Skating '92 (with Katarina Witt and Sandra Bezic, Brian Boitano) Michael Seibert National Tour

Times Square Business Improvement District
Sanitation Workers' Uniforms

1993

My Fair Lady (revival) by Alan Jay Lerner, Frederick Loewe
Directed by Howard Davies
Broadway

1994

The School for Scandal by Richard Brinsley Sheridan
Directed by Joe Dowling
Regional

1996

Picasso at the Lapin Agile by Steve Martin
Directed by Randall Arney
Off Broadway

1998

You Can't Take It With You by George S. Kaufman, Moss Hart
Directed by Douglas C. Wager
Regional

Selected awards/nominations

1965

Tony Award (Winner)	*Fiddler on the Roof*

1967

Tony Award (Winner)	*Cabaret*

1968

Drama Desk Award	*1776*

1969

Tony Award (Nomination)	*Zorba*
American Theatre Wing Design Award	*1776*

1973

Drama Desk Award	*Pippin*
Tony Award (Nomination)	*Pippin*

1975

Tony Award (Nomination)	*Mack & Mabel*

1976

Tony Award (Nomination)	*Chicago*

1983

Tony Award (Nomination)	*Alice in Wonderland*

1984

Tony Award (Nomination) (with Ann Hould-Ward)	*Sunday in the Park with George*

1986

Tony Award (Winner)	*Sweet Charity*

1991

Tony Award (Nomination)	*Shogun: The Musical*
Drama Desk Award	*Shogun: The Musical*
American Theatre Wing Design Award	*Shogun: The Musical*

ACKNOWLEDGMENTS

I am indebted to the family and friends of Patricia Zipprodt for their support and encouragement throughout the research and writing of *If the Song Doesn't Work, Change the Dress*. I am especially grateful to Whitney Blausen and the late Connie Zonka for entrusting me with the task and for opening many doors to other friends and family. Liz Woodman provided the invaluable interviews William Woodman conducted with Patricia. Phyllis Meras and the late Lucia Moffett gave me treasure troves of documents relating to Patricia's life and especially her final months. Jane Ashe, Anstice Carroll, Noelle Clancy, Jonathan Dudley, Michele Elliman, Joel Grey, David Hays, Ann Hould-Ward, Jim Morgan, Sarah Morgan, Austin Pendleton, and Susan Ruddie generously shared deeply personal memories of Patricia. Connie Zonka's children, the late Heidi Sorensen and Milo Zonka, have been especially supportive. I also appreciate the help of Patricia's other nieces and nephews: Kathy Miller (Spielmann), Roger Spielmann, Lynn Huston (Pavlik), and Dan Pavlik. Patricia's friend the late Harvey Stuart gave this project a much-needed spark when he offered support for the illustrations for the book in memory of his late wife, the costume designer Patricia Quinn Stuart, one of Patricia's valued assistants. The Tobin Foundation for the Theatre Arts also provided support for the illustrations, and I appreciate the help of President Mel L. Weingart for facilitating this.

At the Fashion Institute of Technology, Patricia's alma mater, Eileen Costa, Melissa Marra-Alvarez, Patricia Mears, Valerie Steele, and the indefatigable Karen Trivette provided much assistance. At Wellesley College, another of Patricia's alma maters, Margaret Mauruka and Olivia Holbrook of the Alumnae Office were always ready to answer my questions, and Rebecca Goldman, the college archivist, was diligent in finding relevant materials.

At the New York Public Library, I am indebted to Doug Riside, John Calhoun, Jeremy Megraw, Suzanne Lipkin, Jennifer Eberhardt, Tanisha Jones, Linda Murray, and Stephen Bowie at the Performing Arts Library, to Emma Davidson at the Berg Collection, and to Giovanna Pugliese in the Rights and Permissions Office.

I am grateful to the following for their assistance: Robert Beseda, University of North Carolina School of the Arts; Mary Beth Betts, New York City Design Commission; Julia Blaut, Robert Rauschenberg Foundation; Alison Chomet, New York University Library Special Collections; Matthew Clarke, University of Illinois Chicago Library Special Collections; Belzy Day, Kirk Whelen-Foran, United Agents, London; Leo Flaherty, United Scenic Artists, Local USA 829; Marc Happel, New York City Ballet; Andy Harris, University of Texas; Julia Lintott, Stella Richards Management, London; Michael Lobel, Hunter College; Michelle Mulos, University of California at Los Angeles Library, and at the Wisconsin Historical Society, Lee Grady and Lisa Marine.

My thanks for their assistance to Randall Arney, Marc Aronson, Arnold Aronson, Jim Beaver, Jody Blake, Mitch Bloom, the late Betty Brown, Douglas Colby, Gray Coyner, Betsy Crenshaw, William Daniels, the Reverend Robert Davenport, Holly Poe Durbin, Iris Fanger, the late Gerald Freedman, Peggy Gould, Michael Growler, the Reverend Stephen Harding, Martin Izquierdo, Betsy Lee, Arnold Levine, Santo Loquasto, Randy and Cindy Mullett, Jim Nolt, Bobbi Owen, Albert Poland, the late Hal Prince, John Quilty, Martin Rapp, David

Rodger, the late Carl Samrock, John Siffert, Jennifer Stuart, Kathleen Turner, and Barry Weissler. My sister, Reberta Karesh, has been especially supportive.

My gratitude to Dom O'Hanlon and Sam Nicholls at Bloomsbury/Methuen for their enthusiasm about this book, to the project manager Merv Honeywood, and to the meticulous Moira Eagling for her copyediting. Sophie Beardsworth at Bloomsbury has been gracious and supportive.

INDEX

1776, 129

Abbott, George, 75
Addams, Jane, 6
Adler, Ernest, 53, 128
Albert, Eddie, 39
Aldredge, Theoni, 103
Aleichem, Sholem, 89
Allen, Debbie, 146
American Shakespeare Festival, 39
Anatevka (*Fiddler on the Roof*, Amsterdam), 104
Angelou, Maya, 72
Ann-Margaret, 128
Anya, 115
Arena Stage, Washington, DC, 166
Aronson, Boris, 34, 35, 40, 52, 91
Aronson, Lisa, 172
Art Institute of Chicago, 7, 8
Art Students League, 36
Arthur, Bea, 104
Arthur, Sherwood, 45
Artists' Theatre, 28
As You Like It, 29
Ashbery, John, 28
Ashe, Jane, 167
Atkinson, Brooks, 53, 54, 67–8
Axelrod, George, 48
Axelrod, Joan, 48
Azara, Nancy, 79

Back to Methuselah, 51, 53
Baker, Word, 42, 44, 55
Balanchine, George, 25
Balcony, The, 63, 65
Ballard, Lucinda, 48, 80–1
Bancroft, Anne, 119
Barnes, Clive, 140
Barr, Geoffrey, 41
Baruch, Leona Turpin (Aunt Leona), 2
Baruch, Arthur, 2

Baxley, Barbara, 68, 83
Benton & Bowles, 23
Berry, Eric, 136
Bertha The Sewing Machine Girl, 33
Big Deal (musical), 152
Bing, Rudolph, 49
Blacks, The, 72
Blaine, Nell, 28
Blausen, Whitney, vi, vii, 167
Blitzstein, Marc, 39
Blondell, Joan, 51
Bloomer Girl, 38
Bloomgarden, Kermit, 60
Bock, Jerry, 89
Boskamp, Hans, 104
Bradford Junior College, Haverill, MA, 13
Brandeis University, 161
Bridge, Joan, 106
Brizzi, Maria, 79
Broadway Arts Building, 1755 Broadway, NY, 149, 153
Brooklyn Museum Costume Collection, 60, 83
Brooks Costumes, 38, 43, 45, 61
Browne, Roscoe Lee, 72
Burns, Ralph, 152
Burrows, Abe, 42, 43, 44

Cabaret, viii, ix, 107
Call Me Madam, 42
Cambridge, Godfrey, 72
Camino Real, 65–7
Candide (Leonard Bernstein), 41
Capalbo, Carmen, 45
Carmine Street, 24
Carnegie Deli, 131
Carney, Art, 51
Carroll, Anstice, 163, 166, 167
Cassidy, Jack, 83

Casson, Lewis, 46
Cat on a Hot Tin Roof, 179
Cedar Tavern, 26
Chalfant, Kathleen, 172
Chandler Pavilion, Los Angeles, 150
Chapline, Barbara, 16
Chase, Stanley, 45
Chicago (city), 1
Chicago (musical), 141
Chicago City Opera, Civic Opera House, 9
Chorus Line, A, 144
Church of the Holy Comforter, Kenilworth, 3
Circle in the Square, 56
Clancy, Noelle, 175
Cohen, Alexander, 117
Colby, Douglas, 172
Cook, Barbara, 38, 83
Crawford, Cheryl, 38, 71
Crist, Judith, 160
Crouse, Russel, 42
Crucible, The, 55

Daly, James, 68
Daniele, Graciela, 170
Daniels, William, 79
Davenport, Robert, 176
Davidson, Gordon, 128
Davies, Howard, 163, 179
de Nagy, Tibor, 28
Diffen, Ray (Ray Diffen Stage Clothes), 69, 70
Dixon, Jean, 60
Dobyns, Deedee, 23
Donath, Ludwig, 83
Douglas, Melvyn, 60, 62
Dudley, Jonathan, 167, 176
Dudley, William, 181
Dunn, Ralph, 81
Durland's Riding Academy, 38
Durning, Charles, 179
Dysart, Richard, 126

Eaves Costumes, viii, 49, 108
Eckart, William and Jean Eckart, 39, 77, 90
Elgin Hour, 38
Elliman, Michelle, 175
Emerson, Faye, 53
Equity Library Theatre, 29
Evanston, Illinois, 3

Falkenberg, Paul, 107
Fantasticks, The, 63
Fashion Institute of Technology (FIT), 27
Feller, Kate, 97
Feller, Pete, 97
Ferreras, Miguel, 42–3, 118
Fiddler on the Roof, 86, 89
Field, Ron, 107
Fiorentino, Harry, tailor, Philadelphia, 44
Firestone, Idabell, "If I Could Tell You of My Devotion," 38
Fisher, Jules, 141, 170
Fletcher, Robert, 39
Float Night (Wellesley), 15
Fools, 128
Fosse, Bob, 131
Frank E. Campbell Funeral Chapel, 177
Frankel, Gene, 72, 74
Frankenhaler, Helen, 28
Freedman, Gerald, 29
Frey, Leonard, 104
Friedman, Phil, 138
Funny Girl, 91, 115

Gang's All Here, The, 60
Genet, Jean, 63
Gingold, Hermione, 81
Glaser, John, 168
Glassenberg, Fuzzy, 16
Glenwood Park, Middleburg, Virginia, 167
God's Pocket, Martha's Vineyard, 158
Godrone, Charles, 72
Goldman, James, 75
Goldman, William, 75
Good Teeth Council for Children, 17
Goodman Theatre, vi, 9
Gordon, Ruth, 71
Gossett, Louis, 72
Gould, Peggy, 170
Grace Costumes, 79
Graduate, The, 115
Green, Robert L., 163
Grey, Joel, viii, 170
Griffith, Robert, 75
Grooms, Red, 28
Gude, O. J., 23

Haas, Dolly, 107
Hadley, Arthur, 157, 170
Hadley, Jane, 170
Haffenden, Elizabeth, 106

INDEX

Hall, Peter, 51
Hall, Grayson, 63
Hambleton, T. Edward, 76, 79, 170
Haney, Carol, 83
Hansel and Gretel, 9
Happy Hunting, 41, 42
Happy Hill Farm, Virginia, 161
Hardy, Hugh, 42, 44, 166, 170, 174
Harnick, Sheldon, 89
Harris, Bob, 33
Harris, Barbara, 77
Harris, Joseph, 146
Harry Winston Jewelers, 122
Harvey, Anthony, 172
Hays, David, 56, 71, 75, 170
Hays, Leonora, 117, 170
Head, Edith, 115, 118–19
Heeley, Desmond, vi
Hello, Dolly, 81
Henry, Buck, 116
Hicks, Rebecca, 1
Hill, George Roy, 60, 68, 70–1
Hiller, Wendy, 132
Hines, Jerome, 38
Hirschfeld, Al, 107
Hoffman, Dustin, 118
Holliday, Judy, 75
Holliday, Polly, 179
Houghton, Norris, 76
Hould-Ward, Ann, vii, 165, 168
Houseman, John, 40
Hunt, Peter, 129
Hurry, Leslie, vi

Imperial Theatre, 100
Irish, Sally, 176
Izquierdo, Martin, 164, 168

J. Walter Thompson, advertising agency, 20
James, Charles, fashion designer, 30
Jeakins, Dorothy, 11
Jens, Salome, 63
Jewish Daily Forward, 90
Jewison, Norman, 105
Jones, James Earl, 72
Jones, Tom, 63

Kander, John, 75
Kanin, Garson, 71
Karinska, Barbara, 25, 77
Karr, David, 23

Kaufman, George S., 47
Kaye, Nora, 91
Kelly, Daniel Hugh, 179
Kelly, Ellsworth, 28
Kenilworth (Chicago), 1, 3
Kerr, Walter, 140
Kessler, Fran, 177
Kijzer, Paul, 104
Kirkland, Sally, *Life* Magazine, 30
Kirkland, Wallace, 28
Kirstein, Lincoln, 25, 39
Klotz, Florence, 48, 85
Koch, Kenneth, *Little Red Riding Hood*, 28
Kopit, Arthur, 76
Krasner, Norman, 71
Krause, Alvina, 29
Kuchwara, Michael, 183
Kutner, Luis, 20

La Valse, ballet by George Balanchine, 25
Lamas, Fernando, 42
Landau, Jack, 40
Langner, Lawrence, 39, 54
Lansbury, Angela, 37
Lapson, Dvora, 90
Larkin, Peter, 153
Last of the Mobile Hot Shots, 128, 157
Laurette, 75
Lawrence, Jerome, 60, 62
Le Clercq, Tanaquil, 25
Lee, Ming Cho, 42, 44, 55
Lee, Robert E., 60, 62
Lehman, Al, 37
Leighton, Margaret, 126
Lenya, Lotte, 108
Levine, Arnold S., 149
Libin, Paul, 42, 44, 55
Linden, Bella, 167
Lindsay, Howard, 42
Little Foxes, The, 124
Little, Stuart, 65
Louis, Morris, 28
Lowman, Camilla Tyler, 17–19
Lumet, Sidney, 128, 157
Lunsford, Beverly, 52
Lynch, Tim, 171

MacGrath, Leueen, 47–8
Machiz, Herbert, 28
Mack & Mabel, 174

Madame Butterfly, Opera Company of Boston, 90
Madame Rosepettle, 77
Mann, Theodore, 56, 64–5
Marchand, Nancy, 63
Marguerite Gautier, the Lady of the Camellias (*Camino Real*), 67
Marshall, Armina, 54
Marshall, E. G., 126
Martinique Theatre, 55
Mary Crane League Snow Ball (Hull House), 6
Massey, Daniel, 83
Massey, Raymond, 39
Masteroff, Joe, 102
Matchmaker, The, 81
Matera, Barbara Gray, 69, 164
Matera, Arthur, 69
Maximilian Furs, 123
McAndrews, Catherine, 17
McDonald, Marcia K., 182
McDowell, Roddy, 39
McHugh, Gladys, 13
McKenna, Siobhán, 51
McNaughton, James H., 37
McTavish, "Miss," (FIT instructor), 27
Meacham, Anne, 21, 24, 28, 34
Mead, Margaret, 14
Meras, Phyllis, 163
Merchant of Venice, The, 9
Merlin, Joanna, 104
Merlo, Frank, 79
Merman, Ethel, 41, 42
Merrick, David, 42, 71, 72
Merrill, Robert, 38
Miceli, Grace, 79, 96
Mielziner, Jo, 42
Migenes, Julia, 104
Miles, Sylvia, 63
Mili, Gjon, 24, 30, 34, 41, 77, 117
Miller, Arthur, 55, 56
Miller, Betty, 63
Miss Lonelyhearts, 50
Mitchell, Joan, 28
Mitchell, Ruth, viii, 85
Model, Lisette, 25
Moffett, Lucia Evans, 167
Monroe, Marilyn, 48, 55
Morgan, Jim, 173
Morgan, Sarah, 173
Moss, Arnold, 53

Mostel, Zero, 92, 99
Munsel, Patrice, 38
Music Box Theatre, 174
My Fair Lady, 163
Myers, John, 28

Nachman, Jack, 27, 28, 31
Nelson, Inga May, 5
New School for Social Research, 24
New Trier High School, 9
New York City Ballet, 25
New York City Center, 25
New York Public Library, 34
Nichols, Mike, 115
Nidha, Fred, 138
Noland, Kenneth, 28
Norell, Norman, 60
Novellino, Nino, 97

O'Brien, Col. Robert, vi, vii, 19, 20, 161, 166, 167
O'Hara, Frank, 28
Oh, Dad, Poor Dad, Mama's Hung You in the Closet and I'm Feelin' So Sad, 76
Orbach, Jerry, 144
Ostrow, Stuart, 131
Our Lady of Pompeii Church, New York, 24
Our Town, 59

Page, Geraldine, 58
Palance, Jack, 39
Palmer, Leland, 136
Paramount Studios, 116
Paul, Les and Mary Ford, 38
Pauli, Wolfgang, 13
Pendleton, Austin, 77, 104, 126, 171
Period of Adjustment, 68
Peters, Roberta, 38
Phoenix Theatre, 81
Picasso at the Lapin Agile, 166
Pippin, vi, 131
Pitkin, William, 47
Playwrights' Company, The, 51
Plaza Suite, 126
Plummer, Christopher, 39
Polachek, Charles, 38
Pope, Ellie Rand, 32
Potok, Anna Maximilian, 123
Potting Shed, The, 46
Pousse-Café, 115

Power, Tyrone, 53
Prince, Harold (Hal), viii, 75, 81, 91
Promenade Theatre, 166
Pygmalion, 132

Quare Fellow, The, 58, 96
Queen of Spades, 155
Quintero, José, 56, 64, 67

Rainbow Room, Rockefeller Center, 102
Ramirez, Tina, 170
Randolph, Robert
Rapp, Martin, 175
Rauschenberg, Robert, 28
Redford, Robert, 71
Rednor, Josh, 175
Rentner, Maurice, 2
Reuben, Reuben (musical), 39
Riley, Robert, 60, 83
Ritchard, Cyril, 48–9
Robbins, Jerome, 75
Rope Dancers, The, 51
Rosenthal, Jean, 90, 99
Roth, Ann, 41, 43
Rubinstein, John, 132
Ruddie, Susan, 166

Samrock, Victor, 50
Samuel Winston, Inc., clothing manufacturer, 31–2
Scannel, John and Barbara, 158
Scheffler, Carl, 12
Schmidt, Harvey, 63
Schneider, Alan, 50
School for Scandal, The, 166
Schwartz, Stephen, 131
Scott, George C., 126
Scratch, 131
Shakespeare Theatre Company, Washington, DC, 166
Sharaff, Irene, 40, 41, 44, 116
She Loves Me, 83
Shelp, Woody, 164
Sidney, Sylvia, 81
Siepi, Cesare, 38
Six, Robert, 42
Sleighton Farm School, Pennsylvania, 16
Smith, Oliver, 41, 48
Smokenders, 155
sociology, 14
Sorensen, Heidi Zonka, 199

Sousa, John Philip, 2
St. Jacques, Raymond, 72
St. Mark's Playhouse, 65
Stanley, Pat, 71
Stapleton, Maureen, 126
Stark, Ray, 115
Steber, Eleanor, 38
Stein, Joseph, 89
Streisand, Barbra, 91
Stevens, Risë, 38
Stevens, Roger, 39
Strook, Jimmy, 45
Stuart, Patricia Quinn, 126
Stuart, Harvey, vii
Summer and Smoke, 58
Sunday in New York, 71
Sunday in the Park with George, 165
Sweet Charity, 131
Swing, x
Swirl (dress manufacturing firm), 27
Sylbert, Richard, 119

Taylor, Laurette
Ter-Arutunian, Rouben, 40, 60
Tevye (original title of *Fiddler on the Roof*), 89
Tew, Fred, 99
Theatre de Lys, Christopher Street, 28
Thompson, Sada, 81
Thorndyke, Dame Sybil, 46–7
Todd, Mike, 51
Tower Building, Chicago, 7
Trigère, Pauline, 32
Trinity Episcopal Church, Upperville, Virginia, 163, 166
Turman, Lawrence, 116, 121,122, 124
Turner, Kathleen, 179
Turpin, Edward Napoleon Bonaparte, 1, 2
Tyler, Gus, International Ladies' Garment Workers' Union, 34
Tyson, Cicely, 72

United Scenic Artists, USA Local 829, 34

Van Fleet, Jo, 77
Van Gelder, Lawrence, 176
Vanished World, The, 90
Venizelos, Lily, 174
Verdon, Gwen, 131
Vereen, Ben, 140
Vidal, Gore, 48

Visit to a Small Planet, 48
Vivian Beaumont Theatre, Lincoln Center, 124
Voice of Firestone, 37–8

Walton, Tony, vi, 133–4, 141, 172
Watergate, 140
Waterston, Sam, 81
Weaver, Fritz, 50
Webb, Charles, 115
Webster, Margaret, 53
Weissler, Barry and Fran, 179
Wellesley College, 14
Westmoreland, William, 167
Wexler, Connie, 67, 96
Wexler, Peter, 67
White, Miles, 172
William H. Weintraub advertising agency, 23
Williams, Tennessee, 68, 70–1
Wilson, Elizabeth, 121
Winston, Samuel (dress manufacturer), 31
Wishengrad, Morton, 57
Wit, 172
Wolfe, Brian, 97
Wolsky, Albert, 96
Woodman, William, vi
Wrigley Building, Chicago, 17

YIVO Institute, 90
You Can't Take It With You, 166
Ziegfeld Follies, 2

Zipprodt, Inc., 6
Zipprodt, Agnes Irene Turpin, 1
Zipprodt, Herbert E., 2
Zipprodt, Johann Jacob, 3
Zipprodt, Patricia – paper dolls, 9
Zipprodt, Patricia – cancer, 117
Zipprodt, Patricia – loft on University Place, 116
Zipprodt, Patricia – addiction to smoking, alcohol, 156–7
Zipprodt, Patricia – buys God's Pocket on Martha's Vineyard, 157–8
Zipprodt, Patricia – works for Charles James, 31
Zipprodt, Patricia – applies to, begins at FIT, 27
Zipprodt, Patricia – apartment at 23 Carmine Street, 24, 45
Zipprodt, Patricia – marries Col. Robert O'Brien, moves to Virginia, 163
Zipprodt, Patricia – works at American Shakespeare Festival, 39
Zipprodt, Patricia – works for Pauline Trigère, 36
Zipprodt, Patricia – social conscience, 10
Zipprodt, Patricia – begins working at ABC Television, 37
Zipprodt, Patricia – takes Union exam, 36
Zipprodt, Patricia – loft on University Place, 116
Zipprodt, Patricia – "There it was, I thought, it is actually possible to paint with fabric. Everything I was trying to put together, the painting, the paper dolls, clicked into place. I knew for the very first time that I wanted to be a costumer designer more than anything else in the world.", 25
Zipprodt, Patricia – apartment, Central Park South, 45
Zipprodt, Patricia – mantra, "If the song doesn't work, change the dress," 43
Zipprodt-Pavlik, Barbara (sister), 4, 7, 20, 89
Zonka, Constance Zipprodt (Connie, sister), vii, ix, 5, 7, 20, 170
Zonka, Milo, vii